Reservation Policy:
Issues and Implementation

Reservation Policy:
Issues and Implementation

Dr. S.N. Ambedkar

ABD PUBLISHERS
Jaipur ■ New Delhi

ABD PUBLISHERS

Regd. Off. "Bony Residency", Gate No. 2
Opp. Tilak Public School, Vishweswariya Nagar,
Gopalpura Road, Jaipur - 302018, India
Ph: 0141 - 2761280, Telefax: 2761381
Email: abdpublishersjpr@gmail.com

Delhi Office: 102, 1st Floor, Satyam House,
4327/3, Ansari Road, Darya Ganj,
New Delhi - 110002, India
Ph: 011-45652440

visit us: www.oxfordbookcompany.com

Distributed By
KEYA INTERNATIONAL PRESS LLP
E-mail: keyainternationalpressllp@gmail.com

Published in India, 2026

ISBN : 9788183761574

Typeset by Shivangi Computer, Jaipur

Printed and bound in India by Thomson Press Ltd.,
New Delhi

Contents

Preface

The reservation policy in India stands as one of the most debated and deeply rooted socio-political frameworks of modern times. Born out of a historical need to correct centuries of marginalization, discrimination, and social injustice, it seeks to provide fair opportunities to communities that were systemically oppressed. Over the years, this policy has grown to encompass various sections of society—particularly the Scheduled Castes, Scheduled Tribes, and Other Backward Classes—with the intention of building an equitable structure in education, employment, and governance.

Yet, the journey of reservation has never been simple. It exists at the crossroads of justice and resentment, of empowerment and backlash. While it has undoubtedly uplifted many lives and opened doors for representation and dignity, it has also sparked questions about merit, fairness, and unity. These tensions become even more complex in a dynamic democracy like India, where the social, economic, and political layers are deeply intertwined.

This book explores the reservation policy not just as a legal framework, but as a living reality that reflects the socio-cultural complexities of India. It delves into how caste and class influence democratic processes, how historical injustices continue to shape present inequalities, and how institutions function under the weight of such legacy. The text brings forward the intersection of social behavior with political decision-making, and how the power structures maintain or challenge the status quo.

Further, this work discusses the empowerment of marginalized communities in the face of globalization, modern governance, and shifting political narratives. It looks at the challenges of policy implementation and the gap between legislation and ground realities. Equally important, it considers how religion, administration, and democratic practices intersect in shaping public life and opportunity distribution in India.

At its core, this book offers a balanced and research-backed understanding of reservation—not merely as a policy but as a reflection of India's attempt to reconcile its past with its vision of a just future.

This book will be particularly useful for students, researchers, policymakers, and those preparing for civil services or competitive exams. It provides deep insights into the historical, social, and administrative aspects of reservation and development, making it valuable for both academic study and practical understanding of Indian democracy.

– ***S.N. Ambedkar***

1

Social System Influences Political System : A Comparative Study of Sub-continent

Contextual Analysis

Social system of a nation based on local culture. Culture is the practical aspect of a nation's theories. Culture is a way of life including general customs and beliefs of a particular group of people in a particular territory. Social system of sub-continent is a blend of many cultures. Impacts of Dravidians, Aryans, Greece, Mongols, Arabs and Turk Muslims and British cultures are seemed but the Aryan culture looks dominant. One of the most controversial topics regarding the Indian and Pakistani society and culture is its stringent caste system. Caste system is part of our political culture. Components of political culture are attitudes, beliefs, values and behaviour relate to political system. Political Culture is the attitudes, feelings and values which underpin the operation of a particular political system; these were seen as including knowledge and skills about the operation of the political system. Positive and negative emotional feelings towards it.

Every political system has its own culture and political parties work according to the culture. Culture: The set of attitudes, beliefs and sentiments which give order and meaning to a political process and which provide the underlying assumptions and rules that govern behaviour in a political system. It encompasses both the political ideals and operating norms of a polity. Political culture is thus the manifestation in aggregate form of the psychological and subjective dimensions of politics. A political culture is the product of both the collective history of a political system and the life histories of the members of the system and thus it is rooted equally in public events and private experience. This process exists in ever system according to the behaviour of its culture, and the political education. The caste system is a social system in which people are divided into separate communities, known in English as castes and zat\biradari in Pakistan. The word caste is derived from the Portuguese or Spanish word casta, meaning lineage, pure or chaste, breed or race. It can be defined as a rigid social system in which a social hierarchy is maintained generation after generation and allows little mobility out of the position to which a person is born. Castes are further divided into sub-castes, (zat in Pakistan) which are more important in terms of their impact on daily lives of people. The offspring of ancestor belong to the same caste and collection of castes is called biradari.

Those who belongs to Zats form a Biradri, which is the specific socio cultural unit within which caste rules are performed" Biradari (literally 'brotherhood') is commonly argued that 'primordial' group identities such as family, kinship and caste, or membership in a village faction, play a more important role in determining voting behaviour in the sub-continent, than individual political preferences.

Historical Notes

Caste system has existed throughout history and throughout the world. In France as in Britain, if you're born into the working class you'll probably stay there. One of the strongest patterns of Japanese history is its long domination by clans and their leaders. Japanese pride themselves on their group orientation. Almost like a big family. Everyone has a place and must keep it 7.7 but the most well-known caste system today is in Indo-Pak Sub-Contenent.

Around one in 25 people in the world experiences some form of caste discrimination; more than half of these are in India and pakistan. This system dates almost 3600 years back and was formed on the need to form a social order in ancient India. It is still prevalent in Indian and Pakistani societies. Indo-Pak sub-continent is hailed as one of the most productive and dense regions of the world. The history of this region is as ancient as that of human history. Dravidians are the original inhabitants of Indo-Pak. It were Drawards who had laid a foundation of first civilization in ancient India. After Drawards the Aryans came. Aryan means gentle, a farmer and elevated caste. They were cultivators. The Aryans came from Central Asia and so were undoubtedly light skinned.

Gobineau argued that the Aryans had been a nomadic people superior to all other races. The original caste system came into existence when the Aryans migrated from the North to India around 1600.B.C The Aryans were divided into three castes, Brahmana (the priests and the teachers) Khashtriya (administrators and military men) and Vaishya (traders, merchants, businessmen and farmers). The local people were called Shudras.

When Aryan clans came; some groups of the local population had made tribal organizations. Some Aryans mingled in these tribal groups. So, the division of castes among Aryan clans came into existence after the complex blend of native and Aryans. The Aryan discrimination could not be eradicated in the era of the Muslim rulers in India, but the Muslims were also divided into high or low castes.

The Turk, Afghan and Arab division and superiority complex of the ruling Muslims converted the local Muslims into biradaries and these people were divided into many sub-castes related to the names of their fore fathers, which adopted the shape of biradari later. The reality is that people had been bound in social and tribal customs instead of religious regulations. Local Indian Muslims reacted and challenged the so-called superiority of Arabic, Iranian, Afghani and Mughal races.

Newly Muslims were free from the chains of caste and class but their feeling did not end and they adopted new kinds of caste and class system (Biradarism). Muslim society during this period was dominated by the Turkish rulers and nobles who sought to maintain their positions, not only against non-Muslims and Muslims of local origin, but also against other non-Turkish immigrants. Out of the four groups, which had played a prominent part in the establishment of Muslim rule, the Turks, the Tajiks, the

Khaljis and the Afghans, the Tajiks were eliminated from key positions soon after the death of Iltutmish. The Khaljis (apart from the shortlived burst of glory in distant Bengal) did not come into their own until the revelries of Kaiqubad destroyed the fabric of Turkish supremacy, and the Afghans had to wait till the day of the Lodis.

The first hundred years of Delhi Sultanate are a period of Turkish supremacy. The struggle or war of survival became the main cause of biradarism in Muslims. After the Muslims, the English used this social setup in order to prolong their rule in India. The English had not only accepted their social and political status, but also they did their best to make them stronger whatever they could do. For instance, they depended on the loyalty of the clans and communities in lieu of using their class fidelity for their own sake. The British attitude of controlling Punjab politically became the cause of the Biradarism. Colonial policies that distinguished and discriminated along the basis of caste and biradari consideration were also taken into account by colonial administrators while drawing district and sub-district administrative boundaries.

Indian Caste System

The dominating ideology in a society has always been an important determinant in determining the nature of the political system at national as well as at local levels. In India caste plays an important role during election. Its impacts on social and political system of India can be seen on daily lives. Hindu philosopher Kotlia Chankia (Morya era) suggests that ruler should deal everyone according to his caste and people should perform their duties under caste convention.

Caste-based politics still has strong roots in many Indian states. At most times, conversions to other religions like Christianity, or Islam, does not result in end of caste identity due to deep social stratification and lack of social mobility. I.P.Desai had pointed out that conversions to Islam or Christianity did not make any difference to their status at the local level because the dominant upper Hindus castes continued to treat them as before. Under the impact of the centuries old caste system, Indian political system has also followed caste based imperatives. The majority of the Hindu society comprises of 'backward classes', and with the passage of time, the number of these backward categories grew, from 39 in 1875 to 128 in 1950, and 175 by 1960. The lower castes are provided opportunities through a system called "reservations", in which they are provided with quotas in jobs and educations. Between 20-25% of all opportunities in higher education are reserved for the "scheduled castes".

This system has been given legal protection by dividing government jobs into castes in which 22.5 percent quota has been specified for lower castes. This quota is increased in 1990 according to Mandal commission Report 1971, on 49.5 percent, which became the cause of the removal of the government of V.P. Singh. The very important aspect of Indian Political system is Casteism. Castes support their candidates in order to defend their rights in elections and they expect for them the same attitude in legislative assembly. S.N.Roy observes the situation in these words; "Social groups chose their M.P (Members of Parliament) with their support and they, then expect to them that they will bring their demands to the government and secure their benefits such as recruitment and transfer of the local officers, police station, and court for the solution of the local problems.

Their control seems to be active on provincial and especially on district politics. The social base of politics has become significantly broaden. Many of the political parties and groups on national, regional, state and local levels draw their main support from certain segments of Indian society and are in effect political manifestations of deep-rooted social institutions and pratices. Biradarism In Pakistan, especially in Punjab the dominating factor of the social system is biradarism. It impacts the political system at national as well as at local levels. Biradari is a stronger determinant of voting behaviour than party allegiance, except when the two major candidates are from the same biradari. The initial tendency is to treat caste as the primary determinant of voting behaviour. The local bodies' elections are held only on biradari base, so biradari makes decision before, and then the election campaign is begun, and soon after individual annoyed family is compelled to cast their vote to the candidate of biradari.

People in the countryside think in terms of biradaris (tribes and 22 clans); those in urban areas stick to sectarian and ethnic identities. There are also people who view the world divided on religious lines. The problem arises when the state fails to make a balance and plays a role in imposing value system of the one on the other" In local bodies' elections (non-party) biradari plays pivotal role. Major biradaris in Punjab are Jatts, Rajputs, Araiens, Gujjars, Sayads and Baloch Heads of district government in Punjab are from major biradaris.

In northern Punjab, rajput biradari looks dominant. Jatts are in majority in central Punjab and also sharing in southern Punjab. Arains are sharing in central Punjab while Balochs are dominating in southern Punjab. This trend effects the out put of political system of Pakistan. The reason is that local bodies' elections are being held on non-party base. In Britain councilors are commonly members of a party group.

The majority party's leader became the chair of the council. A good deal of biradri "ticket balancing" is done between the candidates for a National Assembly seat and the several provincial assembly constituencies within each. The importance of biradari is most apparent when political parties are selecting National and Provincial Assembly candidates. Zia's policies (non-party elections and local bodies) made it stronger at national, provincial and local level. The non-party elections were held in 1985. This setup of Zia-ul-Haq divided the nation into groups and biradaris. Perhaps, the objects of these elections were to divide the nation into groups and biradaris. In this election the majority of the members of Provincial Assembly (Punjab, 124 out of 240) were from local bodies. Wilder writes about these elections," Local identities and local issues became the substance of Punjab politics.

Political loyalties were increasingly determined by family, faction, and biradari ties, and political power was determined by the amount of patronage at one's disposal. A class system of 'machine politics' developed where politics consisted not of formulating and implementing public policies or concerning oneself with the national interest, but in assisting constituent with thana-katchahry (police station and courtside) problems, introducing local community development schemes, and in doing out patronage in the form of government jobs, welfare funds, contracts, licenses, loans and land. Have a Zia's strategy of diverting political energy from national to local issues had the intended effect.

The political role of biradaris, which had been virtually eliminated in the 1970 elections, again increased in Pakistani politics. And MNAs were converted into glorified councillors, whose days were spent not dealing with national issues, but with writing chits to get their constituents a job or into a hospital, or a Thana." One of General Zia's most durable political legacies, and perhaps the one that has been the most harmful to the political parties, was the 'localization of politics'.

This shifted political attention away from national politics. Local groups became active and participate as a representative of political parties but through dominating bradaries. One of the reasons behind this is the presence of dominant biradaris which dilute the hostility between the political parties. These biradaris are more active and effective than the political parties. Non political powers and martial law's interruption in Pakistan has weaken the political parties and the people depended on groups. Biradari is stronger than any other group, because biradri unity is easy and durable than any ideological unity.

This is why, in making this unity to face financial problems, to get to jails (as politicians faced in Pakistan) and to sacrifice one's life is no matter. Two particles are necessary for the victory of candidate, one is the ticket of major political party and the other is the favour of major biradari. The candidates take the help of biradari, because they want to succeed. They use every method for gaining success and the weapon of biradari is also used for success and on the other hand, the voters or councillors cast their votes voluntarily to their own biradari. Rootless democracy promoted clans politics and local bodies system make it stronger. Ayub's basic, Zia's root less democracy promoted biradarism and by holding party-less local bodies elections strengthen it.

Daily Mashriq write in its column that "Biradari politics is brightened in the non-party elections because the candidates have to take the votes". Dr. Muneer Ahmad examine the party base and non-party base elections in these words; "The candidate says in the party based election that "I am the member of P.P.P. give me the vote or I belong to Pakistan Muslim League, give me the vote", but, in the non-party elections he says that "I am Rajput, I am Jatt or I am Syed, give me the vote". Aabida Ismaail (1991) concludes in her thesis that "The non party elections have been contested in Punjab on the basis of personal, biradari and native level. "The percentage of voters who cast their vote to their biradari in local bodies is 50% and in national/provincial assemblies is 23% and the ratio of people agreed with the statement that non-party elections in Zia era promoted biradarism is 83%.

Review and Reflection

The main concern of this study has been the explanation of the role of culture in local politics with the references of Pakistan and India. Biradarism/casteism as a main component of this culture is discussed briefly. The origin of casteism is also discussed. It is concluded that culture impacts local politics. It is a reality that biradari politics is dominated factor in the political systems of India and Pakistan and it affects the process of political system. Cultural system plays vital role in local bodies system. It is human nature to exercise ethnic preference for their own group in the form of aggression against others.

Political parties are high jacked by biradaries and process of interest aggregation is limited. It presented a negative and aggressive violent style of thinking, behaving and realizing a political objective. Such situations rise if the original problems maintain and no remarkable revolution takes place. In such circumstances, tribal activists continue to appeal to the sense of insecurity of their group and political leaders make use of such a community in their power games. It is concluded that biradari makes decision of every aspect (Political, social) of life and individual is bound of this decision. Individual opinion is nothing in front of biradari.

The prominent biradaries have their hold in political decision making process. The vote is an element of family action. The family is nothing out of biradari. Every caste/biradari does not have equal status in the Pakistani and Indian societies.

Non political powers and non-party elections promoted biradarism in Pakistan and in India these factors are not found but their social system has impacts on Indian political system. Caste system provides security to eminent castes. It gives them an identity and security that not reveal in Western social system. As the Hindu nationalism grew, the Hindu elite class focused increasing attention to religious revival. This led to increase in inter-caste discrimination and this often erupted into violence. The deep rooted impacts of biradarism are seen in Pakistani political system particularly in Punjab. Some advantages of biradarism in Pakistan are also found in the study. Biradarism assumes the status of the central character in non-party elections. It fills the gap of political parties. It is a type of contest which is essential feature of democracy. In Pakistan even the biradari system provides security and power for millions of its members but these biradari groups are a threat to popular government. The continuity in the party base general elections can reduce this tendency. The stability of political system depends on the political socialization which is the most important link between the social and political system by which political culture is maintained and changed. The role of biradaries in 2008 elections in Pakistan is eliminated.

2

Democratic Practice and Social Inequality in India

Ideals, Institutions and Practice

In assessing the past achievements and future potential of Indian democracy, it is useful to distinguish between democratic ideals, democratic institutions, and democratic practice. Democratic ideals represent various aspects of the broad idea of "government of the people, by the people and for the people." They include political characteristics that can be seen to be intrinsically important in terms of the objective of democratic social living, such as freedom of expression, participation of the people in deciding on the factors governing their lives, public accountability of leaders, and an equitable distribution of power. Democratic institutions go beyond these basic intents, and include such instrumental arrangements as constitutional rights, effective courts, responsive electoral systems, functioning parliaments and assemblies, open and free media, and participatory institutions of local governance.

While democratic institutions provide opportunities for achieving democratic ideals, how these opportunities are realized is a matter of democratic practice. The latter depends inter alia on the extent of political participation, the awareness of the public, the vigour of the opposition, the nature of political parties and popular organizations, and various determinants of the distribution of power. Both democratic institutions and democratic practice are important in achieving democracy in the fuller sense, but the presence of the former does not guarantee the latter.

In terms of democratic institutions, India has done reasonably well, and this may look particularly impressive in the international perspective, given the failure of many countries to secure even the most elementary constituents of a democratic institutional structure. Earlier democratic institutions in India—often stretching back in history—were decisively consolidated within the constitutional framework soon after independence in 1947. It is often forgotten how radical the Indian constitution was in those days, especially in light of the limited reach of democracy elsewhere in the world. It is not just that most other developing countries were still under the yoke of colonialism and authoritarianism at that time. Even economically advanced countries still lacked the political freedoms guaranteed by the Indian constitution in many cases. In 1947, when India achieved independence, women were still deprived of universal and equal voting rights in many "developed" countries (Belgium, Canada, Switzerland, and the United States, among others). In Switzerland, women were twenty-four years away from the right to vote. In the United States, African Americans too were effectively deprived of equal voting rights (through systematic denial of the opportunity to register and vote), and state-sponsored racial discrimination (e.g., the prohibition of inter-racial marriages as well as racial segregation in public places) was widespread; it took a protracted civil rights movement, lasting until the late 1960s, to overcome these suppressions of basic democratic freedoms. In other countries of Western Europe and North America, elected parliaments often coexisted uncomfortably with lingering monarchies and also conceded temporal powers to church authorities. These "irregularities" (in terms of democratic norms) continue to this day in many cases, in contrast to India where the constitution made a clean sweep of feudalism and laid solid foundations for a modern secular democracy.

India was also among the first countries to include legislation aimed at affirmative action to combat the lasting influence of past social inequalities. The "reservations" and other priorities for scheduled castes (formerly, the "untouchables") and scheduled tribes expanded the horizon of legal support for social equity, no matter how we judge the exact achievements and failures of this early departure. Affirmative action would not become a serious possibility in the United States for many years after the Indian constitution (which had many affirmative provisions) came into effect in 1950.

What is more, India's democratic institutions have—on the whole—stood the test of time and popular support. In the early stages of Indian independence, there was widespread scepticism about the ability of democratic institutions to survive, let alone flourish, in a poverty-stricken and inequality-ridden country. There was also much pessimism about the potential for democracy in the "third world" as a whole. In both respects, the outlook is much brighter today. India's democratic institutions have proved quite robust (even surviving major challenges such as the imposition of "emergency" in 1975 to 1977, which was reversed by a popular electoral vote), and enjoy wide legitimacy among most sections of the population. The healthy survival of Indian democracy has also given a major boost to the spread of democracy elsewhere in the world.

Furthermore, the institutional basis of democracy in India has retained some dynamism, particularly reflected in the fact that emendations and extensions have been instituted with some regularity. Since the constitution came into effect in 1950, various constitutional amendments have further enlarged the scope of democratic freedoms. For instance, the 73rd and 74th constitutional amendments (the "panchayati raj" amendments), which came into effect in 1993, have consolidated the foundations for local democracy.

Much, of course, remains to be done, and there is scope for further institutional democratization in the future. The right to information, for instance, remains severely restricted, and greater accessibility of official records is a needed step for fuller public accountability. Similarly, provisions for a better political representation of women are needed to address today's blatant male domination of many democratic institutions, from parliament to panchayat (village council). There is also much scope for more equitable electoral rules, better safeguards against human rights violations, more decentralized governance, and so on.

The main limitations of Indian democracy do not, however, relate so much to democratic institutions as to democratic practice.

The performance of democratic institutions is contingent on a wide range of social conditions, from educational levels and political traditions to the nature of social inequalities and popular organizations. Democratic practice in India has often been deeply compromised by a variety of social limitations inherited from the past. To illustrate, consider one of the most basic democratic freedoms-the right to vote. India has an impressive electoral system (monitored by an independent Election Commission), which has proved its credibility and resilience on numerous occasions since independence. Voter turnouts in India are also quite respectable by international standards, especially among underprivileged groups. However, the right to vote is not a momentous freedom when voters are so poorly informed that they are unable to distinguish between different political parties, as is still the case in some areas today. Similarly, while Indian elections are formally "free and fair" in most cases, their effective fairness has been compromised by nepotism, the criminalization of politics, and pervasive inequalities in electoral opportunities as a result of disparities in economic wealth and social privileges.

Another example concerns the legal system. An impartial and efficient judiciary is indispensable for genuine democracy. India's legal system has sound institutional foundations, which incorporate basic democratic principles such as impartiality, secularism, and equality before the law. In practice, however, its functioning is, in many ways, at variance with democratic ideals. For one thing, the legal system is virtually paralyzed by a backlog of millions of "pending cases"-about 30 million according to one estimate (Debroy 2000).

Legal proceedings can take years (if not decades) to be completed, and are often far from intelligible for the average citizen. For this and other reasons, legal protection tends to remain beyond the effective reach of most, especially the poor. In fact, the legal system can also be used as an instrument of harassment (rather than as an efficient means of dispensing justice). Those at the receiving end of the system can end up suffering terrible injustice. For instance, undertria l prisoners (there are some 250,000 of them in India at this time, according to the Home Ministry) often languish in prison for years without any legal recourse.

Similar points can be made about many other components of the democratic institutional structure. The Indian press has much to offer in terms of quality and pluralism, but with less than 10 percent of all households subscribing to a daily newspaper, its contribution to political awareness and public debate remains much below potential. In some states, the legislatures are packed with criminals. Village panchayats are often controlled by the local elite. There are many other failures of democratic practice.

On the positive side, it can indeed be said that there is enormous scope for improving the quality of democracy in India through better democratic practice (and also, to some extent, through expanding democratic institutions). Indeed, democratic practice constantly evolves, as new constituencies are mobilized, new issues come under public scrutiny, and new organizational skills are developed. To illustrate, until recently corruption was not much of a political issue in India. It was accepted as a familiar feature of public life, about which little could be done. In the 1990s, however, corruption became a matter of widespread concern and discussion after a wave of high-profile scams were exposed. Innovative campaigns for public accountability and the right to information sprung up in various parts of the country (Rajasthan, Maharashtra, Kerala, Madhya Pradesh, Orissa, among others), and have gradually developed into a major social movement. This has not, of course, led to an automatic eradication of corruption (far from it), but the issue is at least on the political agenda and there is much scope for securing practical results through harnessing this process. These campaigns, with their innovative focus and techniques (from public hearing to social audit), also signal a transformation of political culture, with much potential in other contexts as well. These developments would have seemed quite unlikely even ten years ago. The nineties have witnessed many other political developments of a similar nature, from pioneering experiments with decentralized planning in Kerala to the growing participation of women in local politics across the country.

As the recent developments show, in various ways, the reach of democratic practice can be radically enhanced in India. But the first step is to see the need for democratic practice as a distinct issue from the existence of democratic institutions. The sense of satisfaction at securing democratic institutions—justified within its context—must not be an excuse for failing to pursue vigorously the strengthening of democratic practice. The great accomplishments in the former do not obviate the need for vigilant pursuit of the latter. There is much scope for making institutionally democratic India more effectively democratic.

Inequality and Empowerment

It is useful to distinguish between different causes of the limitation of democratic practice. Given the democratic institutions, the practice of democracy may be limited for at least three distinct reasons. First, democratic institutions may become dysfunctional due to, say, corruption or inefficiency. Examples include electoral fraud and the paralysis of the legal system through case overload. Second, there may be inadequate use of functional democratic institutions on the part of concerned persons or groups, often due to limited understanding or skill, and sometimes even lack of motivation. Low electoral participation, and the powerlessness of the public in the face of complex legal proceedings, are some illustrations, among many others.

We have already commented briefly on these two deficiencies. We have also touched on the third reason for the failure of democratic practice, viz. the reach and power of antecedent social inequalities, but we must discuss it more. Democratic practice may indeed be thoroughly undermined by social inequalities, even when democratic institutions are all in place. For instance, even if elections are technically free and fair, their effective fairness may be compromised by the role of money and influence in the electoral process. This also applies to the legal system, which is often far from impartial between different classes (even in the absence of any corruption), if only because richer people can afford better lawyers.

At the risk of some over-simplification, the foundations of democratic practice may, thus, be described as facility (functional democratic institutions), involvement (informed public engagement with these institutions), and equity (a fair distribution of power). The central relevance of equity arises from the fact that a fair distribution of power is a basic—indeed fundamental—requirement of democracy. A government "by the people" must ultimately include all the people in a symmetric way, and this is essential also to enable the government to become "of the people and for the people." This is not, of course, a question of the "yes or no" type. In most societies, it is the case that a person's ability to use electoral rights, to obtain legal protection, to express oneself in public, and to take advantage of democratic institutions in general tends to vary with class, education, gender, and related characteristics. In striving for democratic ideals, reducing the asymmetries of power associated with these social inequalities is one of the central challenges of democratic practice in every institutionally democratic country in the world. That challenge is particularly exacting in India, given its historical economic and social inequalities.

It is, however, important to see the reach of inequality in adequately broad terms. The relevant inequalities can be of very different types. In economic analysis, the lion's share of attention tends to go to the inequality of individual income levels. This is indeed an important part of economic inequality. However, economic inequality is a more inclusive—far larger—concept than mere income inequality, and inequality in the fuller sense goes even beyond economic inequality, no matter how broadly the latter may be defined. There are many economic determinants, other than income, of well-being, freedom, and power, and there are social factors—distinct from purely economic ones-that influence inequality between persons and groups.

There has been much discussion in recent years on the discrepancy between measures of income inequality and a broader understanding of the multidimensional nature of economic and social inequality. The contrast can be illustrated through inter-regional comparisons of social inequality in India. For example, the Gini coefficient of the distribution of per-capita expenditures indicates that there is more inequality in Kerala than in, say, Bihar or Uttar Pradesh. In fact, Kerala turns out to be one of the most unequal states in this respect, while Bihar is one of the least unequal. The figures may well be correct as far as they go (even though many conceptual and practical difficulties arise in the computation of these coefficients). But if we were to rely on them for an overall assessment of social disparities in different states, we would be deeply misled. The broader picture of social and economic inequality must also note, inter alia, the fact that Kerala has (1) comparatively low levels of basic gender inequality (reflected, for instance, in a high female-male ratio), (2) relatively equitable educational opportunities (indeed near-universal literacy, especially among the young), (3) extensive social security arrangements (e.g., broad-based entitlements to homestead land, old-age pensions and the public distribution system), (4) limited incidence of caste oppression (e.g., few violent crimes against scheduled castes), and (5) low rural-urban disparities. In all these respects, Kerala does radically better than Bihar and Uttar Pradesh, which are ridden with inequalities between women and men, between child labourers and school-going children, between low castes and high castes, and so on. And yet these states do better than Kerala in terms of indicators of income inequality seen as a factor on its own. As this example illustrates, there is much need for a broad understanding of economic and social inequality.

These distinctions are particularly important in understanding the nature of inequality and also the problems of democratic practice in India. Indeed, indicators of income inequality, seen on their own, can be a very deceptive basis for grasping the far-reaching consequences of inequality on Indian lives and democratic practice. They can also hide the diverse ways in which more equity can be pursued through state policy and public action.

Consider, for instance, the pattern of inequality in Indian society during the last forty years or so. Judging from standard indices of income distribution, there has been little change. The Gini coefficient of per-capita expenditure, for instance, has remained fairly close to .30 in rural areas and .35 in urban areas throughout that period. This is, however, deceptive as a guide to inequality for two distinct reasons.

First, it overlooks the new developments of inequality that have added to the burden of the older, pre-existing ones. For example, the hold of the newly prosperous and socially influential middle classes escapes notice in the constancy of the Gini coefficient of income distribution. Through dominance over the media, political pressure groups and even instruments of knowledge, this flourishing, vocal and (in absolute numbers) fairly large class enjoys new powers that very few groups could have had in the past, in using the levers of democratic politics. The world has been changing, even if the Gini has not.

Second, the remarkable stickiness of the measures of income inequality over a long period suggests a kind of inescapable immutability of inequality which hides the possibility of change and progress through public policy and social action. Indeed, the stationarity of income inequality is often invoked to argue that attempts to achieve greater equality are likely to be futile, and that economic growth (increasing the size of the pie, rather than altering the shares) is the only effective way of raising living standards. But neither the pessimism about altering inequality, nor the faith in economic growth as the only effective means of improving the lot of the deprived, is entailed by the empirical picture of income distribution.

Indeed, even in terms of India's actual experience, the constancy of income inequality indicators during the post-independence period has gone hand in hand with some fairly major changes—often with much positive achievement—in other kinds of economic and social disparities. For instance, upper-caste dominance in the rural economy and society has been decisively challenged with the abolition of zamindari, the introduction of adult franchise, economic progress among the cultivating castes, and various political movements. Correspondingly, there has been a major rise in the economic and political power of the so-called "backward castes" (and, to a lesser extent, of scheduled castes). Similarly, the slow but steady march towards universal elementary education has eroded one of the crucial bases of social stratification in India, namely the exclusion of disadvantaged classes and castes from the schooling system. Even in terms of gender relations (perhaps one of the more resilient domains of social inequalit y in India), there have been some major developments in recent years, involving for instance the emergence of a female advantage in life expectancy (overturning a long history of superior male longevity), a radical diminution of oppressive practices such as child marriage, and growing participation of women in local politics. Other ongoing changes, such as the steady decline of fertility, the accelerated increase in female literacy, and new constitutional provisions for the political representation of women, are likely to facilitate further progress towards more equal gender relations.

No less eminent a sociologist as M.N. Srinivas has even suggested that we are "living in a revolution" (Srinivas 1992). Even if we do not accept such optimism about the recent changes (there are fields of stationarity as well as transformation), the last fifty years have certainly been a time of significant change in India's social structure. There is nothing in the record of India's last half a century that would vindicate the thesis of the futility of changing the hold of antecedent economic and social inequalities in India. The rejection of social fatalism and the cynicism that it generates can be extremely important for motivating attempts to work against pre-existing inequalities and for the enhancement of democratic practice.

One crucial implication of this broader perspective on economic and social inequality is that it points to many different ways of countering inequalities in Indian society. The reduction of income inequality is a difficult challenge in India as elsewhere, partly due to incentive problems (e.g., the possible need for a link between productivity and reward), and partly because of the resistance of privileged classes. But there is no corresponding reason to tolerate widespread gender discrimination, the continued oppression of disadvantaged castes, the persistent divide between the literates and the non-literates, and other destructive economic and social inequalities. Indeed, the dilemmas that arise in reducing economic inequality (in particular, possible conflicts between efficiency and equity) often have little force in addressing these inequalities. In fact, in many circumstances, distributional concerns are highly congruent with other social objectives, including economic efficiency. Reduced gender discrimination, for instance, expands the scope of women's agency, which is an important factor of social change and economic success. The congruence between distributional concerns and other social objectives is also striking in the context of basic education. Indeed, the universalization of elementary education in India would not only reduce educational disparities (and other social inequalities associated with these disparities), but also contribute to a wide range of other economic and social objectives, given the diverse personal and social roles of education.

Achieving greater equity in Indian society depends crucially on political action and the practice of democracy. Indeed, a reduction of inequality both contributes to democratic practice and is strengthened by successful practice of democratic freedoms. There is, in fact, a "virtuous circle" here, the nature of which has to be more adequately reflected in policy analysis and social action in India. There have been, as was noted earlier, significant gains in that respect during the last fifty years, and while reductions of inequality have strengthened the reach of democratic practice, they have often been achieved through determined use of the democratic opportunities that were already available. Indeed, the achievements discussed earlier were often the result, at least in part, of democratic political action.

In some cases, these achievements have been facilitated by economic change. For instance, the rise of the "backward castes" has something to do with their growing economic prosperity, linked inter alia with the "green revolution" (and, before that, the abolition of zamindari). But even here, political action has played an important role, for instance, through farmers' movements as well as direct political participation.

In other cases, political action has succeeded in empowering disadvantaged social groups even in the absence of any significant economic improvement (sometimes even in the face of growing impoverishment). Not so long ago, for instance, tribal communities were routinely displaced by dams and other large projects without any compensation. The situation has radically changed over time, as displaced tribal communities learnt to organize against forced displacement (even though they have not invariably succeeded in changing public policy).

Today, this movement is among the most politically active and best organized in India, and is also a source of much inspiration elsewhere in the world. Whatever position one may take on the projects in question, the force of this movement cannot leave any impartial observer without a major recognition of the power and vigour of organized popular resistance.

Decentralization and Local Democracy

The interconnections between democratic practice and social equity have a strong bearing on recent initiatives to promote local democracy in India. These initiatives have taken place in the framework of the 73rd and 74th constitutional amendments (the "panchayati raj" amendments), which require all the state governments to introduce certain legislative measures geared to the revitalization of local representative institutions. These measures include mandatory elections at regular intervals, reservation of seats in village panchayats for women and members of scheduled castes or tribes, and substantial devolution of government responsibilities to local authorities. The panchayati raj amendments, which took effect in 1993, have led to a range of interesting initiatives in different parts of the country, undertaken not only by state governments but also by political parties, NGQs, grassroots organizations, women's groups, and other activist formations. There is a great deal to learn from recent developments associated with these initiatives.

Achieving greater democracy at the local level must be a crucial component of the broader task of transforming the practice and quality of democracy in India. Indeed, local democracy represents one means of participation in the larger democratic system, which is relatively accessible to the disadvantaged, and can be potentially a stepping-stone towards other forms of democratic participation. Local democracy is also essential as a basis of public accountability, particularly in the context of the need for effective and equitable management of local public services. These services—from schools and health centres to fair price shops and drinking-water facilities—are often crucial for the quality of life. Their effective functioning, however, depends a great deal on the responsiveness of the concerned authorities to popular demands. To illustrate, it is difficult to see how the endemic problem of teacher absenteeism in rural India can be successfully tackled without involving the proximate and informed agency of village communities in general and parental groups in particular. As things stand, there is no mechanism to ensure any kind of accountability of village teachers to the local community or to the parents in large parts of India, and this is an important factor in the persistence of endemic dereliction of duty. The importance of local democracy is not confined, of course, to these and other instrumental roles of participatory politics. Participation can also be seen to have intrinsic value for the quality of life. Indeed, being able to do something through political action—for oneself and for others—is one of the elementary freedoms that people have reason to value. The popular appeal of many social movements in India confirms that this basic capability is highly valued even among people who lead very deprived lives in material terms.

Local democracy is sometimes treated as synonymous with "decentralization," but the two are in fact quite distinct. In particular, decentralization is not necessarily conducive to local democracy. In fact, in situations of sharp local inequalities, decentralization sometimes heightens the concentration of power, and discourages rather than fosters participation among the underprivileged. To illustrate, in some tribal areas where upper-caste landlords and traders dominate village affairs, the devolution of power associated with the panchayati raj amendments has consolidated their hold and reinforced existing biases in the local power structure.

Similarly, top-down decentralization sometimes undermines local democracy by destabilizing traditional institutions of governance and fostering corruption. An interesting example comes from a recent case study of two villages of Uttarakhand, the hill region of Uttar Pradesh (now Uttaranchal, a separate state), discussed by Niraja Jayal (1999b). The study villages earlier had fairly democratic traditional institutions of local governance, based among other things on consensus decision-making and egalitarian contributions to village funds. Then came state-sponsored panchayat elections and "decentralized" development programmes, one effect of which was the integration of these villages into a wider system of prevailing corruption, in which these programmes are embedded. This process undermined local democracy and also created sharp social divisions in the villages studied.

Recognition of these dangers should not be seen as an overall indictment of decentralization. There is undoubtedly much need for decentralized governance in India, especially in relation to the management of local public services, where responsiveness to local conditions is paramount. But we must also recognize that the effects of decentralization are highly context-dependent and circumstance-specific, and that its success depends on decentralization being integrated with other aspects of local democracy. A similar observation applies to the panchayati raj amendments. These amendments, like other democratic institutions, have provided a great opportunity to expand the scope of democracy in Indian society, but their practical results have varied a great deal depending on the extent to which institutional reform has been combined with other types of public action.

Recent studies of the developments associated with the panchayati raj amendments in different parts of the country throw much light and these and related issues. It is, first and foremost, very encouraging to find plentiful evidence of active engagement with the new possibilities of local democracy on the part of the Indian public. By all accounts, panchayat elections elicit keen public interest. Voter turnout rates have been high in most states (even higher than in parliamentary or assembly elections), including among underprivileged groups. This is a sea of change from the days when members of the lower castes were prevented from voting, or when women were not expected to cast an independent vote. Beyond electoral participation, public interest and involvement in local governance has risen markedly during the last few years, even in areas where apathy used to be widespread.

However, the experience so far confirms that the results of state initiatives to promote local democracy are highly contingent on the social context. Indeed, the reforms associated with the panchayati raj amendments have followed very different courses in different states. At one extreme, Bihar has barely reached the stage of organizing panchayat elections. Kerala, on the other hand, has gone far beyond the constitutional requirements and initiated a visionary campaign of "decentralized planning" through panchayati raj institutions. Even among states that have followed a similar course in terms of legislative reform, the practical results have varied a great deal depending on the extent of social preparedness in terms of educational levels, political mobilization, and social equity. The issue of social preparedness has emerged quite clearly in states like Madhya Pradesh, where (unlike Bihar) the state has been constructively active in legislative reforms, yet the practical results have been held back by the antecedent social inequalities, educational backwardness and other bafflers inherited from the past.

The panchayati raj experience highlights the importance of social equity for local democracy, and also the interactive relationship between the two. This can be seen particularly clearly in connection with the issue of political representation of women and disadvantaged castes at the panchayat level. The 73rd amendment stipulates that one-third of all panchayat seats are "reserved" for women, with a similar (overlapping) provision for scheduled castes and tribes. In north India, where caste and gender inequalities are particularly resilient, the local elites have tended to adapt to this requirement by putting up "proxy" candidates from the required group, and continuing to wield power through them. In south and western India, the overall picture is quite different in this respect, with greater success in terms of independent political representation of women and scheduled castes. It must, however, be noted that even in north India, there is considerable evidence that the prevailing patterns of social discrimination and political marginalization are far from immutable.

Local politics, and the different forms of political mobilization and social activism associated with panchayati raj (for example, training programmes for female candidates and political assertion of the scheduled castes), have provided new avenues through which traditional inequalities can be challenged. The fact that these challenges have often been met with violent repression (including even cases of rape of assertive female sarpanchs) is both a telling reminder of the survival of extreme inequality and oppression in Indian society, and an indication that the politics of panchayati raj are perceived as a serious threat by dominant groups. Over time, the forces of repression seem to be losing some ground, with good prospects of further advance in the direction of both greater social equity and more vibrant local democracy in the near future.

These developments illustrate a crucial feature of local democracy—indeed of democracy in general—namely that it involves a certain amount of "learning by doing." Other aspects of this process include the influence of role models (for example, of a successful female sarpanch), the spread of various skills involved in local governance (e.g., the ability to hold orderly meetings or to deal with the bureaucracy), the evolution of a culture of political participation, the creation of new forms of social mobilization, and even changes in public perceptions of the need for as well as scope for foundational change. Given the dynamism of learning by doing, it is important to resist the pessimism arising from observing particular limitations in the current practice of local democracy. The constructive possibilities over time have to be recognized.

In the light of these learning possibilities, the first wave of social change associated with the panchayati raj amendments warrants cautious optimism about the potential for local democracy in India. There are, of course, also matters of concern. These include the frequent derailing of local democracy by social inequality, the limited participation of the public in local governance on a day-today basis, the dormant condition of gram sabhas (village assemblies) in many states, the lack of significant devolution of powers in many fields, and—last but not least—the widespread embezzlement of public resources associated with local development programmes under panchayat auspices. Nevertheless, there are clear signs of a sustained expansion of democratic space at the local level, and also of local politics being an important arena of positive social change. The limitations are best addressed through democratic practice itself, and as far as the potential for the latter is concerned, there is much ground for hope.

Transparency and Corruption

One of the major challenges that democratic practice has to face in India is to eradicate corruption in different fields of civic administration and public life. Among its many terrible consequences, rampant corruption erodes and undermines democratic institutions. Indeed, democratic institutions cannot perform their role adequately if the actions of political leaders, civil servants, police officers, judges and others can be mobilized in defence of private and special interests through illegal inducements. The effect of corruption on ethical codes and social norms also tends to be antithetical to democratic values. And yet democracy itself can be seen as a possible means to fight corruption that can be—and must be—used more effectively. Democratic ideals include the need for transparency and accountability, which are ultimately the principal methods of restraining and dislodging corrupt practices. There is, thus, a two-way relationship between the practice of democracy and the eradication of corruption. The former can help the latter, but the latter, in its turn, can be of great value in extending the force and effectiveness of the former.

In India, the adverse effects of corruption on democracy have come into sharp focus in recent years in connection with issues of local governance and village politics. While there have been promising steps towards local democracy in the nineties (as discussed in the preceding section), one of the major barriers against further progress has been the prevalence of widespread corruption, particularly related to development programmes and electoral processes. To illustrate, consider the issue of panchayat elections.

In most states the main responsibility of a sarpanch (village head) is to oversee various development programmes, such as the Jawahar Rozgar Yojana (local public works) and the Indira Awas Yojana (a subsidized housing scheme). Attached to these schemes, in many cases, is an organized system of loot of public resources, which requires the sarpanch to "redistribute" some of the development funds to various officials, varying from the "gram sevak" (village-level worker) to the Junior Engineer, Block Deve lopment Officer, and others at different steps of the ladder. Often the shares are pre-specified. The sarpanch himself or herself, of course, tends to be one of the principal beneficiaries. The post of village head can be, under these circumstances, highly lucrative. This is one reason why large sums of money are spent in panchayat election campaigns. Where these patterns apply, local electoral politics are thus integrally linked with various development rackets, and can even generate what might be called "competitive corruption."

This nexus undermines local democracy in several ways. First, it raises the up-front cost of election campaigns, making it more difficult for poor candidates to participate. Second, this situation can make it very difficult for an honest person motivated by social concerns to contest panchayat elections.

Indeed, unlike candidates geared to corruption, an aspiring candidate who wants to forgo the opportunity of replenishing his or her coffers after a successful election is financially at a disadvantage in the electoral competition. In addition, honest candidates often face the prospect of official harassment for refusing to cooperate with the system of corruption. Third, the task of plundering public resources, distributing commissions and avoiding scrutiny distracts the panchayats from their primary purpose of working for the public good in the area under their jurisdiction. A sarpanch, for example, often has far more to gain from awarding Indira Awas Yojana subsidies to the highest bidders than from res ponding to the social need for an electricity connection for the village, or from organizing a school enrolment drive.

The "systemic" nature of the corruption arrangements associated with local development is one reason why they are difficult to eradicate: even if one individual culprit is disciplined and punished, another tends to step into his or her shoes. Another barrier to their eradication relates to the fact that the embezzlers (e.g., the sarpanch and private contractor who collude to build a school at half the official cost and pocket the difference) tend to gain at the expense of the public at large.

It has been argued, not without reason, that in such situations (known in the economic literature by the somewhat puzzling name of "corruption with theft") corruption may be particularly hard to eradicate.

Indeed, since the losing group consists of a diffuse and typically unorganized collectivity, the losers may find it difficult to take joint action with adequate effectiveness. Vigilance may, of course, be entrusted to a public agency (on the basis of crosschecks, inspections, audits, and so on), but that supervising agency may often have little incentive to dig deep, which can be bothersome and even dangerous, given the power of the private gainers, compared with the often-inert mass of public losers.

But this is exactly where the remedial use of democracy can be important. The losers may be inactive and hard to mobilize, but once mobilized, the weight of numbers as well as the force of public opinion and open criticism can be quite effective. The practical possibility of such mobilization has been demonstrated in many actual cases. A good illustration comes from the work of such organizations as Mazdoor Kisan Shakti Sangathan (MKSS) in Rajasthan. The movement began in 1987 by organizing underpaid labourers working on drought relief programmes (who can be seen as victims of "corruption without theft," and were to that extent comparatively easy to mobilize). Following this early success, MKSS started mobilizing village communities against the private appropriation of local development funds (corruption with theft), using means such as public hearings and social audits. The organization has considerable popular support and has achieved some striking successes, involving for instance the restitution of e mbezzled funds. Over time, it has inspired many similar initiatives elsewhere, from a campaign to expose corruption in the public distribution system in Surguja (Madhya Pradesh) to recent protests against police harassment of rickshaw-pullers and hawkers in Indian cities. A nation-wide "campaign for the people's right to information," which includes lobbying for adequate legislative reform in this field, has also emerged from these initiatives.

The significance of these movements goes well beyond specific victories such as the restitution of embezzled funds in a particular village, or the introduction of new legislation in a specific state. The demonstration effects can have a much wider reach. Even in areas where no such organizations existed earlier, public initiatives to expose corruption have begun to spread in recent years, with significant results. It has been noted, for instance, that drought relief programmes in Rajasthan in 2000 to 2001 have been remarkably "corruption-free" (at least in comparison with the situation that prevailed in earlier droughts), largely due to greater public vigilance as well as to the improved accessibility of official records-both of which are closely related to the "right to information" movement (Dreze 2001). This is a major achievement, especially in the light of widespread scepticism about the possibility of eradicating corruption in India, and there is a major lesson here about the possibility of achieving wider changes in social norms through local action. In all this, there is reason for hope, since there is some prospect that public vigilance may become an integral part of the political culture in many Indian villages.

Accountability and Countervailing Power

The importance of public vigilance at the village level in curbing corruption, discussed in the last section, is just one example of the general role of vigilance, which can operate at different levels (not just related to local governance), and can be aimed at many different objectives (not just the prevention of corruption). Indeed, even in curbing corruption, vigilance is needed at other levels as well, including non-local politics (involving the operation of organized parties), broader cooperative activities (involving grassroots initiatives), appropriate state policies (involving incentives, monitoring, sanctions, etc.), and so on. Vigilance is crucial to accountability, which in its turn is central to efficiency and equity of public policies in different spheres.

The improvement of living conditions in developing countries depends a great deal on constructive public policies in various fields (basic education, health care, social security, nutritional support, environmental protection, gender equality, among others). And yet there are well-recognized inadequacies from which state actions tend systematically to suffer, as has been noted widely across the world. One problem is, often enough, the presence of persistent inefficiency, reflected in such phenomena as bureaucratic delay, breakdown of public services, lack of timeliness and certainty of delivery, and unusually high costs of operation. Inefficiency, in turn, has much to do with the lack of accountability in the public sector.

If, for example, a public health centre is closed on a work day, the patients may not have any simple means of taking remedial action. Of course, instruments of protest and censure do exist, at least in principle, such as sending a complaint to the local newspaper, or organizing a demonstration, or voting for a rival political party to the one in office, or perhaps even seeking redress from the courts. These means can be widely used, as they indeed are in some parts of India, for example in states such as Kerala (with high levels of education and a long tradition of public activism). But traditions are not easy to establish when they are not already there, and they certainly require a good deal of initiative and acumen.

Our Democratic Polity : Minority and Coalition Governments

India is a constitutional republic consisting of 28 states and seven centre-controlled union territories with New Delhi as the nation's capital. It is the seventh largest and second most populous country with roughly one sixth of the world's population, making it the largest world's democratic country. It is one of the world's oldest civilizations with a rich and varied cultural heritage. It has achieved widespread socio-economic progress during the last 62 years of its independence. From self-sufficiency in agricultural production to space exploration, India is competing effectively with other developed nations.

Indian History in Brief

Indo-Aryans are native inhabitants of south Asia, including present day India, Pakistan and Bangladesh. These Aryans merged with Dravidians, who were the original inhabitants of south India, and gave a dynamic start to Indian classical culture. In the 3rd and 4th century BC, Indian culture reached a peak during the time of Mauryan Empire. The period of the Gupta dynasty from 4th to 6th century AD is considered the Golden Age of India. An Arab invasion in the 8th century and a Turkish invasion in the 12th century was followed by European traders, beginning in the late 15th century. By the 19th century Britain had assumed political control. India won independence after the diligent efforts of Mohandas Karamchand Gandhi better known as father of India MK Gandhi in 1947. The sub-continent was divided into the states of India and Pakistan. Despite impressive economic gains India faces significant problems such as overpopulation, poverty, and religious strife.

India is also known for the highly sophisticated and urbanized culture of the Indus Valley Civilization that thrived in the northwestern part of the sub-continent from about 2600 to 2000 BC.

From that time it was a virtually self-contained political and cultural arena, strongly influenced by Hinduism. Other religions, notably Buddhism, Jainism and Sikhism, originated in India, although their presence is quite small in India relative to both Hinduism and Islam. Throughout past centuries it developed a rich and varied culture with intellectual base in mathematics, medicine, astronomy, and architecture.

Indian Heritage and Culture

Indian culture varies in a similar way to its geography. Indians speak more than a dozen nationally recognized and hundreds of regional languages, dress differently in different parts, follow different religions having numerous castes and eat different food, but are of the same temperament. A festival or a celebration involves the whole community. Likewise, an Indian wedding in every religion is a celebration of union, not only of the bride and groom, but also of two families, and sometimes of cultures and religions.

Government

Constitution

The government of India is framed according to the Constitution. The architects of India's constitution, though drawing on many external sources, were most heavily influenced by the British model of parliamentary democracy. In addition, a number of principles were adopted from the United States Constitution, including the separation of powers among the major branches of government, the establishment of a supreme court, and albeit in modified form, of a federal structure (a constitutional division of power between the union [central] and state governments). The mechanical details for running the central government, however, were largely carried over from the Government of India Act of 1935, passed by the British Parliament, which served as India's governing document in the waning days of British colonial rule. The new constitution took effect on January 26, 1950 and proclaimed India "a sovereign socialist secular democratic republic." With 444 articles, 12 (later 12) schedules (each clarifying and expanding upon a number of articles), and 97 amendments, it is one of the world's longest and most detailed constitutions. The constitution includes a detailed list of "fundamental rights," a lengthy list of "directive principles of state policy" (goals that the state is obligated to promote, though with no specified timetable for their accomplishment), and a much shorter list of "fundamental duties" of the citizen.

The constitution of India draws extensively from Western legal traditions in its outline of the principles of liberal democracy. Unlike many Western constitutions, its principles aspire to end the inequities of traditional social relations and enhance social welfare.

The constitution has fostered an increasing concentration of power in the central government—especially the Office of the Prime Minister. This centralization has occurred in the face of the increasing assertiveness of an array of ethnic and caste groups across Indian society. The government has responded to the resulting tensions by exerting authoritarian, albeit constitutional powers. Together with the public's perception of pervasive corruption among India's politicians, the state's centralization of authority and increasing resort to coercive power have eroded its legitimacy.

Law Commission

After independence, the Constitution's Fundamental Rights and Directive Principles of State Policy gave a new direction to law reform geared to the needs of a democratic legal order in a plural society. Though the Constitution stipulated the continuation of existing Laws pending amendment or repeal, there had been demands in Parliament and outside for establishing a Central Law Commission to recommend updating of the inherited laws to serve the new country. The Government established the First Law Commission of Independent India in 1955. The Ministry of Law reviews the Commission's reports, consulting with the concerned administrative Ministries, submitting them to the Parliament from time to time. They are cited in Courts, in academic and public discourses and are acted upon by concerned Government Departments depending on the Government's recommendations.

The Commission's regular staff consists mostly of research personnel. Priorities are set, topics are identified and preparatory work is assigned to Commission members.

Media

Indian media portray the Indian people and enjoy a monopoly on the people's trust.

Print media originated in 1780. The screening of Auguste and Louis Lumière's films in Bombay in during July, 1895 marked the beginnings of among the oldest and largest film media of the world. Radio broadcasting initiated in 1927. Indian private media has been free and independent throughout most of its history. During the Period of Emergency (1975–1977), declared by Prime Minister Indira Gandhi, the media faced potential government control. India consumed 99 million newspaper copies as of 2007—making it the second largest market in the world for newspapers. By 2008, India had a total of 60,000,000 Internet users—comprising 6.0% of the country's population. 4,010,000 people in India had access to broadband as of 2008, ranking it the 18th largest in the world. In 1997, India ranked 8th worldwide in the number of television broadcast stations.

Factors Affecting Democracy

The success of democracy in India defies many prevailing theories that stipulate preconditions. Indian democracy is best understood by focusing on how power is distributed.

Religion

Religion is a major cultural influence and also plays an important role in politics. Political party support greatly depends upon religion. The main religions are Hinduism and Islam and many political parties are identified by the religion of their supporters. Unlike religions such as Buddhism, Jainism, and Sikhism, Islam is not based on Hinduism. Many national religious issues are the key points of the success in elections. This factor has also led to the formation of many strict laws.

Caste

The caste system crosses religious boundaries to infect both Hindu and Islamic peoples. Hindus have four main castes and hundreds of sub-castes. Many political parties draw supporters from specific castes or sub-castes.

Population

India is the second most populous country of the world after China. The one billion-plus population has challenged the country's ability to provide jobs, health care, and education. Slowing population growth has been a major issue for the government.

Development

India is still an emerging country, making the pace and shape of development a major concern. India began as an explicitly socialist nation and continues with a large public sector and many constraints on private enterprise, although recent governments have reduced some of these restrictions. Their reward has been faster economic growth, particularly through the growth of trade-oriented industry. Some recent governments got removed because economic growth was too low.

Regions

India is very densely populated. Some advocate splitting some twenty eight states and seven union territories.

International Issues

The nation's success in developing an international information technology sector, recent wars with Pakistan, India's role in the world economy and world affairs redefined nationalism in India. People generally support those parties who maintain and enhance India's role in world affairs.

Other Factors

Factors such as education, corruption, women's issues, student politics, criminalization of politics, leadership strategies and the design of political institutions affect national and local politics.

3

Caste, Politics and Votes in India

Nearly sixty years ago Dr. B.R. Ambedkar, who chaired the committee that drafted India's Constitution had warned that our democracy would be in peril if it failed to ensure the political empowerment of the downtrodden classes. Summing up the work of the Constituent Assembly during the final reading of the Constitution in November, 1949, he said castes are "antinational" because they bring about separation in social life and because they generate jealousy and antipathy between caste and caste. "We must overcome all these difficulties if we are to become a nation in reality".

Dr. Ambedkar said so long as people were divided into several thousand castes, we were cherishing a "great delusion" in believing that we were a nation. "The sooner we realize that we are not as yet a nation in the social and psychological sense of the word, the better for us". Only then would we seriously think of ways and means of realizing this goal he said adding that India would gel as a nation only when we make our political democracy a social democracy as well. Political democracy cannot last unless there lies at its base, social democracy. On the social plane we have in India a society based on the principle of graded inequality which means elevation for some and degradation for others. "Without equality, liberty would produce the supremacy of the few over the many". How long shall we continue to deny equality in our social and economic life? If we continue to deny it for long, we will do so only by putting our political democracy in peril. "We must remove this contradiction at the earliest possible moment or else those who suffer from inequality will blow up the structure of political democracy which this assembly has so laboriously built up" he warned. A year earlier, while introducing the Draft Constitution in the Constituent Assembly in November, 1948, Dr. Ambedkar told the assembly that constitutional morality was not a natural sentiment. It was something that had to be cultivated. "Democracy in India" he had warned was only "a top-dressing on an Indian Soil, which is essentially undemocratic".

It is difficult to find a more perceptive mind that could honestly discuss the social and political situation in the immediacy of India's freedom and draw out the road map for the survival of democracy in the country. There can be no doubt that the creation of a fair and just political system depended on the equalisation of political opportunity in the country.

I wish to tell Dr.Ambedkar, where ever he is now, that to a large measure we have, more by accident than design, succeeded in converting our political democracy into a social democracy. The formation of regional and caste-based parties and the splintering of major political parties like the Congress Party and the Janata Dal over the last three decades have ensured the political empowerment of many castes and classes which were hitherto in the hinterland of political power. All this has also meant the translation of social diversity into political diversity and brought about a dramatic change in the social composition of our democratic bodies. For example, there were just 12 political parties in the Second Lok Sabha in 1957. This has now risen to 42 political parties in the year 2007.

The emergence of new parties signify the political empowerment of neglected groups. Secondly, the Lok Sabha is today a far more representative body than it was a half a century ago. For example in the First Lok Sabha which came into existence in 1952, 51 per cent of the members were lawyers, doctors, journalists and writers. Lawyers had such a big share of seats (more than one-third of the House) that one wondered whether the India of the 1950s was a nation of lawyers. Similarly, traders and industrialists had won 12 per cent of the seats while agriculturists (though India's economy was mostly agrarian) had just 22.50 per cent of the seats. All this has changed over the years and we now see the occupational democratization of the Lower House of our Parliament. For example, the number of lawyers, doctors, journalists and writers in the Lok Sabha had fallen to 14 per cent in recent years. Traders and industrialists are down to about 2 per cent whereas agriculturists had come to occupy half the seats in the House. Though the Lok Sabha Secretariat does not maintain caste-wise data of members, the rising political empowerment of persons practicing different occupations is an indicator of the growing assertiveness of the intermediate castes and the Dalits and their rising strength in democratic bodies.

These statistics indicate the equalization of political opportunity and the rising empowerment of hitherto underprivileged social groups. However what buttresses the statistical analysis is the political ground reality. India has seen the emergence of a large number of new political parties – some regional, some caste-based-over the last three decades and the new parties have made our democracy more participatory. Everyone is now getting sucked into the democratic circus, thus reducing the scope for disillusionment with democracy.

Among the new political parties are Ms.Mayawati's Bahujan Samaj Party, representing Dalit interests, the Lok Janshakti Party of Mr.Ram Vilas promoting the interests of Dalits in Bihar, the Rashtriya Janata Dal floated by Mr.Lalu Prasad Yadav to safeguard the interests of backward castes like Yadavas in Bihar and a couple of political parties floated in Andhra Pradesh and Assam to safeguard Muslim interests. In addition, we have the Janata Dal (Secular) headed by Mr.Deve Gowda in Karnataka, which has a strong Vokkaliga vote base, the Telugu Desam launched by the late Mr.N.T.Rama Rao in Andhra Pradesh, which has a strong Kamma vote base and the Janata Dal (United) in Bihar which has politically empowered people from castes such as Kurmis and Keoris. There are also regional parties with influence across castes like the Trinamool Congress of Ms.Mamata Bannerjee in West Bengal and the Telengana Rashtra Samithi in the Telengana region of Andhra Pradesh. These developments have helped draw different caste and social groups into electoral politics and ensured them seats in democratic bodies. Though the splintering of political parties and the emergence of caste-based parties has put a question mark of governance and political stability, there can be no denying that the participation of more and more groups across the social spectrum in the democratic process has enhanced the chances of survival of the democratic system itself.

Apart from backward castes, the growth of regional parties and the end of one-party rule at the federal level and in the states has meant greater participation of people from different regions of India. This is put an end to centrifugal tendencies in states like Tamil Nadu where the people felt that the dominance of politicians from the Hindi heartland deprived them of a legitimate share in political power at the Centre. The end of one-party rule has also meant the advent of the coalition era and political power at the federal level for many regional outfits like the Dravida Munnetra Kazhagam and the Telugu Desam. These developments have put the brakes of anti-Hindi sentiments in the non-Hindi speaking areas and contributed in no small measure to the political integration of India.

But in all this, I regard the success of the Bahujan Samaj Party (BSP) in the recent election to the Uttar Pradesh Assembly as the most significant and as an event that has far reaching implications for the future of democracy in India. The success of the B S P in this election symbolizes the political empowerment of one of the most oppressed and disadvantaged social groups any where in the world. It constitutes the bloodless and peaceful transfer of political power from a class of people who were considered to be oppressors to a class of people who were the oppressed. This must truly be the most remarkable story of the triumph of democracy.

Though the Dalits have had reservations in democratic bodies, government jobs and educational institutions, the reins of political power have never been in their hands. Every political party pays lip sympathy to the cause of Scheduled Castes but the levers of power have invariably been with the Hindu Upper Castes and dominant Middle Castes. Therefore, a clear majority in the recent election to the Uttar Pradesh Assembly for the BSP, symbolizes the first-ever clear transfer of power from the Hindu upper crust to one of the most oppressed and disadvantaged social groups in the world. However belated this development may seem, it is certainly a significant milestone in India's democratic journey over the last six decades and will hopefully minimize the bitterness amongst this section of the country's population over the tardy efforts of the Indian State to equalize opportunities.

Ironically, though Dr.Ambedkar made the first attempt to politically mobilize the dalits, he met with little success whether it was the Labour Party that he launched in the 1930s or the Republican Party which he founded much later. The idea eventually took off in the mid 1980s, a good 30 years after Dr.Ambedkar's death when the late Mr.Kanshiram decided to try it out. Mr. Kanshiram, who founded the BSP, prepared the ground for a Dalit political party through the Backward and Minority Communities Employees Federation (BAMCEF) that was established about three decades ago. As this organization grew in strength, Kanshiram took the first step towards formation of a political party when he established the Dalit Shoshit Samaj Sangarsh Samithi (D S– 4) in the early 1980s. DS-4 became a code for Dalit political empowerment and it made its presence felt for the first time in Uttar Pradesh prior to the Lok Sabha election held in 1984. During that election, as the Congress Party rode a massive sympathy wave consequent to the assassination of Indira Gandhi, Dalit youth painted the walls in Eastern and Central Uttar Pradesh with this secret code that stood for Dalit political aspirations and bonding. DS-4 metamorphosed into a full-fledged political party in 1985. Initially the party's two top leaders –Mr.Kashiram and Ms.Mayawati – focused on consolidation of Dalit votes. Once this was achieved, they roped in the Muslims and the BSP was promoted as a Dalit-Muslim party. This strategy paid off because in the Lok Sabha election held in 1999, the party secured 14 seats and 22.08 per cent of the vote in the state. But, while the BSP had a firm grip on the Dalit vote, it found that it had to share the Muslim vote with the Samajwadi Party. The division in the Muslim vote did not give the BSP the clear lead it was looking for over the Samajwadi Party and the Bharatiya Janata Party (BJP). Its share of the popular vote in the state remained in the 22-24 per cent band, which was inadequate for it to gain a clear majority in the assembly elections.

In the First-Past-The-Post System, whenever there are two major political parties or coalitions and a few smaller parties in the fray, a party or coalition will need around 42-45 per cent of the popular vote to secure a clear majority in the legislature. Over the last two decades, the political scene has got crowded with the emergence of several regional and caste-based parties with vote banks big enough to take on the biggies like the Congress and the BJP. This has led to triangular and quadrangular contests and has substantially brought down the percentage of votes needed by a party or coalition to secure a clear majority. For example in Uttar Pradesh where you have four prominent parties in the contest, the threshold could be as low as 30 per cent. Aware of this relationship between votes and seats, the BSP decided over a year ago to enlarge its social base just enough to cross this threshold. Though the party was built on a hate-Upper Castes slogan, Ms.Mayawati offered the live branch to the Brahmins because she perceived the newly-empowered Other Backward Castes as the bigger evil. The party held several Brahmin Sammelans and laid the ground for the Dalit-Muslim-Brahmin vote base that eventually helped the party in the recent election. It also took BSP's vote share from the 22-24 per cent band to just over 30 per cent – enough in a quadrangular electoral battle to obtain a clear majority.

We are indeed lucky to see the transfer of political power in the country's largest state to the Dalits with our democratic system and Constitution still intact because Maoists and other radical left groups have been tempting Dalits for a long time to join them in wrecking the democratic system. Despite this, the commitment of a majority of the Dalits to the democratic process speaks volumes of the patience and resilience among a people who have put up with some of the worst humiliations that man can inflict on man. Their endurance is indeed remarkable because even in 1949 Dr.Ambedkar had declared that the downtrodden classes were "tired of being governed" and were therefore "impatient to govern themselves", In his view, the sooner room is made for the realization of their aspiration, the better for the country, for its independence and for the continuance of its democratic structure. "This urge for self-realisation in the downtrodden classes must not be allowed to devolve into a class struggle or class war" he had warned..

It has taken the Dalits 60 years to get the opportunity "to govern themselves", at least in one state. Fortunately, the Dalit party has come to power riding on a rainbow coalition. This electoral success of the BSP can have considerable social and political implications. It can now offer to extend this coalition experiment to other states provided the Brahmins and others who are at the top of the Hindu caste hierarchy are willing to work with it to eliminate social inequalities. Apart from Uttar Pradesh, the BSP has been making its presence felt in Madhya Pradesh, Punjab, Jammu and Kashmir and Haryana. As we go along, it could set its sights on other states like Rajasthan, Bihar and Karnataka. If this happens, the BSP could become the first "regional" party to acquire a national footprint and unsettle national parties like the Congress and the BJP, which have never factored in the prospect of having another contender for the pan-Indian vote.

Therefore, willy-nilly we appear to have addressed the concerns voiced by Dr.Ambedkar while drafting India's Constitution and ensured that political democracy also becomes a social democracy. The flip side of all this is of course fears of instability but that seems a bit exaggerated if one sees the remarkable manner in which over a dozen or even two dozen political parties have combined to offer the country stable coalitions at the national level since 1998.

Caste System : A Unique Feature of Indian Society

The caste system of India is a particularly unique feature of its society. As a dominant principle of social organisation, caste is deeply rooted in both Hindu tradition and religion. Although it has been argued that caste's influence is slowly on the decline, its importance can still be seen in all areas of Indian life – socially, politically and economically. These spheres are all influenced by caste to different extents, as the caste system does not uniformly carry out the same role in all areas. A system so heavily ingrained in the culture cannot simply be eroded after a couple of decades, and while the system may be lessening in its rigidity, there is evidence that indicates that caste is still a significant force in daily life.

There are numerous theories as to why the caste system developed in India. All of these, however, seem to draw to the same conclusion – that caste developed as a means of organizing

Hindu social space. A widely accepted explanation for the development of caste in India is the socio-historical theory. This claims that characteristics of caste were present in Indian society as early as 3rd century BC. The system was more rigidly established with the arrival of the fair-skinned Aryans, who used caste (or more specifically, the four classes, or varnas) to keep the dark-skinned indigenous peoples in a state of permanent subordinance. There is evidence from 1500 BC of conquerors inter-marrying with non-Aryans. However gradually, the upper sections of the Aryan groups (i.e. priests and warriors) resented this due to their loss of power and privilege. This led to marriage being confined to occupational groups, with a change in ancestral vocation as socially barred, and thus the system was established as it is still distinctly seen today.

The influence of caste can be particularly seen in Indian politics. Different regions of India have been influenced politically by caste to different extents. There is a great difference, for example, between South and North India when considering caste's political influence-South India is seen with more caste-based politics than other regions. However, there is one universal concept that can be seen throughout India. Although both socially and economically, caste can be seen as a tool of subjugation, politically, lower castes may use their universal franchise as a means of empowerment simply due to sheer numbers.

Lower castes have increasingly begun to use their numbers to their own electoral advantage. Elections held between 1996 and 1999 in India are evidence that lower caste parties are gaining increasing support, achieving 18 to 20 percent of the national vote. This result, when compared to India's largest political party, the Bharatiya Janata Party (BJP) (who gained 20 to 25 percent of the national vote), shows that lower caste parties have a significant standing in Indian politics. Thus it has also been realized by other political parties the importance of the lower caste vote, and policies of various parties have changed accordingly.

This shift of electoral power has subsequently seen a change of direction in Indian politics, as parties compete for lower caste support. The BJP, with a history of support mainly stemming from upper castes, has changed its direction as a result of this (Baldauf

2001). BJP has attempted to gain lower caste support by changing its policies to become more 'lower caste friendly'. At the expense of potentially alienating its grassroots support, BJP's new suggested policies include the creation of a new category of Most Backward Classes, with this group being given extra access to government jobs. Thus as the lower caste vote becomes increasingly important, caste's influence over Indian politics can be seen as significant, forcing political parties to take notice of members of society disregarded by most.

Although caste is a great social influence over Indian society, it has been argued that its stronghold on the people is gradually loosening. Caste, as particularly perceived by a growing educated middle class, is increasingly being viewed as outdated and irrelevant to contemporary society. The importance of the caste system, however, should not be dismissed. It is not disappearing, but rather can be viewed as undergoing significant alteration due to the dynamic nature of a changing society.

The influences of caste on social interaction are seen through many facets. Physical contact between members of different castes, forms of greeting, modes of dress and physical posture all indicate a ritual hierarchy. However, the increasing modernization of society has contributed to the changing role of the caste system. Due to modern means of production and communication, caste rituals once strictly adhered to may be more difficult to perform. The system has changed in the sense that it is less rigid, with structural differences between castes and also sub-divisions of castes being reduced. Religious and ritual barriers are being loosened, with ideas on purity and pollution and segregation between castes becoming more relaxed. This however is seen to a much greater extent in the metropolitan areas of India, and has affected rural areas to a lesser extent.

India's society is mainly agriculturally based, with most of the population still living in villages. It thus should be noted that caste still plays a considerable role when concerned with social interaction in these areas. This can be seen as housing patterns within villages are affected by caste. Members of higher castes live in the centre of the village, middle castes live beyond the higher castes at a distance, and lower castes live on the periphery in small clusters. The patterns of social interaction among people of different castes is subsequently influenced, and also determined by caste. There has been resistance to the system though, as lower castes gain power through ownership of land. These members are more reluctant to participate in old traditions that are clearly degrading – displaying an increasing class mobility due to economic power that affects the way in which caste operates.

The acceptance of the caste system, especially by those who are disadvantaged to a certain extent by its operation, can be linked to its religious justification. This can explain why the caste system has survived since its early beginnings, and still has an influence over contemporary Indian society. Through such major Hindu concepts such as karma (every action has an effect that must be accounted for in other lifetimes), a person's place in the caste system is justified. This fatalistic characteristic of Hinduism sees members of Hindu society accepting their place in the caste hierarchy; as to disrupt the order of caste is to disrupt the order of the universe. As the caste system is therefore so deeply rooted in the culture and religion, it will continue to influence India's social sphere both directly and indirectly, through the shaping of people's values, attitudes and morals.

The influence of caste over India's economic activities is seen by many to be on the decline. In contemporary Indian society, people are becoming more inclined to form alliances that may not be within their caste in order to serve their own personal economic interests. In the past, a strong positive correlation existed between caste and property ownership. However, Singh argues that over time, caste will have increasingly less influence on property status, political power, education status and occupational status.

The industrialization of Indian society has contributed to a change in the influence of caste over economic behaviour. D. Lal argues that the introduction of non-traditional sources of economic power, increased commercialization of agriculture and introduction of property rights has contributed to the caste system becoming less influential. Although in rural areas caste still influences economic interaction to a larger extent, the introduction of methods such as cash payments in replacement of traditional caste-based bartering of services are contributing to a decline in its role.

Another significant factor for the decreasing economic role of caste is the diminishing importance of occupation specialization based on caste. This argument has been acknowledged by scholars such as D. Gupta, who even suggests that members of traditional castes have been performing non-traditional occupations since 1891. There is also evidence indicating that although members of a particular occupational caste have held family names, many have been performing different tasks, seen even in rural India, the nation's most traditional area. Thus it can be seen that the influence of caste over economic activity is on the decline, or as D. Quigley suggests, already has a limited role in economic life.

In conclusion, caste's influence over contemporary Indian society is apparent socially, politically and economically. Although these spheres are influenced by caste to different extents, caste's influence can still be observed in all three areas, thus playing a significant role in daily life. As society continues to change, the role of caste will change with it. The modernization of society has seen the loosening of the system's rigid structure and rules, in order to become more relevant to contemporary Indian life. However, this does not compromise caste's importance as a social structure, as caste will continue to operate as the basic structural feature of Hindu society for years to come.

4

Reservation in Educational Institution

The Union HRD Ministry's proposal of 27 per cent reservation for OBC students in Centrally-funded universities has re-ignited the merit vs caste debate in the education sector, reviving the furore the Mandal commission recommendation raised in 1991.

Opinions are clearly divided between those who feel that the reservations are nothing but a political gimmick and should be opposed at all costs, and those who say the move will genuinely help lift the status of the backward classes.

The proposed reservation is expected to affect premier education institutions like the Indian Institutes of Technology (IITs) and Indian Institutes of Management (IIMs), which have already reserved 22.5 per cent seats for scheduled castes and tribes. If the new recommendations come into place, "general category" students will have access to just half the seats in these institutions.

Basically I wanted to comment to that article but I came with some suggestion so I believe this will be good to publish on legalserviceindia where people will understand more that I want to say about.

I am not against reservation but I am against this type of reservation. Reservations should not be based on caste. Indeed government has duty to provide education equally to everybody but when government is asking for reservation in education, it is actually showing its inability to give education to everybody with present educational infrastructure. I accept that India is going through very difficult period where it is expanding its economy. To sustain economy, educated and skilled labour is necessary. So in my view government policy should be promoting education for youth and children. The question is not if subsidy is necessary or not but the question here is to whom and how government should provide subsidy and how it should give thrust to education among youth.

Article 15(4) of Indian Constitution read as "Nothing in this article or in clause (2) of article 29 shall prevent the State from making any special provision for the advancement of any socially and educationally backward classes of citizens or for the Scheduled Castes and the Scheduled Tribes." This article was added by the Constitution (First Amendment) Act, 1951.

To start reforms, parliament need to change 55 years old Article 15(4) of Indian Constitution and replace it with something like this-"Nothing in this article or in clause (2) of article 29 shall prevent the State from making any special provision for the advancement of any socially, educationally and economically backward classes of citizens without depriving other classes of citizen's equality of opportunity."

If you read my proposal carefully I have added "economically backward class" in the proposed article and remove "or for the Scheduled Castes and the Scheduled Tribes." Also I have added "without depriving other classes of citizen's equality of opportunity" in end. Let me explain all three proposed change.

(1) By adding "economically backward class", I am making provision for government to give subsidy to poor people regardless of their caste.

(2) By removing "or for the Scheduled Castes and the Scheduled Tribes", I want to remove caste politics from India. It will not allow rich but Scheduled Castes and the Scheduled Tribes citizen of India to get subsidy, as I have seen so many SCST people having big properties but still getting aid from government on the name of caste, and I also have seen so many general class people who even dont have enough resource to earn as much money to feed

themselves. I don't want to remove aid from poor people. That is why I added "economically backward class" in article 15(4).

(3) By adding "without depriving other classes of citizen's equality of opportunity", I am disabling government to make law that can give unequal privileges to poor people. Instead government will only have option to provide financial aid to poor people who want to do something. Government can give them full aid from study to rent of house for study.

By this way those needy people can get protection by government but they will have to show merit. If after getting aid, they failed in college or school, their aid can be stopped.

On educational system, I would say that government needs to spent more money on educational infrastructure as classrooms in colleges are less then needed. Government needs to open more universities and more colleges or at least give supports who are trying to open new colleges and universities. India today needs more professional education without degrading primary education. Private institutions are good option. It is Indias primary educational system that is enabling Indian graduate ahead of other foreign graduate at aboard. Definitely we need to improve our primary educational system too. We need to give our children an environment where then can stand and speak in front of people.

We need to give aid to deprived citizens, but we should not deprive others who have merit. Recent proposal of OBC quota is one similar to proposal of the than HRD minister of BJP government Mr. Murlimanohar Joshi. My suggestion is, give financial aid on basis of performance instead of seat reservation.

Background to Reservations in India

Since the establishment of the Indian Constitution special provisions were created for those castes that were earlier called 'untouchables." These castes are now called scheduled castes on account of the fact that they are listed in the schedule of the constitution. Over a number of years provisions regarding positive discrimination favouring these castes gradually took shape in the form of reservations. These reservations exist in the form of quotas and they pertain only to government jobs and educational institutions so far. The percentage reserved for Scheduled Castes (SC) is 17.5 % in these state institutions, which is roughly proportional to their demographic presence in the country.

The SCs were, and still continue to be, preponderantly rural based. Barring rare exceptions, the SCs do not own land but till the lands of others as agricultural labourers.

Within the village they are humiliated on a daily basis in a number of ways. Their children find it difficult to attend schools, they are not allowed to visit the main village temple, and on many occasions are barred from gathering in the village square with other castes. Though there has been a marked decline in the persecution of rural SCs today, one of the reasons is probably the efficacy of reservations for this category that has allowed many of them to leave the village and find better jobs in cities and towns. For the SCs the village is not where they can realize their ambitions, in fact, it is a place that would like to escape from.

Reservations in government institutions have given many SCs a chance to live an alternative life outside rural confines. As a category they are far more oppressed in the village than in the city as individual biographies can now be de-coupled from family histories in urban locales. In the village where memory is strong, all interactions are informed by it regardless of an individual's personal attributes. This kind of depth personal knowledge is impossible to sustain in a town or city.

In this presentation, the term reservation and affirmative action will be used synonymously though technically there are differences between the two. These differences will be dealt with when we discuss the differences between the United States and India on how these democracies have handled the question of the historically underprivileged in their respective democracies. Though it has many detractors, affirmative action is one such normative intervention that can enhance the quality of modernity in contemporary life.

Properly understood, affirmative action programmes have all the potentialities of initiating and developing a "minimum set of resemblances" between people by deliberate policy decisions. This not only makes citizenship substantive, but would also make the past less and less relevant to the future and to how people relate to one another.

Yet, reservations and affirmative action have many detractors who argue from within Liberal premises. Their opinions are forceful, well-elaborated, and based on respectable foundational principles that are not intrinsically anti-democratic in character..It is, therefore, important to take these ideas on board while arguing in favour of affirmative action for they will help to finesse our position on the meaning of democratic fraternity and, eventually, of citizenship too.

Reservation in India

Reservation in Indian law is a term used to describe the governmental policy whereby a percentage of seats are reserved in the Parliament of India, State Legislative Assemblies, Central and State Civil Services, Public Sector Units, Central and State Governmental Departments and in all Public and Private Educational Institutions, except in the Minority and Religious Educational Institutions, for the socially and educationally backward classes of citizens or/and for the Scheduled Castes and the Scheduled Tribes who are perceived by the Government to be inadequately represented in these services and institutions.

Reservation is a phenomenon unique to India and is different from affirmative action which is practised in many other countries. The main difference between the two is that in affirmative action the amount of concessions to be made in order to increase representation in an under represented group is at the discretion of individual organizations, whereas the reservation system in India is based on statutory quota that must be met.

Purpose: Reservations are intended to increase the social diversity in campuses and workplaces by lowering the entry criteria for certain identifiable groups that are grossly under-represented in proportion to their numbers in general population. However caste is most used criteria to identify under represented groups. There are other identifiable under represented groups like Gender

(Women are under represented), State of domicile (North Eastern States, Bihar, Uttar Pradesh are under represented), rural people etc. as revealed by Government of India sponsored National Family Health and National Sample surveys.

The underlying theory is that the under-representation of the identifiable groups is a legacy of the Indian caste system. After India gained independence, the Constitution of India listed some erstwhile groups as Scheduled castes (SC) and Scheduled Tribes (ST). The Constitution laid down that 15% and 7.5% of vacancies to government aided educational institutes and for jobs in the government/ public sector, as reserved quota for the SC and ST candidates respectively.

Later reservations were introduced for other sections as well. The supreme court ruling that reservations cannot exceed 50% (that would be violative of equality guaranteed by the constitution) has put a cap on reservations, but there are state laws that exceed this 50% limit and these are under litigation in the supreme court. For example, the caste based reservation fraction stands at 69% and is applicable to about 87% of the population in the state of Tamil Nadu.

Types of Reservation: Seats in Educational institutions and jobs are reserved based on a variety of criteria. The quota system sets aside a proportion of all possible positions for members of a specific group. Those not belonging to the designated communities can compete only for the remaining positions, while members of the designated communities can compete for all positions (reserved and open). For example when 2 position out of 10 clerical in Railways are reserved for Ex-Servicemen, those who have served in Army can compete both in the General Category as well as in the Specific Quota.

Caste: Seats are reserved for Schedules Castes, Scheduled Tribes, Most backward Castes, Backward Castes, Other Backward Castes in varying ratio by the Central Government and State Government. This caste is decided based on birth, so it will never get changed. The advantage of this system is that this cannot be changed. While a person can change his religion, and his economic status can fluctuate, the caste is permanent. In Central government-funded higher education institutions: 22.5% for scheduled caste (dalit) and scheduled tribe (adivasi) students. (15% for SC and 7.5% for ST) It has been proposed to raising this to 49.5%, by including 27% reservation for OBCs also.. In AIIMS 14% reserved for SC, 8% for ST. In addition, SC/ST students with only 50% scores are eligible. This ratio is followed even in Parliament and all elections where few constituencies are earmarked for those from Certain communities. In few states like Tamil Nadu, the percentage of reservation is 18% for SC and 1% for ST and this is based on the population. In Andhra Pradesh educational institutes and government jobs 25% for BCs, 15% for SCs, 6% for STs and 5% to Muslims, total: 51% (Note: 5% Muslim Quota is under the purview of the Court)

The post of Temple priest in most (not all) of Hindu temples is reserved only for a man from Brahmin Caste.

Religion: Jobs in few departments like Hindu Religious & Charitable Endowments Department are 100% reserved for Hindus. Government of Andhra Pradesh has introduced a law enabling 5% reservations for Muslims which has been contested in the court. Kerala Public Service Commission Muslim quota: 12%. (Religious) Minority status education institutes have also 50% reservation for their particular religion.

State of Domicile: Usually Jobs under State Government are 100% reserved to those who are domicile under that government with few exceptions. In PEC Chandigarh, earlier 80% of seats were reserved for Chandigarh domiciles and now it is 50%.

College of Undergraduation: Admission to Post Graduate courses in Delhi Medical Colleges is 100% reserved for those who have studied MBBS in Delhi. Institutes like JIPMER have a policy of reserving Post Graduate seats for those who completed their MBBS in JIPMER. AIIMS used to reserve 33% of its 120 Postgraduation seats for the 40 Undergraduate students (meaning everyone who has completed MBBS in AIIMS are assured of a PG Seat) which was held illegal by a Court.

Other: Some reservations are also made for:

- Gender (Around 30% seats reserved for females in many institutions)

- Sons/Daughters/Grandsons/Grand daughters of Freedom Fighters
- Physically handicapped
- Sports Personalities
- Non-Resident Indians (NRIs)
- Candidates sponsored by various organisations
- Those who have served in the armed forces (Ex-Servicemen quota) in jobs
- Dependants of armed forces personnel killed in action
- repartriates
- Those born from inter-caste marriages
- Widows and deserted women

Relaxations: Many times, the selection criteria for those coming under reservation are relaxed (some times they are altogether done away with.) The criteria that is relaxed are:

1. The minimum high school marks criteria are relaxed for reserved seats. For example in IIT JEE Reserved category candidates scoring about 65% of the last admitted general category candidate are directly offered admission. Candidates not meeting this cutoff but scoring as low as half of this are offered admission to a one year preparatory course. In AIIMS, for example SC/ST students are eligible only if they score 50%. But this 50% is not mandatory for the Institute Quota and in occasion the Honouranle High Court of Delhi had found that "AIIMS students, who had secured as low as 14% or 19% or 22% in the (all-India) entrance examination got admission to PG courses
2. Age
3. Fees, Hostel Room Rent etc.

Tuition fees and room rent is waived.

But the final marks needed to clear the exam and gain the degree is never relaxed.

History of the Practice: India is divided into many endogamous groups, or castes and sub-castes, as a result of centuries of practicing a form of social hierarchy called the caste system. Proponents of reservation policy says that traditional caste system, as it is practised, leads to severe oppression and segregation of the lower castes and limited their access to various freedoms, including education. Caste, according to ancient scriptures such as "Manu Smriti", is "Varnasrama Dharma", which translates to "offices given according to colour". The practice of caste in India followed this rule.

- 1921-Madras Presidency introduces reservation of 44 per cent for non-Brahmins, 16 per cent for Brahmins, 16 per cent for Muslims, 16 per cent for Anglo-Indians/ Christians and eight per cent for Scheduled Castes.
- 1935-Indian national congress passes resolution called Poona Pact to allocate separate electoral constituencies for depressed classes.
- 1942-B.R.Ambedkar established the All India Depressed Classes federation to support the advancement of the scheduled castes. He also demanded reservations for the Scheduled castes in government services and education.
- 1947-India obtained Independence. Dr. Ambedkar was appointed chairman of the drafting committee for Indian Constitution. The Indian constitution prohibits any discrimination based on religion, race, caste, sex and place of birth. But, while providing equality of opportunity for all citizens, the constitution also contains special clauses to ensure reservation, "for the advancement of any socially and educationally backward classes of citizens or for the Scheduled Castes and the Scheduled Tribes". Separate constituencies allocated to Scheduled Castes and Tribes to ensure their political representation for 10 years. (These were subsequently extended for every 10 years through constitutional amendments).
- 1979 Mandal Commission was established to assess the situation of the socially and educationally backward. The commission didn't have exact figures for a sub-caste, known as the Other Backward Class (OBC), and used the 1930 census data to estimate the OBC population at 52%, and further classified 1257 communities as backward.

- 1980, the commission submitted a report, and recommended changes to the existing quotas, increasing them from 22% to 49.5%. As of 2006 number of castes in Backward class list went up to 2297 which is the increase of 60% from community list prepared by Mandal commission.
- 1990, Mandal commission recommendations were implemented in Government Jobs. Student Organisations launched nationwide agitations. Rajiv Goswami Delhi university student attempted self immolation. Many students followed suit.
- 1991 Narasimha rao Government introduced 10% separate reservation for Poor Among Forward Castes.
- 1992 Supreme court upheld reservations to Other backward classes.
- 1998, Central Government conducted large nationwide survey for the first time to estimate economical and educational status of various social groups.. The National Sample Survey puts the figure at 32%. There is substantial debate over the exact number of OBC's in India, with census data compromised by partisan politics. It is generally estimated to be sizable, but lower than the figures quoted by either the Mandal Commission or and national Sample Survey. Mandal commission has been criticised of fabricating the data. National surveys indicated that status of OBC is comparable to Forward castes in many areas.
- 2005 93rd Constitutional amendment brought for ensuring reservations to other backward classes and Scheduled castes and Tribes in Private Educational institutions
- 2006 Reservations introduced for Other backward classes in Central Government Educational Institutions. Total Reservation went up to 49.5%.

Constitutional Rights and Administrative Discretion with Reference to Scheduled Tribes in India

There are more than 84 million people of the scheduled tribes in India today; more than 15 per cent of them have been displaced without any comprehensive programme of rehabilitation in order to make way for development projects such as dams, manufacturing industries, and mines. The traditional access of the tribal people to forest and minor forest resources has made them victims of the contractor-forest official nexus. These circumstances have forced many Adivasi people into contract labour gangs and even to bonded labour and many atrocities are being committed on them.

Despite elaborate provisions in the Constitution and other laws, it is an unfortunate reality that social injustice and exploitation of Scheduled Castes and Scheduled Tribes and other weaker sections persist.

There are reports in the press about atrocities against persons belonging to these groups and the frequency with which they occur is a cause for disquiet. Tribes are given special mentioning and emphasis in our constitution. Articles 244 and 244(A) of the constitution make special provision for the administration and control of the Scheduled areas and Scheduled tribes in any State by the application of the Fifth and Sixth Schedules. This expression "administration and control" in Art. 244 (1) extends to administration and control by the exercise of Governmental powers of every description – executive, judicial and legislative.

Art. 32 or Section 91 and order I, Rule 8 of the CPC can be used to fight for the causes related to the marginalized class of scheduled and non-scheduled tribes. But, there are hardly any cases regarding that. Be it, the legislative or executive or judiciary, nobody has come up with properly utilizing the doctrine of Affirmative Action so that the benefit reaches to the needy. The paper thus analyses some major issues related to the tribes in India. Be it, their education, their land rights, the policies framed by the government on papers, the commissions set up, the cases decided, the all-time media and polity spoof of reservation etc. etc.

Constitutional Rights of Scheduled Tribes

Recognizing the special needs of STs, the Constitution of India made certain special safeguards to protect these communities from all the possible exploitation and thus ensure social justice. While Article 14 confers equal rights and opportunities to all, Article 15 prohibit discrimination against any citizen on the grounds of sex, religion, race, caste etc; Art. 15(4) enjoins upon the State to make special provisions for the advancement of any socially and educationally backward classes; Article 16(4) empowers the State to make provisions for reservation in appointments or posts in favour of any backward class of citizens, which in the opinion of the State, is not adequately represented in the services under the State; Article 46 enjoins upon the State to promote with special care the educational and economic interests of the weaker sections of the people and, in particular, ... the STs and promises to protect them from social injustice and all forms of exploitation. Further, while Art. 275(1) promises grant-in-aid for promoting the welfare of STs and for raising the level of administration of the Scheduled Areas, Articles 330, 332 and 335 stipulate reservation of seats for STs in the Lok Sabha and in the State Legislative Assemblies and in services.

Finally, the Constitution also empowers the State to appoint a Commission to investigate the conditions of the socially and educationally backward classes and to specify those Tribes or Tribal Communities deemed to be as STs. The Fifth Schedule to the Constitution lays down certain prescriptions about the Scheduled Areas as well as the Scheduled Tribes in states other than Assam, Meghalaya, Tripura and Mizoram by ensuring submission of Annual Reports by the Governors to the President of India regarding the Administration of the Scheduled Areas and setting up of Tribal Advisory Councils to advise on matters pertaining to the welfare and advancement of the STs. Likewise, the Sixth Schedule to the Constitution also refers to the administration of Tribal Areas in the states of Assam, Meghalaya, Tripura and Mizoram by designating certain tribal regions and also by constituting District Councils and Regional Councils (Article 244(2)).

To ensure effective participation of the tribals in the process of planning and decision-making, the 73rd and 74th Amendments of the constitution are being extended to the Scheduled Areas through the Panchayats (Extension to the Scheduled Areas) Act, 1996. In spite of so many constitutional safeguards, hardly any right has literally on ground level has actually reached the deprived tribes. The next portion shall analyse the same apathy.

Major Tribulations of the Marginalized Tribes

The Misfortune of Educational Deprivation

In *Unni Krishnan v. State of A.* the court has recognized a fundamental right to education in the right to life under Article 21. Taking help from Article 41 and 45 it has held that 'every child/ citizen of this country has a right to free education until he completes the age of fourteen years'.

In spite of right to education being the fundamental right now, the very ambitious Sarva Shiksha Abhiyan aimed at universalisation and promotion of education in real sense, still, is unreachable for tribes. In spite of getting motivation to continue their education tribal students are often discouraged at local level by teachers & upper caste groups. Various studies to analyse the causes of poor educational status of tribal prove that the present scenario of education in remote tribal areas seems responsible for such higher date of dropouts in primary & upper primary level. Tribal & Dalit children are forced to sit at a distance from upper caste students. Teacher pays no attention towards their education. Tribal students are forced to do work like cleaning school, wash utensils etc in place of studying. They want to study; they are often discouraged even by teachers saying that they cannot learn it as they (tribal) do not mind to learn. Such frequent discrimination in the school compels the tribal to leave their education.

The Administrative Inefficacy in Implementing the Imperfect Legislations/Policies

The Scheduled Castes and Scheduled Tribes (Prevention of Atrocities) Act (POA) has been on the statute books since 1989. There are however hardly any convictions under this Act. Dalit activists say that there are many loopholes in the law which help offenders slip out of both the Atrocities Act as well as the Penal Code. An activist made particular mention of sec. 3 (iv) and (v) of the Act.Section 4 of the POA clearly establishes the punishment for government servants who neglect or willfully neglect his/her duty. However, it has been noted that the state ministry of home has taken such provisions in a very casual manner. Therefore, they have failed to ensure the proper implementation of the concerned section of the SC/ST Act.

The U.N. Committee recommended that the State party, in accordance with article 17 of its Constitution and article 2 of the Convention, take all necessary steps to abolish the discriminatory practice of "untouchability", prevent caste-and tribe-motivated abuse, and prosecute State and private actors who are responsible for such practices or abuses. Moreover, in compliance with article 46 of the Constitution, the State party is encouraged to implement, inter alia, special measures to advance and protect these groups. The Committee further recommended the full implementation of the 1989 POA, the 1995 Scheduled Castes and Scheduled Tribes Rules (Prevention of Atrocities) and the Employment of Manual Scavengers and Construction of Dry Latrines (Prohibition) Act, 1993.

The so Called 'Promising' National Commissions

Indra Sawhney case, suggested establishment of a commission, which has experts to determine, identify and specify the reservation issues with respect to backward classes. Chandrachud, C.J. in *K.C. Vasant Kumar Case,* there should be a periodic revision of these lists to exclude those who have ceased to be backward or for inclusion of new classes, as the case may be. Can the apathy be more explicit when we confront the fact that The first National Commission for Scheduled Tribes (NCST) was constituted in March, 2004, 57 years after independence. The purpose of the National commission is to IMPLEMENT adequately the policies and benefits conferred upon the Sts. But, following are certain recommendations that the NCST gave in its recent report.

Recommendations of NCST

a) Strengthening the role of the Commission as a truly independent watchdog body with punitive powers.

b) The qualifications of the Chairperson and Members should be publicly available, and there should be an effort to involve people from different professions concerned with Scheduled Tribes.

c) In October 1999 a Ministry of Tribal Affairs was created by the Government of India through the bifurcation of the Ministry of Social Justice and Empowerment. The objective was to ensure more focused attention on integrated socio-economic development of the most under-privileged section of Indian society, the Scheduled Tribes in a Coordinated and planned manner. The overlap with the Ministry of Tribal Affairs needs to be examined, and the independence of the Commission vis-à-vis MOTA asserted.

d) The Commission is short staffed, as well as underfunded and therefore unable to deal satisfactorily with the volume of cases. The Regional offices need to be strengthened, along with an independent investigating mechanism. This should replace the standard procedure of asking for clarification as the dominant mode of functioning. After such a late commencement of the process of reaching to the tribes through commissions, these recommendations shows the lacunas still prevalent in the establishment, or, the so called a very 'promising' institutions.

Tribes! The Worst Hit in the Cases of Development Induced Displacement

National Tribal Policy, and the Scheduled Tribes and Other Traditional Forest Dwellers (Recognition of Forest Rights) Act, passed in December 2006, grants tribes some measure of ownership in forest lands and produce, emphasizing that tribal rights are increasingly figuring as a prominent national concern. The term Scheduled Areas denotes the tribal regions to which either the Fifth Schedule or the Sixth Schedule applies.

Article 10 of UN DRIPS clearly states that indigenous people shall not be forcibly removed from their lands or territories. No relocation shall take place without the free, prior and informed consent of the indigenous peoples concerned and after agreement on just and fair compensation and, where possible, with the option of return. As per Article 20 (2) of DRIPS, indigenous peoples, if deprived of their means of subsistence and development, are entitled to just and fair redress. The local institutions engaged in the task are known by different names in different states. The philosophy of Joint Forest Management (JFM) in essence aims at involving people in resource generation activities through motivation, and eliciting their participation in forest management and the sharing of benefits through adequate institutional arrangements. The most significant principle underlying the Land Acquisition Act, 1894 is the doctrine of eminent domain, according to which the state can acquire land from private citizens for public purposes.

The state's powerful right of eminent domain is nearly impossible to challenge legally, and thus the PAPs are left with no mechanism by which to resist the state's acquisition of their land. In *Bandhua Mukti Morcha* with respect to Article 21, the apex court explicitly laid down that –'It *is the fundamental right of everyone in this country...to live with human dignity.'* Then, Indian Supreme Court in *Olga Tellis v. Bombay Municipal Corporation* expanded the socio-economic dimension of right to life under Article 21 to the persons who are forcibly evicted, in terms of *'right to livelihood'.* In addition, Article 39 also directs the state to secure its citizens with the 'right to an adequate means of livelihood' thereby leading to the preservation of the right to work.

The clause 'public purpose' in LAA is one of the most controversial of all because it is nowhere defined. The Supreme Court in various cases has lain that not only is "Public Purpose" hard to define; the Government is the best judge to decide whether a purpose falls under this definition. This implies the court has already transferred the discretion of determining the benefits of particular project that whether they are for the public purpose or no.

The Constitution of India provides for a comprehensive framework for the socio-economic development of Scheduled Tribes and for preventing their exploitation by other groups of society. It provides the necessary safeguards for the rights of tribal peoples in Articles 15(4), 16(4), 17 and 23 of the Constitution. Plus, Article 46 states: *"The State shall promote with special care the educational and economic interests of the weaker sections of the people, and, in particular, of the Scheduled Castes and the Scheduled Tribes, and shall protect them from social injustice and all forms of exploitation."* As was held by the Hon'ble Supreme Court, *"Agriculture is the only source of livelihood for scheduled tribes, apart from collection and sale of minor forest produce to supplement their income. Land is their most important natural and valuable asset and imperishable endowment from which the tribal derive their sustenance, social status, economic and social equality, equality of status and dignity of person and permanent place of abode and work and living and tribes too have great emotional attachment of their lands."*

In *Board of Trustees, Court of Bombay v Dilip Kumar Nadkarni* it was ruled by the Hon'ble Supreme Court that the right to life will include the right to livelihood. Right to livelihood is an essential part of Right to life. Tribal are emotionally attached to their land and is strongly linked to their dignity. In spite of all this, mining rights are being granted to the corporations mostly over tribal lands. Nearly 4 million people in India live inside protected areas and are dependent on their resources for survival. "Bona-fide livelihood needs" means fulfilment of sustenance needs of self and family through production or sale of produce resulting from self-cultivation of forest land as provided under clauses (a), (c) and (d) of sub-section (1) of section 3 of the Act. Their survival is inextricably linked to the forest land resources because forest provides them resource for survival.

Recently, the Orissa government's agreement with Vedanta Alumina to allow mining of bauxite deposits in the Niyamgiri hills, the home of the Dongaria Kondha tribe, is an example of how corporate interests backed by state support are trampling on tribal livelihoods and threatening an ecologically rich and important region.

Article 12(1) of ICCPR provides for the 'right to liberty of movement and freedom to choose his residence.' Similarly, arbitrary interference with privacy, family, honour and reputation is been protected under Article 17(1). International law comes to the rescue to those as well whose right to an adequate standard of living, including adequate food, clothing, and housing or right to work is violated or snatched by the draconian policies. States should refrain, to the maximum possible extent, from compulsorily acquiring housing or land, unless such acts are legitimate and necessary and designed to facilitate the enjoyment of human rights through, for instance, measures of land reform or redistribution.

Further, Article 12(1) of ILO Convention 107 states that indigenous people "shall not be removed without their free consent from their habitual territories." While ILO Convention 107 goes reasonably far in promoting indigenous peoples' right to their territories, it accepts forced resettlement if necessary to secure national economic development. But, even if ILO Convention 107 accepts forced resettlement for such reasons, Articles 12(2) and 12(3) provide land of quality at least equal to that of the land previously occupied by the displaced, as well as full compensation for any resulting loss or injury. In India usually the eviction done for the purpose of development is by using force and as far as 'quality' Resettlement and Rehabilitation (R&R) is concerned, it seems to be a virtual impossibility if the past experiences are to be taken into consideration. Rights under I.L.O. convention are available to members of tribal or semi-tribal populations in independent countries whose social and economic conditions are at a less advanced stage than the stage reached by the other sections of the national community, and whose status is regulated wholly or partially by their own customs or traditions or by special laws or regulations The provisions of Fifth Schedule apply to the Scheduled Areas and Scheduled Tribes in any state other than the states of Assam, Meghalaya, Tripura and Mizoram. According to Part B of Fifth Schedule, normal laws are not applicable to Scheduled areas and empower the Governor to make special laws for the administration of such areas. India is signatory to I.L.O. As per Article 51 (c) of the Constitution of India. In the case of *P.U.C.L. Union of India*: *"Rules of customary International law are incorporated into national law and considered to be part of the national law, unless they are in conflict with an Act of Parliament."*

International Law treaties recognize tribal land rights and such rights have acquired the status of human rights in International arena because such rights are inalienable and inherent for the tribal. Due to general and consistent practice followed by the states from a sense of legal obligations, rights of tribal to hold collective ownership of the land has now become rule of customary international law. The Convention on Elimination of Racial Discrimination requires state parties 'to recognize and protect the rights of indigenous and tribal peoples to own, develop, control and use their communal lands'. Right to land of tribal is collective human rights. In the case of *Ominiyak v. Canada*, the Human Rights Committee held that the state sponsored encroachments on the lands traditionally used by the indigenous people for hunting, fishing, herding or other means of earning their livelihood may violate Article 27 of I.C.C.P.R.

The Persisting Reservation Dilemma

When the first Backward Classes Commission was constituted on 29th January, 1953 under the chairmanship of *Kakasaheb Kalelkar*, he wanted economic backwardness to be the criterion and not caste in deciding backwardness. But he had to fail to the majority of the members who wanted caste to be the criterion, to decide the backwardness The government on an average spends about 3% of GDP on education while countries that have developed at a fast pace have spent about 6% of their GDP on education. Pertinently, even the Right to education till the age of 14 was made compulsory after the intervention of the court. The two most contentious issues in the application of Article 15(4) as well as Article 16(4) have been-(i) determination of backward classes and (ii) extent or quantum of reservation.Apart from reservations in educational institutions and now even in private enterprises, Scheduled tribes also enjoy (on paper) the benefit of reservation in legislature.

It is not that the backward have not progressed but the percentage is less because those who have already availed reservation and progressed keep getting it again. This results in the formation of the creamy layer. Instead of having a reservation policy we feel the emphasis of the government should be to build good schools in the rural as well as urban areas so that the poor have an opportunity to study. All kinds of encouragement from the government should be there in the implementation of such policies. The mid day meal program was a successful one and we should see more of such schemes which encourage the poor to study. The current debate is for awarding reservation in the private sector as globalization has resulted in a boom in the private sector while there has been shrinkage in the jobs being generated by the public sector entities. But is this nation only for the backward? Why is it that every time the politicians are interested in the issues of the backward classes? The higher casts over the generations may have been very suppressive but that does not mean that tools for empowerment like reservation are misused. It has increasingly been the case with the politicians. When every election nears then they have some kind of reservation or the other being announced which I think is just a mechanism to get votes.

It is the very malfunctioning of the reservation system that has made it reaches this stage where a need has arisen for reservation in the private sector. If the whole reservation policy would have been successful then reservation should have ended in the educational institutions itself, as those who would have got into these institutions would have developed their skills whereby they could work as professionals or join the public sector depending upon their interest.

If real empowerment is the aim the backward should exhort the government to make good schools and world class institutions for higher education and make conditions conducive for availing of the reservation. This would go a long way in solving the problems faced by the backward. If the backward rely on the politicians completely and think reservations would help them out then they would be repeating the mistake that they have been repeating all these years. It would only help in the concentration of power in a few among this class which is not the purpose of giving reservation. In our view, reservation, in principle, is an effective means of improving the condition of socially and economically backward classes. Further, since wrongs were done against SC/STs in the name of caste system, we believe that they should be meaningfully compensated. However, it must be alienated from politics for truly benefiting these classes. It must be ensured that this benefit goes to the really deserving people and not to those who have already availed its benefit. The objective of reservation should be to bring an end to reservation itself by uplifting every one of the backward classes.

Suggestions & Conclusion

Thus, we perceive that how blatantly the blasphemy of gross neglect in cases of innocent yet victimized tribes in India is perpetuated. Their most basic human rights of education, livelihood, representation and dignity are literally snatched away. Snatch! We say because when the Constitution itself promises various benefits then who are we to block them and not allowing them to reach to the needy? We can only snatch in that case, and that too to fulfill our own selfish purposes of playing cheap politics and diverting the funds that come for their recourse. It will be late if adequate steps are not taken as soon as possible. In cases of land expropriation laws we have the following expositions to mark-

1. Independent Body Constitution.
2. Substitute for cash compensation.
3. Policy Innovations.

In majority of rest of the cases, we can only make a plea to the government and its administrative organs to get awake in the sunlight of rectitude, probity and selflessness as soon as possible. Better for them, better for tribes and moreover-Better for Nation. Apart from this, if in case governmental agencies genuinely want to help the displaced but they lack in co-ordination and accessories to do so it is again advisable to involve more and more Non-Governmental Organizations in the R&R operations. Plus, their contribution should also be in the policy making regarding the same. The so called independent bodies which the proposed models claim are actually no more than puppets in the hands of government because their appointment is in the 'appropriate government's' hand. Thus, if NGOs and the affected people are involved in the policy framing process, it can definitely bear more fruits and be more effective, therefore leading to fewer antagonisms and frictions between the citizens and the governments.

Government Policy and Legislative Framework Regarding Ethnic Groups

The Constitution of India provides specific measures for the protection and promotion of the social and economic interests of the Scheduled Tribes (STs). These include: reservation of seats in the legislature, educational institutions, services and posts, a tribal development program and provisions for autonomy.

Reservation in the Legislature: The Constitution of India ensures the political representation of Scheduled Tribes in the Lower House (*Lok Sabha*) of the Parliament and in the State Legislative Assemblies through reserved seats. Reservation in Educational Institutions and Services: Article 15(4) of the Indian

Constitution provides for the reservation of seats for Scheduled Tribes in educational institutions. In order to improve the social situation of the tribal people, the government has, in addition to quotas in education, also designed a reservation policy for employment in government services. Depending on the respective positions, posts reserved for members of "Scheduled Tribes" are either in proportion to the tribal population of the state in question, or – in most cases – comprise 7.5% of the total number of government jobs.

Constitutional Provisions for Tribal Self Rule: Geographical areas designated as Fifth and Sixth Scheduled areas by independent India are identical to those already delineated by the British as Scheduled Areas. Article 244(i) provides for a *Fifth Schedule* that can be applied to any state other than those of North-East India. This Schedule has been termed a "Constitution within the Constitution". Under this Schedule, the governors of the states in question have been given extensive powers, and may prevent or amend any law enacted in the parliament or the state assembly that could harm the tribals' interests. The *Sixth Schedule* is supposed to be informed by the ethos of self-management. The Schedule currently operates in the tribal-dominated areas of North-East India: Karbi Anglong and North Cachar districts in Assam; Khasi Hills, Jaintia Hills and Garo Hills districts in Meghalaya; Chakma, Lai and Mara districts in Mizoram; and Tripura tribal areas in Tripura state. Each Scheduled Tribe area covered by the Sixth Schedule has an Autonomous District Council with legislative, executive and judicial powers.

Provisions of the Panchayats (Extension to the Scheduled Areas) Act, 1996: This act is aimed primarily at promoting village-level democracy through the Panchayat Raj institutions. It includes changes aimed at adapting the generally established system for use in the Scheduled Areas, which have a different socio-economic and politico-administrative setting.

The National Commission for Scheduled Castes and Tribes: Article 338 of the Constitution provides for the appointment of a Special Officer for Scheduled Tribes and Castes by the President, who is commissioned to investigate and report to the President on all matters relating to the constitutional safeguards on Scheduled

Tribes and Castes. A National Commission for Scheduled Castes and Scheduled Tribes was subsequently created to take over these responsibilities.

Promotion of the economic and educational interests of the Scheduled Tribes and their protection from social injustice and exploitation are enshrined as a national goal in article 46 of the Constitution. Realizing that earlier programs under the central government's Five-Year Plans had failed to address the development needs, marginalization and exploitation of tribal communities, the *Tribal Sub-Plan (TSP)* was devised as a new strategy in the Fifth Five-Year Plan in 1973. It is still the approach that guides development programs in tribal areas. Its main objectives are to eliminate exploitation, to speed up social and economic development, and to promote and improve the organisational capacity of tribal people.

Wide-ranging *sector programs in tribal areas* have been implemented since the launch of the TSP by the different line agencies, with both state and central government funds. The focus has thus far clearly been on the development of physical infrastructure and on establishing and improving service institutions.

On a state level, the departments in charge of tribal affairs vary, i.e. a separate department has not been created in all cases but tribal issues usually come under the Ministry of Welfare. On a national level, a separate ministry, the Ministry of Tribal Affairs, has been created.

In December 2006 a *Forest Rights Bill* was passed by the Parliament and a few days later ratified by the Upper House of the Parliament. It is now pending at the office of the President for final approval. Under this Bill, the forest dwellers will receive ownership rights, including the right to farm on small plots and to sell forest produce such as honey, wax, medicinal plants and herbs. The passing of the Bill is seen as a victory of the people, especially the Indigenous Peoples, but not without a flaw that has the potential of becoming fatal. The final decision to recognize the forest dwellers lies with the bureaucrats not with the Village Council (*Gram Sabha*) as recommended by the Joint Parliamentary

Committee (JPC). Other recommendations of the JPC were also not taken into consideration, the most fatal of them being the deletion of the rights of the forest dwellers to fuelwood. This is seen by the people as a way of asking people to leave the forest. The traditional right to hunting wild animals and fishing have met the same fate.

The Right Pathway to Higher Education

With as many as 265 universities, 13,150 colleges, 8.821 million students, and 0.427 million teachers during 2001-02 as against 32 universities, 695 colleges, and 0.174 million students during 1950-51, India has developed one of the largest higher education systems in the world.

However, as the website of the Foundation for Academic Excellence and Access has rightly pointed out in India there is a chasm between what the education system is expected to achieve and what it is, in fact, accomplishing, and each of its main objectives remains to be accomplished. As the website would have, education was to be the medium through which equality of opportunity was to be made concrete, yet it remains an endlessly deferred dream for many; investment in education was meant to be a path of greater productivity and growth, yet its potential contribution to economy remains unrealised; education was to be an aspiration for better experience of excellence in all fields, yet it continues to remain a mere aspiration.

India's gross expenditure on education now, by the state and central governments combined, is nearly Rupees one lakh crore or 3.52 percent of the GDP. The Government of India's spending on education is expected to double by next year and go up to three times by 2009-10, from the current level to Rupees 1.82 lakh crore first and Rupees 238,835 crore subsequently.

Though the increase in spending will fulfill the promise of the Congress-led United Progressive Alliance ruling at the Centre to allocate six percent of the GDP to education, it will still be a case of the little done and a lot undone.

If the dropout and survival rates and the literacy and illiteracy rates of the broad social categories are any indication, India has not done much for democratisation of access even at the primary level. Going by the Census 2001, India has about 41 million illiterates in the 7-13 age group, 16 million illiterates in the 14-17 age group, and 33 million illiterates in the 18-24 age group. The illiterates account for about 27 percent, 25 percent, and 35 percent respectively of the total population of the relevant age groups. Of those enrolled at the primary level, about 40 percent drop out by the time they reach the fourth year of schooling.

In each age cohort the illiteracy rate is much higher among the traditionally backward Scheduled Castes, Scheduled Tribes, and Muslims (accounting for about 47 percent of India's population), and among women in each social group. Thus, if India has a long way to go to achieve basic education for all, its distance to achieve universal higher education may be infinity.

Despite the rapid and massive growth of higher education, India has only about 8 to 9 percent of its relevant age group enrolled for higher education, as against 50-85 percent in developed countries.

The problems of Indian education centers around financing, equity and excellence in access and outturn. As these problems have been confounded by the rapid speed of globalization under which society needs only educated manpower, the deprived in India are now victims of double whammy. Their traditional deprivation keeps them away from education; and the demands of a knowledge-driven society under globalization leave them out of the mainstream as social misfits – as the disposable people of society-because of their lack of education.

Instead of seeing the problems in perspective, governance in India seems to be choosing cheap populist options. Though satisfying to the politicians, these options can do no good, and in the long run can do a lot of harm to the rising generation, in particular, the historically deprived social groups, which are still victims of entrenched backwardness.

The reference is to the Bill passed by Indian Parliament on 22 December 2005 extending reservation (the principal form of affirmative action in India) of seats to the Scheduled Castes, Scheduled Tribes, and Other Socially and Educationally Backward

Classes in higher education institutions under private management. The provision of reservation cannot benefit students from the deprived groups in a big way, though it may still be necessary. If reservation for more than fifty years in State-run institutions has not benefited them much, it is naïve to expect that the State's mandate for reservation in private institutions will benefit them. One indication of the inadequacy of reservation to meet the educational needs of the deprived sections is the share of degree holders from them.

Going by the Census 2001, the overall share of Graduates in the 20-24 age-group population in India is about 8 percent. Of the six categories into which the Census 2001 has classified the Indian population, the degree holders in the 20-24 age group account for only 2.3 percent of the total population in this age group among the Scheduled Tribes, 3.6 percent among the Scheduled Castes, 4 percent among the Muslims, 7.4 percent among the Buddhists, 7.6 percent among the Sikhs, 9.8 percent among the caste-Hindus (Hindus excluding the SCs and STs), and 11 percent among the Christians.

Given this dismal scenario, it is only too obvious that the State has so far failed to grapple with the reality of the enormous task of educating India's rising generation in socially equitable and globally competitive ways, the problem that many parents are too poor that they would like their children to be wage-earners, and that even if they want to have their children educated-which I am confident, most of them want-the prohibitive cost of education and failure of their children to get admission discourage them from doing so.

To place higher education on a fast track, the most important need is to foster existing institutions by ensuring equity and fairness in their intake, by strengthening their basic and infrastructure needs including, and especially of qualified teachers, and by grounding these institutions in disciplinary diversity and excellence in quality. The institutions cannot generally address these issues in the absence of active intervention by educationists from outside.

Educationists, on their part, can justify their intervention only by providing adequate financial support and orientation to the institutions, backed by institution-friendly monitoring mechanisms.

When institutions become convinced that the support from educationists are genuine and reliable, they will be eager to identify and admit more and more students from the deprived groups, and use the capacity building facilities-though primarily given to meet the special needs of the deprived-to the greater good.

The FAEA's Pathways Programme is one such innovative package comprising admission of carefully selected students from deprived social groups, administering scholarships and bursaries, providing institutional support, and arranging outreach programmes and regular meetings of cluster colleges. At the instance of the FAEA, college principals and others, involved in the Programme, from different parts of the India exchange their experiences, learn from each other's work and try to systematically augment the scope of the Programme, so as to make it gradually self-sustaining.

Founded in a modest way, in just a few years, the Programme has already become a household name among the poor in India, despite its limited resources. When the spirit of commitment is combined with dedicated work, and a new innovative system of education evolves as it is happening in the case of the FAEA Programme, the outcome in terms of access, equity, and excellence, can be profound.

Dr. K.R. Narayanan, former President of India, who hailed from one of the most backward and deprived social groups, was the FAEA patron till his death recently. Professor V.R. Mehta, an eminent political scientist, who was vice-chancellor of at least three universities-including the Delhi University-at a young age, is the brain behind the FAEA. Mehta has built up an excellent team committed to the cause of education; and core-teams to help the FAEA in the day-to-day administration of the Programme, and for periodic meetings, reviews, and brainstorming.

While there cannot be many Mehtas and many FAEAs, it is certainly possible to expand the scope and reach of the FAEA itself. For that, the FAEA needs a lot of money, from well-meaning institutions. The Ford Foundation has already been one. In fact, it is with a generous grant from the Ford Foundation that the FAEA has been managing its Programme. While the Ford

Foundation could renew its grant generously for enabling the FAEA Programme to sustain its momentum, other well-meaning institutions should also pitch in and turn the FAEA momentum into a lofty national movement, without in any way interfering with the autonomy of the FAEA. The Government of India on its part should draw lessons from the FAEA Programme and work for strengthening and replicating it.

Action-oriented Learning to Identify Issues Important to Women

Sustainable Tribal Empowerment Project (STEP) works to empower the marginalized tribal communities of Andhra Pradesh. The cornerstone of the project is the Action Oriented Learning process, which involves communities as active partners in assessing their own socio-economic conditions, prioritizing their needs and working towards realization of their rights collectively. The guiding principles are inclusion/participation, access to information, and building local organizations capacity for ensuring transparency and accountability both at the community level as well as the government level.

The successive, bottom-to-top, consultative and participatory learning process of 'Action Oriented Learning' (AOL), which enables the tribal community to critically reflect, analyse and understand their socio-economic realities, followed by taking initiatives to make changes or actions. During the process the issues that affected most families were given priority and taken up irrespective of whether it was a women or men's issue.

Gender equity is a cross cutting theme and is incorporated in all the project interventions. The project has consciously tried to include women as active participants in all interventions like the community planning process and also in the affairs of all the community-based organizations, along with specific interventions like grain banks, drinking water projects, and land and water management initiatives.

Context

The NGO partner has been working in the tribal region of Visakhapatnam and Vizianagaram of Andhra Pradesh since 1992.

People here live as close-knit rural communities, but organizing them for political action is very difficult primarily due to remoteness, lack of information and education, and living in a cocoon. This has made tribal regions vulnerable and open to exploitation and subjected tribal people to repression of the worst kind. There were different issues of exploitation, poverty, and social exclusion in the region. Government development policies had displaced tribal peoples, threatened their traditional livelihoods and pushed them into abject poverty and hunger. As a result, many are forced to migrate. Other issues included transfer of land and mining leases to the private companies without consulting the communities that would be affected. NATURE's major concern was collectivizing the community, giving them voice and building leadership assert their rights.

The village selected to measure changes in women's empowerment as a result of these interventions is 10 kms from a main road, with no bus service. There are 72 households with a total population of 320. Most of the people earn their living growing vegetables, turmeric, corn etc., using a form of shifting cultivation in the jungles and mountains that is illegal. This village was compared with a village with government-led community interaction.

How Empowerment is Defined Locally

Empowerment for the researchers was seen as developing positive types of power, as opposed to one person having power over another, which is often legitimized by society through norms, rules customs, etc. Power within, refers to self-esteem, self-respect and belief in one's own ability to take action. Power to refers to expanding one's boundaries through the development of skills, negotiating and learning. Power with refers to collective action, whereby women learn from each other, recognize their strengths and weakness, reflect on their situation and come up with strategies for change. Power is thus relational, situational, and structural as well as individual issue, and empowerment is a process as well as an outcome.

Using Action Oriented Learning (AOL), women identified the following issues as important for women.

- Water
- Food for children
- Money in the hands of women
- Rice grinding mill
- Toilets for women
- Transport so that women could transport their produce to markets
- Common place for a meeting specially since meeting during rains is very difficult, the whole place is very water logged
- Pension for widows
- Proper drainage system.

The key study questions focus on five broad indicators of empowerment:

- What are the women's perceptions about the most significant changes in their lives in the last five years and how it relates to indicators of empowerment?
- What has been the impact on women's decision-making and influence within family and community
- What has been the impact on gender equity in distribution and management of resources within the community?
- What types of collective actions have women taken to influence wider social/political issues within the community?
- How do initiatives taken up by collectives impact social dialogue and development partnerships between tribal people and government agencies.

Research Methodology and Tools

The inquiry involved interactions with PNGO staff, staff from STEP and NGO partner NATURE, teachers, community leaders, and community members. Appropriate qualitative methods were adopted in order to gather insights using checklists developed to gather information.

Research hypothesis: Community planning contributes to

confidence, awareness, decision making and overall women's empowerment in tribal communities. Women's representation in Community Action Groups contributes to women's issues being prioritized at community level. Being members of SHG have improved participation in Panchayats.

Focus Group Discussions were conducted with members of the women's groups in each of the sites. Additionally, individual interviews for in-depth investigation of selected areas of inquiry and getting the perspective of other key stakeholders (non members, brothers, sons and daughters, husbands, community leaders, PRI members, etc) about the impact on women's empowerment. Every facilitator ensured that the women selected for the individual interviews were both vocal as well as non-vocal, new members as well as old members, young and old women etc.

Indicators of Empowerment

The research findings were organized around the constructs of Agency, Relationships and Structure, which relate back to the researchers' definitions of power.

Agency

Self: Women said they felt more confident, do not hesitate to meet strangers, can call for meetings and are more knowledgeable on issues. The also reported greater mobility, starting individual enterprises, making decisions about crops grown on their own land, and increased participation in family and community decision-making.

Group: There is greater bondage among community members of different economic and social status, and resources are given to the neediest irrespective of caste. Decisions about community resources are decided through community participation processes, and women serve on local water committees. The entire community, including women, comes together to fight for their rights and demand public hearings.

Community behaviour and practices: There is increased health seeking behaviour, family planning (vasectomies for men), personal cleanliness. Girls no longer get married before age 18 and formerly rampant alchoholism has been addressed and curbed. People wear better clothing and men and women participate jointly in community festivals.

Relationships

Community Planning Process: Everyone interviewed had participated in the community planning process and felt it had enabled them identify their needs, problems and the village resources. The community grain banks are widely appreciated and community ownership and management is high. The initiative has helped arrest distress migration and ensured food security for members for 3-4 weeks during the lean periods. Lack of transport remains an unsolved problem, but the community planning process has greatly impacted gender equity in distribution and management of resources within the community and building solidarity.

Structural

Linkages with key institutions: The women feel closer to many institutions. They first learned about different institutions and their importance through the micro planning process and training. They were sent to learn about Grain Banks management and developed one for their own village. By being involved in the Forest Protection Committee, they were brought closer to the forest department. They are very close to the PHC because they get all the facilities. The school has been brought closer to them because of their participation in School Education Committee. The Panchayat headquarter is physically far from the village but the community felt it was closer now as they have started attending the meetings and also accessing resources for their village.

Participation: Women now participate in Gram Sabha meetings and learn about schemes and sanctions that they discuss in their villages and bring back proposals. Voting during elections has become a community-wide consultative process, based on negotiations with the candidates on issues that are of utmost importance to the community. The women said that constant negotiation with men have resulted in greater bargaining power in them. The community reported increasing visits by government officials to learn and replicate the efforts in other areas. The government officials visited the village to look at the grain bank and the water sources created and also study the systems that were put in place to ensure participation and ownership of the community to maintain these structures.

Enabled social action: A new teacher was appointed by the community and paid with community contributions, after the government-appointed teacher was found to be unsatisfactory. This salary was later negotiated for from the education department. Alcoholism was increasing the incidence of violence against women; the community was able to address the problem through local community organizations, by framing rules and assigning roles and responsibilities.

The women of the village took a vow to abstain from alcohol and women compelled men to give up alcohol. Several men interviewed stated that alcoholism is a thing of the past in the village. The village floods during the monsoons. During planning, the community identified the urgent need for drainage and have now successfully built a drainage system through joint efforts of both men and women. The community is now pressing for toilets and dreams of having a good road and a village bus. One woman even envisioned the day when the children will go to college for a degree.

Lessons Learned, Conclusions

- The evidence indicates an increase in women's capabilities (Power to) and (Power with) due to the collective mobilisation of women. This has impacted the agency-related indicators of women's empowerment, 'enhanced quality of participation, control over resources and decision-making, shift in critical consciousness and understanding, of women within the group'.
- There is ample evidence to suggest that STEP has impacted Structures, they have been able bring about a change in the education system where the community has now started playing an active role in ensuring education for their children. Their active participation in Panchayats and negotiation with political leaders for initiating community development processes can be linked to the rights based approach and information on various projects and schemes disseminated by the staff.

- A unique feature of the project has been the ability to affect changes in the inequitable structures by building mutual support through community planning processes. This has greatly impacted the livelihood security and also ensured inclusion of excluded groups.
- Working with both men and women in mixed groups has brought about a bigger change in women because of their constant involvement and negotiations with men in the groups.
- The project has a very explicit conceptualisation of gender inequity and this is reflected in the processes used in the project. Rather than simply taking women as vulnerable groups and doing individual empowerment, the program aimed at addressing cultural stereotypes that affect women's ability to be empowered.
- The teams' (staff and partner) experience, assumptions and beliefs on women's empowerment have contributed greatly to the strategies used to address social exclusion and power relations. The program has been successful in strategically using collective power to negotiate for the rights of the community and promoting partnerships with government agencies/departments.

The SII study highlights the importance of having a concrete empowerment strategy to address the many challenges and obstacles faced by organizations working in difficult areas. Moreover, since the ultimate goal of STEP was to empower poor women, gender issues has been understood from a perspective that looked at underlying causes of power that determined outcomes of interventions. It looked at poverty and vulnerability as products of the inequitable distribution of power over resources and designed interventions using the equity lens.

The project targets women as members and decision-makers of both community resources and village planning committees. The decision to encourage the full participation of women in this project is based on the fact that women in the project areas are major economic contributors to their households. Not only are women involved in subsistence agriculture, participating in production and post harvest activities, but they are also petty traders of snacks and meals prepared at home, and vegetables from their gardens. Another reason to include women is to protect and develop women's economic interests in the project and address issues of, access and control over resources, participation in decision making and qualitative participation in different public forums. The increased sense of self-confidence and esteem being felt by many women in the community, the close bonding between members and the participation of groups in local markets and political forums are encouraging signs and reveal the change in gender dynamics.

Women's empowerment has been stated as an explicit goal and outcomes and focuses explicitly mention impact on women in some of the key result areas but STEP does not have an articulated gender strategy. There are very few female staff members in the district in the project. There is a need to do gender relation analyses using the power relations' analysis at CBO level to enable the project to strengthen and sustain it initiatives.

The study also throws light on the need for greater organizational commitment and support structures to mainstream gender, rights and governance in its programs. High degree of collaboration, teamwork is lost when there are no clear guidelines on resource allocation and utilization. For the future the program should focus on monitoring the functioning of women and consciously strengthening the links between women leaders, non-government resource providers and government departments. The program could be further strengthened if internal work around gender and diversity is consciously promoted and supported by the organization to further performance on gender outcomes and impacts.

5

Dalit Empowerment

Caste System in India

The Indian caste system describes the social stratification and social restrictions in the Indian subcontinent, in which social classes are defined by thousands of endogamous hereditary groups, often termed as *jatis* or castes. Within a jati, there exist exogamous groups known as gotras, the lineage or clan of an individual, although in a handful of sub-castes like Shakadvipi, endogamy within a gotra is permitted and alternative mechanisms of restricting endogamy are used (e.g. banning endogamy within a surname). Although generally identified with Hinduism, the caste system was also observed among followers of other religions in the Indian subcontinent, including some groups of Muslims and Christians. The Indian Constitution has outlawed caste-based discrimination, in keeping with the socialist, secular, democratic principles that founded the nation. Caste barriers have mostly broken down in large cities, though they persist in rural areas of the country, where 72% of India's population resides. Nevertheless, the caste system, in various forms, continues to survive in modern India strengthened by a combination of social perceptions and divisive politics.

History

There is no universally accepted theory about the origin of the Indian caste system. The Indian classes are similar to the ancient Iranian classes ("*pistras*"), wherein the priests are Athravans, the warriors are Rathaestha, the merchants are Vastriya, and the artisans are Huiti.

Origin

The origin of the caste system as it is today is still obscure.

A 2001 genetic study, led by Michael Bamshad of University of Utah, found that the genetic affinity of Indians making their way to Europeans is proportionate to caste rank, the upper castes being most similar to Europeans, whereas lower castes are more like Asians. The researchers believe that the Indo-European speakers entered India from the Northwest, admixing with or displacing the proto-Dravidian speakers. Subsequently they may have established a caste system and placed themselves primarily in higher castes.

The study concludes that the Indian castes "are most likely to be of proto-Asian origin with West Eurasian admixture resulting in rank-related and sex-specific differences in the genetic affinities of castes to Asians and Europeans.". Because the Indian samples for this study were taken from a single geographical area, it remains to be investigated whether its findings can be safely generalized. However the findings of this study is considered controversial since the study was limited to one state, Andhra Pradesh, in India during the regime of a Chief Minister who was reprimanded several times by the Indian courts for Anti-Hindu activities. At the end of this article, the acknowledgments state that it incorporates contributions from an anonymous reviewer and because of its financial support, it has to be classified as an *advertisement. The publication costs of this article were defrayed in part by payment of page charges. This article must therefore be hereby marked "advertisement" in accordance with 18 USC section 1734 solely to indicate this fact.* The findings of this article is also in contradiction to later Human Genetic studies conducted with larger samples.

An earlier 1995 study by Joanna L. Mountain et al. of Stanford University had concluded that there was "no clear separation into three genetically distinct groups along caste lines", although "an inferred tree revealed some clustering according to caste affiliation".

A 2002-03 study by T. Kivisild et al. concluded that the "Indian tribal and caste populations derive largely from the same genetic heritage of Pleistocene southern and western Asians and have received limited gene flow from external regions since the

Holocene." A 2006 genetic study by the National Institute of Biologicals in India, testing a sample of men from 32 tribal and 45 caste groups, concluded that the Indians have acquired very few genes from Indo-European speakers.

According to a 2006 study by Ismail Thanseem et al. of Centre for Cellular and Molecular Biology (India) "the vast majority (>98%) of the Indian maternal gene pool, consisting of Indo-European and Dravidian speakers, is genetically more or less uniform", while the invasions after the late Pleistocene settlement might have been mostly male-mediated. The study concluded that the "lower caste groups might have originated with the hierarchical divisions that arose within the tribal groups with the spread of Neolithic agriculturalists, much earlier than the arrival of Aryan speakers", and "the Indo-Europeans established themselves as upper castes among this already developed caste-like class structure within the tribes." The study indicated that the Indian caste system may have its roots much before the arrival of the Indo-Aryan immigrants; a rudimentary version of the caste system may have emerged with the shift towards cultivation and settlements, and the divisions may have become more well-defined and intensified with the arrival of Indo-Aryans. More recent studies have also debunked the British claims that so-called "Aryans" and "Dravidians" have a "racial divide". A study conducted by the Centre for Cellular and Molecular Biology in 2009 (in collaboration with Harvard Medical School, Harvard School of Public Health and the Broad Institute of Harvard and MIT) analysed half a million genetic markers across the genomes of 132 individuals from 25 ethnic groups from 13 states in India across multiple caste groups. The study establishes, based on the impossibility of identifying any genetic indicators across caste lines, that castes in South Asia grew out of traditional tribal organizations during the formation of Indian society, and was not the product of any mythical "Aryan Invasion" and "subjugation" of Dravidian people.

Hindu Scriptures

Although the Hindu scriptures contain some passages that can be interpreted to sanction the caste system, they also contain indications that the caste system is not an essential part of the

Hindu religion, and both sides in the debate are able to find sections in scriptures that support their views.

The most ancient scriptures—the *Shruti* texts, or Vedas, place very little importance on the caste system, mentioning caste only rarely and in a cursory manner. A hymn from the Rig Veda seems to indicate that one's caste is not necessarily determined by that of one's family:

Rig Veda 9.112.3

—I am a bard, my father is a physician, my mother's job is to grind the corn.

In the Vedic period, there also seems to no discrimination against the Shudras (which later became an ensemble of the so-called low-castes) on the issue of hearing the sacred words of the Vedas and fully participating in all religious rights, something which became totally banned in the later times.

Later scriptures such as *Bhagavad Gita* and *Manusmriti* state that the four varnas are created by God. However, at the same time, the Gita says that one's varna is to be understood from one's personal qualities and one's *karma* (work), not one's birth. Some scholars believe that, in its initial period, the caste system was flexible and it was merit and job based.

One could migrate from one caste to other caste by changing one's profession. This view is supported by records of sages who became Brahmins. For example, the sage Vishwamitra belonged to a Kshatriya caste, and only later became recognized as a great Brahmin sage, indicating that his caste was not determined by birth. Similarly, Valmiki, once a low-caste robber, became a great sage. Veda Vyasa, another sage, was the son of a fisherwoman. Vasishtha was a shudra and he became sage later.

Manusmriti, dated between 200 B.C.E. and 100 A.D., contains some laws that codified the caste system. Varna is mentioned as caste equivalent in Manusmriti. Manusmriti and some other shastras mention four varnas: The Brahmins (teachers, scholars and priests), the Kshatriyas (kings and warriors), the Vaishyas (traders, landowners and some artisan groups), and Shudras (agriculturists, service providers, and some artisan groups).

Another group of untouchables excluded from the main society was called Parjanya or Antyaja. A varna can be viewed as a group of castes or a social division that consists of various sub-castes called *jatis*.

Passages in Manusmriti and other scriptures suggest that the Indian caste system was originally non-hereditary:

ManuSmriti X:65

— As the son of Shudra can attain the rank of a Brahman, the son of Brahman can attain rank of a Shudra. Even so with him who is born of a Vaishya or a Kshatriya

The various smritis, like the Yagnavalkyasmriti and the Manusmriti strongly disapprove of marrying outside one's caste. The smritis also argue that new, despicable castes are formed out of such cases. According to these smritis, the chamars were born out of the union of a vaideha and a nishada, the chandals were born out of the sexual relations between a Brahmin and a Shudra.

Emergence of Rigid Caste Structures

Megasthenes, the Greek ambassador to Chandragupta Maurya's court in India classified people of India into seven classes: philosophers, peasants, herdsmen, craftsmen and traders, soldiers, government officials and councillors.

In its later stages, the caste system is said to have become rigid, and caste began to be inherited rather than acquired by merit. In the past, members of different castes would not partake in various activities, such as dining and religious gatherings, together. In addition, the performance of religious rites and rituals were restricted to Brahmins, who were the designated priesthood. The "Pandaram" priests are an example of an order of Dravidian tamil priests, based in Nepal and South India. The Pandaram maintain the same tradition as the Brahmin priests, including the use of the Sanskrit language (traditionally reserved for the Brahmins) for the rituals. While they are not generally as well trained as the Brahmin priests, they are highly respected within their community and are addressed with reverence.

According to the Manusmriti, every caste belongs to one of the four varnas (Brahmin, Kshtriya, Vaishya, and Shudra). However, there have been many disputes about the varna of many castes, such as castes being considered Kshatriya by some scholars, while described as Shudra by others. While texts such as the Manusmriti attempted to rationalize ambiguous castes by placing them in varna-sankaras (i.e. mixed varna), the fact remains that Indian society was, and is, composed of numerous geographically diversified but endogamous groups. With many occupational groups practicing endogamy within a particular region, as well as numerous sub-divisions within the four main castes, a more complex system of subcastes and jatis is evident. The jatis have broken up into clans like Agarwal, Iyer, etc.

Mobility Across the Castes

The view of the caste system as "static and unchanging" has been disputed by many scholars. For instance, sociolgists such as Bernard Buber and Marriott McKim describe how the perception of the caste system as a static and textual stratification has given way to the perception of the caste system as a more processual, empirical and contextual stratification. Other sociologists such as Y.B Damle have applied theoretical models to explain mobility and flexibility in the caste system in India.. According to these scholars, groups of lower-caste individuals could seek to elevate the status of their caste by attempting to emulate the practices of higher castes.

Some scholars believe that the relative ranking of other castes was fluid or differed from one place to another prior to the arrival of the British.

The distinctions, particularly between the Brahmans and the other castes, were in theory sharper, but in practice it now appears that social restrictions were not so rigid. Brahmans often lived off the land and founded dynasties. Most of the groups claiming Kshatriya status had only recently acquired it. The conscious reference to being Kshatriya, a characteristic among Rajputs, is a noticeable feature in post-Gupta politics. The fact that many of these dynasties were of obscure origin suggests some social mobility: a person of any caste, having once acquired political power, could also acquire a genealogy connecting him with the traditional lineages and conferring Kshatriya status. A number of new castes, such as the Kayasthas (scribes) and Khatris (traders), are mentioned in the sources of this period. According to the Brahmanic sources, they originated from intercaste marriages, but this is clearly an attempt at rationalizing their rank in the hierarchy. Many of these new castes played a major role in society. The hierarchy of castes did not have a uniform distribution throughout the country.

Flexibility in caste laws permitted very low-caste religious clerics such as Valmiki to compose the Ramayana, which became a central work of Hindu scripture.

According to some psychologists, mobility across broad caste lines may have been "minimal", though sub-castes (jatis) may change their social status over the generations by fission, re-location, and adoption of new rituals..

Sociologist M. N. Srinivas has also debated the question of rigidity in Caste. In an ethnographic study of the Coorgs of Karnataka, he observed considerable flexibility and mobility in their caste hierarchies. He asserts that the caste system is far from a rigid system in which the position of each component caste is fixed for all time.

Movement has always been possible, and especially in the middle regions of the hierarchy. It was always possible for groups born into a lower caste to "rise to a higher position by adopting vegetarianism and teetotalism" i.e adopt the customs of the higher castes. While theoretically "forbidden", the process was not uncommon in practice. The concept of sanskritization, or the adoption of upper-caste norms by the lower castes, addressed the actual complexity and fluidity of caste relations.

Historical examples of mobility in the Indian Caste System among Hindus have been researched. There is also precedent of certain Shudra families within the temples of the Shrivaishava sect in South India elevating their caste.

Historical Advantages of the Caste System

Historically, the caste system offered several advantages to the population of the Indian subcontinent. While Caste is nowadays seen by instances that render it anachronistic, in its original form the caste system served as an important instrument of order in a society in which mutual consent rather than compulsion ruled ; where the ritual rights as well as the economic obligations of members of one caste or sub-caste were strictly circumscribed in relation to those of any other caste or sub-caste; where one was born into one's caste and retained one's station in society for life; where merit was inherited, where equality existed within the caste, but inter-caste relations were unequal and hierarchical. A well-defined system of mutual interdependence through a division of labour created security within a community.

1. Preservation of order in society through the use of institutional stratification of social groups.
2. Integration of foreigners and invading forces into Indian culture by assigning a caste to them (a process that historian Jawaharlal Nehru referred to as "Indianization"): India has faced repeated invasions from outside the region, dating back to the Macedonian invasion by Alexander the Great. Most invaders were swiftly assimilated into ancient Indian society by assigning them specific castes. Examples include the Kambojas, believed to be of Indo-Scythian descent, who were retroactively assigned a social position in the Manusmriti.
3. The Varna system, with its normative interpretation as a division of labour, had and continues to have a heavy bias towards spiritual evolution. The deep religious proclivities and the urge for spiritual uplift had induced the people to search for simpler and effective ways to achieve the spiritual goal which led to innovations like the Bhakti movement which had a powerful impact on the socio-cultural-spiritual life of the people even at mass level without distinctions of caste or class or other social differences. It is these deeply run cultural roots which caused an abiding following for Hinduism even in the face of unrelenting assaults by other religions and had in fact continued to influence the lives of people even after their conversion to other faiths. Thus, the caste system can be said to have preserved ancient cultural values in Indian society.

4. The caste system played an influential role in shaping economic activities. The caste system functioned much like medieval European guilds, ensuring the division of labour, providing for the training of apprentices and, in some cases, allowing manufacturers to achieve narrow specialisation. For instance, in certain regions, producing each variety of cloth was the speciality of a particular sub-caste.
5. Philosophers argue that the majority of people would be comfortable in stratified endogamous groups and have been in ancient times. Membership in a particular caste, with its associated narrative, history and genealogy would instill in its members a sense of group accomplishment and cultural pride. Such sentiments are routinely expressed by the Marathas, for instance.

British Rule

The caste system was first exposed to the modern Western world during the Portuguese occupation and rule of sections of India. The word 'caste' in this context is derived from the Portuguese, 'casta'. Later, other European empires, including the British, occupied parts of the subcontinent.

The earliest use of caste as a basis for interpreting social and demographic data arose from British officials' concern to stamp out female infanticide. Later, the use of caste to classify the population formed a basis for British attempts at social engineering. According to certain British laws (such as the Criminal Tribes Act of 1871), many castes and tribes were described as habitually criminal, and adult male members of such groups forced to report weekly to the local police. The caste-based classification (moneylending, agricultural or martial) was also used for other purposes such as legislation controlling land transfers, the grant of proprietary rights, the regulation of rents, recruitment to the armed forces etc. British anthropologist Herbert Risley's *The Tribes and Castes of Bengal*, published in 1892, was one of the first works on the caste system in India written by a Western scholar.

The earliest forms of classification in the British censuses of India (1865, 1872 and 1881) were based on the varna system, with the population being divided into Brahmins, Kshatriyas, Vaishyas and Shudras. Denzil Ibbetson, in his introduction to the 1881 census of the Punjab, argued that the Indian caste system was more of a social than a religious institution, and that conversion from Hinduism to Islam had not necessarily the slightest effect upon caste. He stated that the varnas had "no present significance". The 1891 census was based primarily on castes as occupational guilds instead of the varnas.

Some scholars state that the caste system was broken up greatly during British Raj in India. However, some other historians suggest that the impact of British reforms has been greatly exaggerated.

Initially, the British strengthened the caste system. They gave the Brahmins back special privileges the Muslim rulers had taken away. During the initial days of British East India Company's rules, caste privileges and customs were encouraged in the Bengal Army. But, British law courts disagreed with the discrimination against the lower castes. Many believe that the lack of British respect for sepoys' caste traditions was one of the reasons behind the Indian Rebellion of 1857. During British rule, the reservation of seats for the "Depressed Classes" was incorporated into the Government of India Act 1935, which went into force in 1937. The Act brought the term "Scheduled castes" into use, which was later clarified in The Government of India (Scheduled Castes) Order, 1936 which contained a list of scheduled castes.

British Census Officers determined caste hierarchy based on the principle, e.g. someone who accepts food and water from another person but the other person does not reciprocate the same way, then the other person is superior to the former. It was contested at many places (a notable example is that the Koeris of UP who said they won't accept water from Brahmins, and so should be placed higher than them). Because it was met with rampant controversies, arbitration was very common during those days. The most notable arbitration stories are:

1. Caste status of Kayastha
2. Caste status of Kurmi.

It raised more questions than it answered and subsequent census records varied radically, making it free for all, after some time.

Major Caste Groups

According to the 1891 census data, the major caste groups in India were following (listed in the order of population):

Caste-group	Example	Population %
Cultivators	Maurya, Kurmi, Mali, Lodha, Kushwaha	20%
Village Menials	Chamar, Dosadh, Dom	13%
Military	Jat, Rajput, Nairs, Maratha	12%
Artisans	Lohar, Sunar, Julaha	12%
Pastoral	Ahir, Gaderia, Dhangar	7%
Forest tribes	Santhal, Gond, Bhil	7%
Professionals	Namboothiri, Brahmbhatt, Kayasth	6%
Services	Nai, Dhobi, Kandoi	6%
Merchants	Agrawal, Khatri, Balija, Barnwal	5%
Labourers	Musahar, Bagdi, Bawari	3%
Fishers	Kahar, Mallah	3%
Other professionals	Vaidya, Mirasi, Bhand	2%
Vagrants	Waddar, Nat, Beldar	1%

Reform Movements

There have been cases of upper caste Hindus warming to the Dalits and Hindu priests, demoted to outcaste ranks, who continued practising the religion. An example of the latter was Dnyaneshwar, who was excommunicated from society in the 13th century, but continued to compose the Dnyaneshwari, a Dharmic commentary on the Bhagavad Gita. Other excommunicated Brahmins, such as Eknath, fought for the rights of untouchables during the Bhakti period. Historical examples of Dalit priests include Chokhamela in the 14th Century, who was India's first recorded Dalit poet, Raidas, born into Dalit cobblers, and others. The 15th century saint Ramananda also accepted all castes, including untouchables, into his fold. Most of these saints subscribed to the Bhakti movements in Hinduism during the medieval period that rejected casteism. Nandanar, a low-caste Hindu cleric, also rejected casteism and accepted Dalits.

Many movements in Hinduism have welcomed Dalits into their fold, the foremost being the Bhakti movements of the medieval period. Early Dalit politics involved many Hindu reform movements which arose primarily as a reaction to the tactics of Christian Missionaries in India and their attempts to mass-convert Dalits to Christianity under the allure of escaping the caste system (unfortunately, there is Caste system among Indian Christians among large sections of Indian Christians).

In the 19th Century, the Brahmo Samaj under Raja Ram Mohan Roy, actively campaigned against untouchability. The Arya Samaj founded by Swami Dayanand also renounced discrimination against Dalits. Sri Ramakrishna Paramahamsa founded the Ramakrishna Mission that participated in the emancipation of Dalits.

Upper caste Hindus, such as Mannathu Padmanabhan also participated in movements to abolish Untouchability against Dalits, opening his family temple for Dalits to worship. While there always have been places for Dalits to worship, the first "upper-caste" temple to openly welcome Dalits into their fold was the Laxminarayan Temple in Wardha in the year 1928 (the move was spearheaded by reformer Jamnalal Bajaj). Also, the Satnami movement was founded by Guru Ghasidas a Dalit himself.

Other reformers, such as Mahatma Jyotirao Phule also worked for the emancipation of Dalits. Another example of Dalit emancipation was the Temple Entry Proclamation issued by the last Maharaja of Travancore in the Indian state of Kerala in the year 1936. The Maharaja proclaimed that "outcastes should not be denied the consolations and the solace of the Hindu faith". Even today, the Sri Padmanabhaswamy temple that first welcomed Dalits in the state of Kerala is revered by the Dalit Hindu community. The 1930s saw key struggles between Mahatma Gandhi and B.R. Ambedkar, most notably over whether Dalits would have separate electorates or joint electorates with reserved seats.

The Indian National Congress was the only national organisation with a large Dalit following, but Gandhi failed to gain their commitment. Ambedkar, a Dalit himself, developed a deeper analysis of Untouchability, but lacked a workable political strategy: his conversion to Buddhism in 1956, along with millions of followers, highlighted the failure of his political endeavours. India's first Prime Minister, Jawaharlal Nehru, based on his own relationship with Dalit reformer Ambedkar, also spread information about the dire need to eradicate untouchability for the benefit of the Dalit community.

In more contemporary times, India has had an elected Dalit president, K. R. Narayanan, who has stated that he was well-treated in his community of largely upper-caste Hindus (24 July 2002). Another popular Harijan includes Babaji Palwankar Baloo, who joined the Hindu Mahasabha and was both a politician and a cricketer. He was an independence fighter. In addition, other Hindu groups have reached out to the Dalit community in an effort to reconcile with them, with productive results. On August 2006, Dalit activist Namdeo Dhasal engaged in dialogue with the Rashtriya Swayamsevak Sangh in an attempt to "bury the hatchet".

Also, the "Pandaram" are an order of Dravidian Tamil Hindu priests (a task traditionally reserved for the Brahmins) based largely in Nepal and parts of South India. These Pandaram priests maintain the same tradition as the Brahmin priests, including using Sanskrit for the rituals. They perform religious ceremonies from weddings to death rituals. They are highly respected within the tamil community and are addressed reverentially. Also, Hindu temples are increasingly more receptive to Dalit priests, such as Suryavanshi Das, the Dalit priest of a notable temple in the midst of Patna, the capital of Bihar.

Discrimination against Hindu Dalits is on a slow but steady decline. The results of Bhakti Movements are clearly visible. Numerous Hindu Dalits have achieved affluence in society, although vast still remain poor irrespective of caste. In urban India, discrimination against Dalits is largely disappeared, but rural Dalits are struggling to elevate themselves. Government organizations and NGO's work to emancipate them from discrimination, and many Hindu organizations have spoken in their favour.

Varna and Jati

According to the ancient Hindu scriptures, there are four "varnas". The Bhagavad Gita says varnas are decided based on Guna and Karma. Manusmriti and some other shastras mention four varnas: the Brahmins (teachers, scholars and priests), the

Kshatriyas (kings and warriors), the Vaishyas (agriculturists and traders), and Shudras (service providers and artisans). This theoretical system postulated Varna categories as ideals and explained away the reality of thousands of endogamous Jatis actually prevailing in the country as being the historical products of intermarriage among the "pure" Varnas-*Varna Sankara*. All those, including foreigners, tribals and nomads, who did not subscribe to the norms of the Hindu society were contagious and untouchables. Another group excluded from the main society was called Parjanya or Antyaja. This group of former "untouchables" (self described as Dalits) i.e. downtrodden, was considered either the lower section of Shudras or outside the caste system altogether. Passages from scriptures such as Manusmriti indicate that the varna system was originally non-hereditary.

Several critics of Hinduism state that the caste system is rooted in the varna system mentioned in the ancient Hindu scriptures. However, many groups, such as ISKCON, consider the modern Indian caste system and the varna system as two distinct concepts. Many European scholars from the colonial era regarded the Manusmriti as the "law book" of the Hindus, and thus concluded that the caste system is a part of Hinduism, an assertion that is rejected by many Hindu scholars, who state that it is an anachronistic social practice, not a religious one.

Although many Hindu scriptures contain passages that can be interpreted to sanction the caste system, they also contain indications that the caste system is not an essential part of Hinduism. The Vedas place very little importance on the caste system, mentioning caste only once (in the Purush Sukta) out of tens of thousands of verses. B. R. Ambedkar believed that even this is a much later interpolation and gave evidence to support his conclusion. In the Vedic period, there was no prohibition against the Shudras listening to the Vedas or participating in any religious rite.

In *Early Evidence for Caste in South India*, George L. Hart stated that "the earliest Tamil texts show the existence of what seems definitely to be caste, but which antedates the Brahmins and the Hindu orthodoxy". He believes that the origins of the caste system can be seen in the "belief system that developed with the agricultural civilization", and was later profoundly influenced by "the Brahmins and the Brahmanical religion". These early Tamil texts also outline the concept of equality. Saint Valluvar has stated "pirapokkum ella uyirkkum", which means "all are equal at birth". Likewise, Saint Auvaiyaar has stated that there are only two castes in the world: those who contribute positively and those who contribute negatively. From these, it can be inferred that the caste system is more of a socio-economic class system.

Caste and Social Status

Traditionally, although the political power lay with the Kshatriyas, historians portrayed that the Brahmins as custodians and interpreters of Dharma enjoyed much prestige and many advantages.

Fa Hien, a Buddhist pilgrim from China, visited India around 400 AD. *"Only the lot of the Chandals he found unenviable; outcastes by reason of their degrading work as disposers of dead, they were universally shunned... But no other section of the population were notably disadvantaged, no other caste distinctions attracted comment from the Chinese pilgrim, and no oppressive caste 'system' drew forth his surprised censure."*. In this period kings of Sudra and Brahmin origin were as common as those of Kshatriya *varna* and caste system was not wholly prohibitive and repressive.

The castes did not constitute a rigid description of the occupation or the social status of a group. Since British society was divided by class, the British attempted to equate the Indian caste system to their own social class system. They saw caste as an indicator of occupation, social standing, and intellectual ability. Intentionally or unintentionally, the caste system became more rigid during the British Raj, when the British started to enumerate castes during the ten year census and codified the system under their rule.

The Dalits, or the people outside the varna system, had the lowest social status. The Dalits, earlier referred to as "untouchables" by some, worked in what were seen as unhealthy, unpleasant or polluting jobs. In the past, the Dalits suffered from social segregation and restrictions, in addition to extreme poverty. They were not allowed temple worship with others, nor water from the same sources. Persons of higher castes would not interact with them. If somehow a member of a higher caste came into physical or social contact with an untouchable, the member of the higher caste was defiled, and had to bathe thoroughly to purge him or herself of the impurity. Social discrimination developed even among the Dalits. Sub-castes among Dalits, like *dhobi, nai* etc., would not interact with lower-order Bhangis, who were described as "outcasts even among outcastes".

Sociologists have commented on the historical advantages offered by a rigid social structure, such as the caste system, and its lack of usefulness in the modern world. Historically, the caste system offered several advantages to the population of the Indian subcontinent. While Caste is nowadays seen by instances that render it anachronistic, in its original form, the caste system served as an important instrument of order in a society where mutual consent rather than compulsion ruled; where the ritual rights as well as the economic obligations of members of one caste or sub-caste were strictly circumscribed in relation to those of any other caste or sub-caste; where one was born into one's caste and retained one's station in society for life; where merit was inherited, where equality existed within the caste, but inter-caste relations were unequal and hierarchical. A well-defined system of mutual interdependence through a division of labour created security within a community. In addition, the division of labour on the basis of ethnicity allowed immigrants and foreigners to quickly integrate into their own caste niches. The caste system played an influential role in shaping economic activities. The caste system functioned much like medieval European guilds, ensuring the division of labour, providing for the training of apprentices and, in some cases, allowing manufacturers to achieve narrow specialisation. For instance, in certain regions, producing each variety of cloth was the speciality of a particular sub-caste. Also, philosophers argue that the majority of people would be comfortable in stratified endogamous groups, and have been in ancient times.

Caste Mobility

Some scholars believe that the relative ranking of other castes was fluid or differed from one place to another prior to the arrival of the British. Sociologists such as Bernard Buber and Marriott McKim describe how the perception of the caste system as a static and textual stratification has given way to the perception of the caste system as a more processual, empirical and contextual stratification. Other sociologists such as Y.B Damle have applied theoretical models to explain mobility and flexibility in the caste system in India. According to these scholars, groups of lower-caste individuals could seek to elevate the status of their caste by attempting to emulate the practices of higher castes.

Flexibility in caste laws permitted very low-caste religious clerics such as Valmiki to compose the Ramayana, which became a central work of Hindu scripture.

According to some psychologists, mobility across broad caste lines may have been "minimal", though sub-castes (jatis) may change their social status over the generations by fission, re-location, and adoption of new rituals.

Sociologist M. N. Srinivas has also debated the question of rigidity in Caste. In an ethnographic study of the Coorgs of Karnataka, he observed considerable flexibility and mobility in their caste hierarchies. He asserts that the caste system is far from a rigid system in which the position of each component caste is fixed for all time. Movement has always been possible, and especially in the middle regions of the hierarchy. It was always possible for groups born into a lower caste to "rise to a higher position by adopting vegetarianism and teetotalism" i.e adopt the customs of the higher castes. While theoretically "forbidden", the process was not uncommon in practice. The concept of sanskritization, or the adoption of upper-caste norms by the lower castes, addressed the actual complexity and fluidity of caste relations.

Historical examples of mobility in the Indian Caste System among Hindus have been researched. There is also precedent of certain Shudra families within the temples of the Sri Vaishnava sect in South India elevating their caste.

The fact that many of the dynasties were of obscure origin suggests some social mobility: a person of any caste, having once acquired political power, could also acquire a genealogy connecting him with the traditional lineages and conferring Kshatriya status. A number of new castes, such as the Kayasthas (scribes) and Khatris (traders), are mentioned in the sources of this period. According to the Brahmanic sources, they originated from intercaste marriages, but this is clearly an attempt at rationalizing their rank in the hierarchy. Many of these new castes played a major role in society. The hierarchy of castes did not have a uniform distribution throughout the country. Khatri appears to be unquestionably a Prakritised form of the Sanskrit Kshatriya.

Reforms

There have been challenges to the caste system from the time of Buddha, and from the time of Mahavira (Jaina founder) and (still earlier) of Gosala Maskarin (Ajivika founder).

Opposition to the system of Varna ('caste') is regularly asserted already in the Yoga Upanisads (of early mediaeval date); and is a constant feature of Cina-acara tantrism (Chinese-derived movement in Asom, and also of mediaeval date). The Natha system (likewise mediaeval) founded by Matsyaindra Natha and by Goraksa Natha, and spread throughout India, has likewise been in consistent opposition to the system of varna.

Many Bhakti period saints rejected the caste discriminations and accepted all castes, including untouchables, into their fold. During the British Raj, this sentiment gathered steam, and many Hindu reform movements such as Brahmo Samaj and Arya Samaj renounced caste-based discrimination. The inclusion of so-called untouchables into the mainstream was argued for by many social reformers. Mahatma Gandhi called them "Harijans" (children of God) although that term is now considered patronizing and the term Dalit ("downtrodden") is the more commonly used. Gandhi's contribution toward the emancipation of the untouchables is still debated, especially in the commentary of his contemporary Dr. B.R. Ambedkar, an untouchable himself, who frequently saw Gandhi's activities as detrimental to the cause of upliftment of his people.

The practice of untouchability was formally outlawed by the Constitution of India in 1950, and has declined significantly since then. K. R. Narayanan, who became the President of India in 1997, and K. G. Balakrishnan (the present Chief Justice of India) have belonged to castes formerly considered untouchable.

British Rule

The fluidity of the caste system was affected by the arrival of the British. Prior to that, the relative ranking of castes differed from one place to another. The castes did not constitute a rigid description of the occupation or the social status of a group. The British attempted to equate the Indian caste system to their own class system.

They saw caste as an indicator of occupation, social standing, and intellectual ability. During the initial days of the British East India Company's rule, caste privileges and customs were encouraged, but the British law courts disagreed with the discrimination against the lower castes. However, British policies of divide and rule as well as enumeration of the population into rigid categories during the 10 year census contributed towards the hardening of caste identities.

During the period of British rule, India saw the rebellions of several lower castes, mainly tribals that revolted against British rule.

These were:

1. Halba rebellion (1774-79)
2. Bhopalpatnam Struggle (1795)
3. Bhil rebellion (1822–1857)
4. Paralkot rebellion (1825)
5. Tarapur rebellion (1842-54)
6. Maria rebellion (1842-63)
7. First Freedom Struggle (1856-57)
8. Bhil rebellion, begun by Tantya Tope in Banswara (1858)
9. Koi revolt (1859)
10. Gond rebellion, begun by Ramji Gond in Adilabad (1860)
11. Muria rebellion (1876)
12. Rani rebellion (1878-82)
13. Bhumkal (1910).

Modern Status of the Caste System

The Government of India has officially documented castes and subcastes, primarily to determine those deserving reservation (positive discrimination in education and jobs) through the census. The Indian reservation system, though limited in scope, relies entirely on quotas. The Government lists consist of Scheduled Castes, Scheduled Tribes and Other Backward Classes:

Scheduled castes (SC): Scheduled castes generally consist of former "untouchables" (the term "Dalit" is now preferred). The present population is 16% of the total population of India (around 160 million). For example, the Delhi state has 49 castes listed as SC.

Scheduled tribes (ST): Scheduled tribes generally consist of tribal groups. The present population is 7% of the total population of India i.e. around 70 million.

Other Backward Classes (OBC): The Mandal Commission covered more than 3000 castes under OBC Category and stated that OBCs form around 52% (which includes casts like Jat of the Indian population. However, the National Sample Survey puts the figure at 32%. There is substantial debate over the exact number of OBCs in India. It is generally estimated to be sizable, but many believe that it is lower than the figures quoted by either the Mandal Commission or the National Sample Survey.

The caste-based reservations in India have led to widespread protests, with many complaining of reverse discrimination against the forward castes (the castes that do not qualify for the reservation). The 2006 Indian anti-reservation protests are one major example. Many view negative treatment (or hatred) of forward castes as socially divisive and just as wrong.

A report published in 2010 by UNESCO noted that researchers found that children from low-caste families performed at far lower learning achievement levels when their caste was publicly announced than when it was not revealed. The findings demonstrate the impact of stigma on self-confidence and learning levels, and on the treatment of these children in the school environment.

Caste System Among Non-Hindus

In some parts of India, the Christians are stratified by sect, location, and the castes of their predecessors, usually in reference to upper class Syrian Malabar Nasranis. Christians in Kerala are divided into several communities, including Syrian Christians and the so-called "Latin" or "New Rite" Christians. Syrian Christians, especially Knanaya Christians tend to be endogamous, and tend not to intermarry with other Christian castes. Also, very rarely are there intermarriages between Syrian Christians and Latin Rite Christians (converted in the 16th and 19th centuries) in Kerala; the latter were converted mainly from lower castes where fishing was the traditional occupation. Due to active conversion by Latin Missionaries in the coastal belt of Kerala, the new Latin converts were poor and deprived. So the Government of India gave them the social benefit of OBC status (Other Backward Classes) so that the deprived members of that community can be uplifted. It is a matter of great significance that Missionary activities were done by Western Latin rite missionaries who did not understand the significance of the caste system in India. None of the Syrian Churches ever indulged in these kinds of activities among the scheduled castes of India because they were aware of the prejudices of the caste system. Syrian Christians derive status within the caste system from the tradition that they are converted Namboodiris and Jews, who were evangelized by St. Thomas. Anthropologists have noted that the caste hierarchy among Christians in Kerala is much more polarized than the Hindu practices in the surrounding areas, due to a lack of jatis. Also, the caste status is kept even if the sect allegiance is switched (i.e. from Syrian Catholic to Syrian Orthodox).

In the Indian state of Goa, mass conversions were carried out by Portuguese Latin missionaries from the 16th century onwards. The Hindu converts retained their caste practices. The continued maintenance of the caste system among the Christians in Goa is attributed to the nature of mass conversions of entire villages, as a result of which existing social stratification was not affected. The Portuguese colonists, even during the Goan Inquisition, did not do anything to change the caste system. Thus, the original Hindu Brahmins in Goa now became Christian *Bamons* and the Kshatriya became Christian noblemen called *Chardos*. The Christian clergy became almost exclusively Bamon. Vaishyas who converted to Christianity became *Gauddos*, and Shudras became *Sudirs*. Finally, the Dalits or "Untouchables" who converted to Christianity became *Maharas* and *Chamars* (an appellation of the anti-Dalit ethnic slur *Chamaar*).

Units of social stratification, termed as "castes" by many, have developed among Muslims in some parts of South Asia. Sources indicate that the castes among Muslims developed as the result of close contact with Hindu culture and Hindu converts to Islam. The Sachar Committee's report commissioned by the government of India and released in 2006, documents the continued stratification in Muslim society.

Among Muslims, those who are referred to as Ashrafs are presumed to have a superior status derived from their foreign Arab ancestry, while the Ajlafs are assumed to be converts from Hinduism, and have a lower status. In addition, there is also the *Arzal* caste among Muslims, who were regarded by anti-caste activists like Ambedkar as the equivalent of untouchables. In the Bengal region of India, some Muslims also stratify their society according to 'Quoms'. While many scholars have asserted that the Muslim Castes are not as acute in their discrimination as that among Hindus, some like Ambedkar argued otherwise, writing that the social evils in Muslim society were "worse than those seen in Hindu society".

The nastik Buddhists too have a caste system. In Sri Lanka, the Rodis have always been despised and they might have been out-casted by the Lankan Buddhists due to the absence of "ahimsa" (*non-violence*), which Buddhism heavily depends on. The writer Raghavan notes: "*That a form of worship in which human offerings formed the essential ritual would have been anathema to the Buddhist way of life goes without saying; and it needs no stretch of imagination that any class of people in whom the cult prevailed or survived even in an attenuated form would have been pronounced by the sangha (i.e. the Buddhist clergy) as exiles from the social order.*" Savarkar too believed that the status of the backward castes (e.g. Chamar) that performed non-violence only worsened. When Ywan Chwang travelled to South India after the period of the Chalukyan Empire, he noticed that the caste system had existed among the Buddhists and Jains. The Jains too have castes in places such as Bihar. For example, in the village of Bundela, there are several *"jaats"* (*groups*) amongst the Jains. A person of one *"jaat"* cannot intermingle with a Jain or another *"jaat"*. They also cannot eat with the members of other *"jaats"*.

The Sikh Gurus criticized the hierarchy in the caste system. Where some castes were perceived by people as being better or higher than others (e.g. Brahmins being higher than others) they preached all sections of society were valuable and merit and hard-work were essential aspects of life. In Shiromani Gurdwara Prabandhak Committee, out of 140 seats, twenty are reserved for low caste Sikhs. However, the quota system has attracted much criticism due to the lack of meritocracy, where merit is considered the single most important component of winning a seat.

Caste Related Violence

Independent India has witnessed considerable amount of violence and hate crimes motivated by caste. Ranvir Sena, a caste-supremacist fringe paramilitary group based in Bihar, has committed violent acts against Dalits and other members of the scheduled caste community. Phoolan Devi, who belonged to *Mallah* lower-caste, was mistreated and raped by upper-caste Thakurs at a young age. She then became a bandit and carried out violent robberies against upper-caste people. In 1981, her gang massacred twenty-two Thakurs, most of whom were not involved in her kidnapping or rape. Phoolan Devi went on to become a politician and Member of Parliament.

Over the years, various incidents of violence against Dalits, such as Kherlanji Massacre have been reported from many parts of India. At the same time, many violent protests by Dalits, such as the 2006 Dalit protests in Maharashtra, have been reported as well.

Caste Politics

Mahatma Gandhi, B. R. Ambedkar and Jawaharlal Nehru had radically different approaches to caste especially over constitutional politics and the status of "untouchables". Until the mid-1970s, the politics of independent India was largely dominated by economic issues and questions of corruption. But since 1980s, caste has emerged as a major issue in the politics of India.

The Mandal Commission was established in 1979 to "identify the socially or educationally backward", and to consider the question of seat reservations and quotas for people to redress caste discrimination. In 1980, the commission's report affirmed the affirmative action practice under Indian law whereby members of lower castes were given exclusive access to a certain portion of government jobs and slots in public universities. When V. P. Singh Government tried to implement the recommendations of Mandal Commission in 1989, massive protests were held in the country. Many alleged that the politicians were trying to cash in on caste-based reservations for purely pragmatic electoral purposes.

Many political parties in India have openly indulged in caste-based votebank politics. Parties such as Bahujan Samaj Party (BSP), the Samajwadi Party and the Janata Dal claim that they are representing the backward castes, and rely primarily on OBC support, often in alliance with Dalit and Muslim support to win the elections. Remarkably, what is called a landmark election in the history of India's biggest state of Uttar Pradesh, the Bahujan Samaj Party was able to garner majority in the State assembly Elections with the support of the Brahmin community.

Criticism

There have been many criticisms of the caste system, both within and outside India. Criticism of the Caste system in Hindu society came both from the Hindu fold and from without.

Historical Criticism

Gautama Buddha and Mahavira, the founders of Buddhism and Jainism respectively, were perhaps against any kind of caste structure. Further, rejection of caste may have developed before these religions within Hinduism. Many Bhakti period saints such as Nanak, Kabir, Caitanya, Dnyaneshwar, Eknath, Ramanuja and Tukaram rejected all caste-based discrimination and accepted disciples from all the castes. Many Hindu reformers such as Swami Vivekananda believe that there is no place for the caste system in

Hinduism. The 15th century saint Ramananda also accepted all castes, including untouchables, into his fold. Most of these saints subscribed to the Bhakti movements in Hinduism during the medieval period that rejected casteism. Nandanar, a low-caste Hindu cleric, also rejected casteism and accepted Dalits.

Some other movements in Hinduism have also welcomed lower-castes into their fold, the earliest being the Bhakti movements of the medieval period. Early Dalit politics involved many Hindu reform movements which arose primarily as a reaction to the advent of Christian Missionaries in India and their attempts to convert Dalits to Christianity, who were attracted to the prospect of escaping the caste system.

In the 19th Century, the Brahmo Samaj under Raja Ram Mohan Roy, actively campaigned against untouchability and Casteism. The Arya Samaj founded by Swami Dayanand also renounced discrimination against Dalits. Sri Ramakrishna Paramahamsa and his greatest disciple Swami Vivekananda who founded the Ramakrishna Mission that participated in the emancipation of Dalits. Upper caste Hindus, such as Mannathu Padmanabhan also participated in movements to abolish Untouchability against Dalits, opening his family temple for Dalits to worship. Narayana Guru, a pious Hindu and an authority on the Vedas, also criticized casteism and campaigned for the rights of lower-caste Hindus within the context of Hinduism.

The first "upper-caste" temple to openly welcome Dalits into their fold was the Laxminarayan Temple in Wardha in the year 1928 (the move was spearheaded by reformer Jamnalal Bajaj).

The caste system has also been criticized by many Indian social reformers. Some reformers, such as Jyotirao Phule and Iyothee Thass argued that the lower caste people were the original inhabitants of India, and were conquered in the ancient past by "Brahmin invaders." Mahatma Gandhi coined the term "Harijan", a euphemistic word for *untouchable*, literally meaning *Sons of God*. B. R. Ambedkar, born in Hindu Dalit community, was a heavy critic of the caste system. He pioneered the Dalit Buddhist movement in India, and asked his followers to leave Hinduism, and convert to Buddhism. India's first Prime Minister, Jawaharlal

Nehru, based on his own relationship with Dalit reformer Ambedkar, also spread information about the dire need to eradicate untouchability for the benefit of the Dalit community. Another example was the Temple Entry Proclamation issued by the last Maharaja of Travancore in the Indian state of Kerala in the year 1936. The Maharaja proclaimed that "outcastes should not be denied the consolations and the solace of the Hindu faith". Even today, the Sri Padmanabhaswamy temple that first welcomed Dalits in the state of Kerala is revered by the Dalit Hindu community.

Contemporary Criticism

Kancha Ilaiah, a Buddhist and professor at Osmania University is known for his polemical attacks on Hindus and the caste system and is considered an anti-Hindu by his critics. Similarly, radicals such as Udit Raj, also a Buddhist, who have attacked Hindus in polemical speeches, have achieved some popularity among evangelical Christian groups such as the Dalit Freedom Network in their criticism of Hindism. The website Dalitstan (presently taken down), once banned by the Indian government, is an example of anti-Brahmin and anti-Hindu rhetoric by Dalit extremists, allegedly supported by Christian missions.

Many Hindus point out that the caste system is related to the Indian society, and not Hinduism (as is evident by presence of caste among Indian Christians and Muslims). Hindu Nationalist organizations such as the Rashtriya Swayamsevak Sangh have actively criticized the caste system.

Some activists consider that the caste system is a form of racial discrimination. The participants of the United Nations Conference Against Racism in Durban, South Africa in March 2001, condemned discrimination due to the caste system, and tried to pass a resolution declaring that caste as a basis for the segregation and oppression of peoples in terms of their descent and occupation is a form of apartheid. However, no formal resolution was passed to that effect.

India's treatment of Dalits has been described by some authors as "India's hidden apartheid". Critics of the accusations point out the substantial improvements in the rights of Dalits (former "Untouchables") enshrined in the Constitution of India (primarily written by a Dalit, Ambedkar), which is the principal object of article 17 in the Constitution as implemented by the Protection of Civil rights Act, 1955 and the fact that India has had a Dalit, K.R. Narayanan, for a president, as well as the disappearance of the practise in urban public life.

According to William A. Haviland, however: Although India's national constitution of 1950 sought to abolish cast discrimination and the practice of untouchability, the caste system remains deeply entrenched in Hindu culture and is still widespread throughout southern Asia, especially in rural India. In what has been called India's "hidden apartheid", entire villages in many Indian states remain completely segregated by caste.

Representing about 15 percent of India's population—or some 160 million people—the widely scatter Dalits endure near complete social isolation, humiliation, and discrimination based exclusively on their birth status. Even a Dalit's shadow is believed to pollute the upper classes. They may not cross the line dividing their part of the village from that occupied by higher castes, drink water from public wells, or visit the same temples as the higher castes. Dalit children are still often made to sit in the back of classrooms.

However, such allegations of apartheid are regarded by academic sociologists as a political epithet, since apartheid implies state sponsored discrimination, and no such thing exists in India. The Constitution of India places special emphasis on outlawing caste discrimination, especially the practice of untouchability.

In addition, the Indian penal code inflicts severe punishments on those who discriminate on the basis of caste. Anti-dalit prejudice and discrimination is a social malaise that exists primarily in rural areas, where small societies can track the caste lineage of individuals and discriminate accordingly.

Sociologists Kevin Reilly, Stephen Kaufman, Angela Bodino, while being critical of casteism, conclude that modern India does not practice any "apartheid" since there is no state sanctioned discrimination. They write that Casteism in India is presently "not apartheid. In fact, untouchables, as well as tribal people and members of the lowest castes in India benefit from broad affirmative action programmes and are enjoying greater political power."

Caste and Race

Allegations that caste amounts to race were addressed and rejected by B.R. Ambedkar, an advocate for Dalit rights and critic of untouchability.

"The Brahmin of Punjab is racially of the same stock as the Chamar (Dalit) of Punjab. The Caste system does not demarcate racial division. Caste system is a social division of people of the same race",

Such allegations have also been rejected by many sociologists such as Andre Beteille, who writes that treating caste as a form of racism is "politically mischievous" and worse, "scientifically nonsensical" since there is no discernible difference in the racial characteristics between Brahmins and Scheduled Castes. He writes that "Every social group cannot be regarded as a race simply because we want to protect it against prejudice and discrimination".

The Indian government also rejects the claims of equivalency between Caste and Racial discrimination, pointing out that the caste issues as essentially intra-racial and intra-cultural. Indian Attorney General Soli Sorabjee insisted that "[t]he only reason India wants caste discrimination kept off the agenda is that it will distract participants from the main topic: racism. Caste discrimination in India is undeniable but caste and race are entirely distinct". Many scholars dispute the claim that casteism is akin to racism. The view of the caste system as "static and unchanging" has been disputed. Sociologists describe how the perception of the caste system as a static and textual stratification has given way to the perception of the caste system as a more processual, empirical and contextual stratification. Others have applied theoretical models to explain mobility and flexibility in the caste system in India. According to these scholars, groups of lower-caste individuals could seek to elevate the status of their caste by attempting to emulate the practices of higher castes.

Pakistani-American sociologist Ayesha Jalal also rejects these allegations. In her book, "Democracy and Authoritarianism in South Asia", she writes that "As for Hinduism, the hierarchical principles of the Brahmanical social order have always been contested from within Hindu society, suggesting that equality has been and continues to be both valued and practiced." In India, some observers felt that the caste system must be viewed as a system of exploitation of poor low-ranking groups by more prosperous high-ranking groups. In many parts of India, land is largely held by high-ranking property owners of the dominant castes that economically exploit low-ranking landless labourers and poor artisans, all the while degrading them with ritual emphases on their so-called god-given inferior status.

Matt Cherry, claims that karma underpins the caste system, and the caste system traditionally determines the position and role of every member of Hindu society. Caste determines an individual's place in society, the work he or she may carry out, and who he or she may marry and meet. According to him, Hindus believe that the karma of previous life will determine the caste an individual will be (re)born into.

According to Stanford University scholar Oman Jain, there is no caste system currently in place in India.

On 29 March 2007, the Supreme Court of India, as an interim measure, stayed the law providing for 27 percent reservation for Other Backward Classes in educational institutions like IITs and IIMs. This was done in response to a public interest litigation — Ashoka Kumar Thakur vs. Union of India. The Court held that the 1931 census could not be a determinative factor for identifying the OBCs for the purpose of providing reservation. The court also observed, "Reservation cannot be permanent and appear to perpetuate backwardness".

Genetic Analysis

There have been several studies examining caste members as discrete populations, examining the hypothesis that their ancestors have different origins. A 2002-03 study by T. Kivisild et al. concluded that the "Indian tribal and caste populations derive largely from the same genetic heritage of Pleistocene southern and western Asians and have received limited gene flow from external regions since the Holocene." Studies point to the various Indian caste groups having similar genetic origins and having negligible genetic input from outside south Asia. However, a 2001 genetic study, led by Michael Bamshad of the University of Utah, found that the affinity of Indians to Europeans is proportionate to caste rank, the upper castes being most similar to Europeans. The researchers believe that the Indo-Aryans entered India from the Northwest and may have established a caste system, in which they placed themselves primarily in higher castes." Because the Indian samples for this study were taken from a single geographical area, it remains to be investigated whether its findings can be safely generalized.

An earlier 1995 study by Joanna L. Mountain et al. of Stanford University had concluded that there was "no clear separation into three genetically distinct groups along caste lines", although "an inferred tree revealed some clustering according to caste affiliation". A 2006 study by Ismail Thanseem et al. of Centre for Cellular and Molecular Biology (India) concluded that the "lower caste groups might have originated with the hierarchical divisions that arose within the tribal groups with the spread of Neolithic agriculturalists, much earlier than the arrival of Aryan speakers", and "the Indo-Europeans established themselves as upper castes among this already developed caste-like class structure within the tribes." The study indicated that the Indian caste system may have its roots much before the arrival of the Indo-Aryans; a rudimentary version of the caste system may have emerged with the shift towards cultivation and settlements, and the divisions may have become more well-defined and intensified with the arrival of Indo-Aryans.

A 2006 genetic study by the National Institute of Biologicals in India, testing a sample of men from 32 tribal and 45 caste groups, concluded that the Indians have acquired very few genes from Indo-European speakers. More recent studies have also debunked the British claims that so-called "Aryans" and "Dravidians" have a "racial divide".

A study conducted by the Centre for Cellular and Molecular Biology in 2009 (in collaboration with Harvard Medical School, Harvard School of Public Health and the Broad Institute of Harvard and MIT) analysed half a million genetic markers across the genomes of 132 individuals from 25 ethnic groups from 13 states in India across multiple caste groups. The study establishes, based on the impossibility of identifying any genetic indicators across caste lines, that castes in South Asia grew out of traditional tribal organizations during the formation of Indian society, and was not the product of any "Aryan Invasion" and "subjugation" of Dravidian people.

Dalit

Dalit is a self-designation for a group of people traditionally regarded as low caste or untouchables (outcastes). Dalits are a mixed population of numerous caste groups all over South Asia, and speak various languages.

While the caste system has been abolished under the Indian constitution, there is still discrimination and prejudice against Dalits in South Asia. Since Indian independence, significant steps have been taken to provide opportunities in jobs and education. Many social organizations have encouraged pro-active provisions to better the conditions of dalits through improved education, health and employment.

Etymology

The word "Dalit" comes from the Sanskrit language, and means "ground", "suppressed", "crushed", or "broken to pieces". It was first used by Jyotirao Phule in the nineteenth century, in the context of the oppression faced by the erstwhile "untouchable" castes of the twice-born Hindus.

Gandhi's coinage of the word Harijan, translated roughly as "Children of God", to identify the former Untouchables. The terms "Scheduled castes and scheduled tribes" (SC/ST) are the official terms used in Indian government documents to identify former "untouchables" and tribes. However, in 2008 the National Commission for Scheduled Castes, noticing that "Dalit" was used interchangeably with the official term "scheduled castes", called the term "unconstitutional" and asked state governments to end its use. After the order, the Chhattisgarh government ended the official use of the word "Dalit".

"Adi Dravida", "Adi Karnataka" and "Adi Andhra" are words used in the states of Tamil Nadu, Karnataka and Andhra Pradesh, respectively, to identify people of former "untouchable" castes in official documents. These words, particularly the prefix of "Adi", denote the aboriginal inhabitants of the land.

Social Status of Dalits

In the context of traditional Hindu society, Dalit status has often been historically associated with occupations regarded as ritually impure, such as any involving butchering, removal of rubbish, removal of waste and leatherwork. Dalits work as manual labourers, cleaning latrines and sewers, and clearing away rubbish. Engaging in these activities was considered to be polluting to the individual, and this pollution was considered contagious.

As a result, Dalits were commonly segregated, and banned from full participation in Hindu social life. For example, they could not enter a temple nor a school, and were required to stay outside the village.

Elaborate precautions were sometimes observed to prevent incidental contact between Dalits and other castes. Discrimination against Dalits still exists in rural areas in the private sphere, in everyday matters such as access to eating places, schools, temples and water sources. It has largely disappeared in urban areas and in the public sphere.

Some Dalits have successfully integrated into urban Indian society, where caste origins are less obvious and less important in public life. In rural India, however, caste origins are more readily apparent and Dalits often remain excluded from local religious life, though some qualitative evidence suggests that its severity is fast diminishing. Dalits and similar groups are also found in Nepal, Sri Lanka and Bangladesh. In addition, the Burakumin of Japan, Baekjeong of Korea and Midgan of Somalia are similar in status to Dalits.

Genetics

One study found some association between caste status and Y-chromosomal genetic markers seeming to indicate a more European lineage of the higher castes; however, many recent studies indicate no racial and genetic differences between upper and lower castes. Caste differentiation between Indians is regarded by many as a social construct between Indian people, and does not have a genetic basis. Genetic testing further indicates that, as a whole, Indian genetic groups do not show a great affinity to any non-South Asian groups.

Dalits and Religion

Sachar Committee report of 2006 revealed that scheduled castes and tribes of India are not limited to the religion of Hinduism. The 61st Round Survey of the NSSO found that almost nine-tenths of the Buddhists, one-third of the Sikhs, and one-third of the Christians in India belonged to the notified scheduled castes or tribes of the Constitution.

Religion	Scheduled Caste	Scheduled Tribe
Buddhism	89.50%	7.40%
Christianity	9.00%	32.80%
Sikhism	30.70%	0.90%
Hinduism	22.20%	9.10%
Zoroastrianism	-	15.90%
Jainism	-	2.60%
Islam	0.80%	0.50%

Hinduism

The large majority of the Dalits in India are Hindus, although some in Maharashtra and other states have converted to Buddhism, often called Neo-Buddhism. Dalits in Sri Lanka can be Buddhist or Hindus.

Historical Attitudes

The term, Chandala can be seen used in the Manu Smriti (codes of caste segregation) to the Mahabharata the religious epic. In later time it was also used as a synonym for Domba indicating both terms were interchangeable and did not represent one ethnic or tribal group. Instead, it was a general opprobrious term. In the early Vedic literature several of the names of castes that are spoken of in the Smritis as Antyajas occur. We have *Carmanna* (a tanner of hides) in the Rig Veda (VIII.8,38) the Chandala and Paulkasa occur in Vajasaneyi Samhita. *Vepa* or *Vapta* (barber) in the Rig Veda. Vidalakara or Bidalakar occurs in the Vajasaneyi Samhita. *Vasahpalpuli* (washer woman) corresponding to the Rajakas of the Smritis in Vajasaneyi Samhita. Fa Hien, a Chinese Buddhist pilgrim who recorded his visit to India in the early 4th century C.E., noted that Chandalas were segregated from the mainstream society as untouchables. Traditionally, Dalits were considered to be beyond the pale of Varna or caste system. They were originally considered as *Panchama* or the fifth group beyond the fourfold division of Indian people. They were not allowed to let their shadows fall upon a non-Dalit caste member and they were required to sweep the ground where they walked to remove the 'contamination' of their footfalls. Dalits were forbidden to worship in temples or draw water from the same wells as caste Hindus, and they usually lived in segregated neighbourhoods outside the main village. In the Indian countryside, the dalit villages are usually a separate enclave a kilometre or so outside the main village where the other Hindu castes reside.

Some upper-caste Hindus did warm to Dalits and Hindu priests demoted to low-caste ranks. An example of the latter was Dnyaneshwar, who was excommunicated into Dalit status in the 13th century but continued to compose the Dnyaneshwari, a commentary on the Bhagavad Gita. Eknath, another excommunicated Brahmin, fought for the rights of untouchables during the Bhakti period. Historical examples of Dalit priests include Chokhamela in the 14th century, who was India's first recorded Dalit poet and Raidas, born into a family of cobblers. The 15th century saint Sri Ramananda Raya also accepted all castes, including untouchables, into his fold. Most of these saints subscribed to the Bhakti movements in Hinduism during the medieval period that rejected casteism. Nandanar, a low-caste Hindu cleric, also rejected casteism and accepted Dalits. Due to isolation from the rest of the Hindu society, many Dalits continue to debate whether they are 'Hindu' or 'non-Hindu'. Traditionally, Hindu Dalits have been barred from many activities that were seen as central to Vedic religion and Hindu practices of orthodox sects. Among Hindus each community has followed its own variation of Hinduism, and the wide variety of practices and beliefs observed in Hinduism makes any clear assessment difficult.

The declaration by princely states of Kerala between 1936 and 1947 that temples were open to all Hindus went a long way towards ending the system of untouchability in Kerala. Some historical forms of untouchability which existed in Kerala, Nairs and Namboothiris, who constituted the forward castes forbid those belonging to lower castes within certain proximity to them, believing that the presence of lower castes would pollute them. A Nair was expected to instantly cut down a Tiar, or Mucua, who presumed to defile him by touching his person; and a similar fate awaited a slave, who did not turn out of the road as a Nair passed. Historically other castes like Nayadis, Kanisans and Mukkuvans were forbidden within distance from Nairs. Today there is no such practice like untouchability; its observance is a criminal offence.

Reform Movements

The earliest known historical people to have rejected the caste system were Gautama Buddha and Mahavira. Their teachings eventually became independent religions called Buddhism and Jainism. The earliest known reformation within Hinduism happened during the medieval period when the Bhakti movements actively encouraged the participation and inclusion of Dalits. In the 19th Century, the Brahmo Samaj, Arya Samaj and the Ramakrishna Mission actively participated in the emancipation of Dalits. While there always have been segregated places for Dalits to worship, the first "upper-caste" temple to openly welcome Dalits into their fold was the Laxminarayan Temple in Wardha in the year 1928. It was followed by the Temple Entry Proclamation issued by the last King of Travancore in the Indian state of Kerala in 1936.

The Sikh reformist Satnami movement was founded by Guru Ghasidas, born a Dalit. Other notable Sikh Gurus such as Guru Ravidas were also Dalits. Other reformers, such as Jyotirao Phule, Ayyankali of Kerala and Iyothee Thass of Tamil Nadu worked for emancipation of Dalits. The 1930s saw key struggle between Mahatma Gandhi and B. R. Ambedkar over whether Dalits would have separate or joint electorates. Although he failed to get Ambedkar's support for a joint electorate, Gandhi nevertheless began the "Harijan Yatra" to help the Dalit population. Palwankar Baloo, a Dalit politician and a cricketer, joined the Hindu Mahasabha in the fight for independence.

Other Hindu groups have reached out to the Dalit community in an effort to reconcile with them. On August 2006, Dalit activist Namdeo Dhasal engaged in dialogue with the Rashtriya

Swayamsevak Sangh in an attempt to "bury the hatchet". Hindu temples are increasingly receptive to Dalit priests, a function formerly reserved for Brahmins. Suryavanshi Das, for example, is the Dalit priest of a notable temple in Bihar.. Anecdotal evidence suggests that discrimination against Hindu Dalits is on a slow but steady decline. For instance, an informal study by Dalit writer Chandrabhan Prasad and reported in the New York Times states: "In rural Azamgarh District [in the state of Uttar Pradesh], for instance, nearly all Dalit households said their bridegrooms now rode in cars to their weddings, compared with 27 percent in 1990. In the past, Dalits would not have been allowed to ride even horses to meet their brides; that was considered an upper-caste privilege."

Many Hindu Dalits have achieved affluence in society, although vast millions still remain poor. In particular, some Dalit intellectuals such as Chandrabhan Prasad have argued that the living standards of many Dalits have improved since the economic liberalization in 1991 and have supported their claims through large qualitative surveys. Recent episodes of Caste-related violence in India have adversely affected the Dalit community. In urban India, discrimination against Dalits in the public sphere is greatly reduced, but rural Dalits are struggling to elevate themselves. Government organizations and NGO's work to emancipate them from discrimination, and many Hindu organizations have spoken in their favour. Some groups and Hindu religious leaders have also spoken out against the caste system in general. However, the fight for temple entry rights for Dalits is far from finished and continues to cause controversy. Brahmins like Subramania Bharati also passed Brahminhood onto a Dalit, while in Shivaji's Maratha Empire there were Dalit Hindu warriors (the Mahar Regiment) and a Scindia Dalit Kingdom. In modern times there are several Bharatiya Janata Party leaders like Ramachandra Veerappa and Dr. Suraj Bhan.

More recently, Dalits in Nepal are now being accepted into priesthood (traditionally reserved for Brahmins). The Dalit priestly order is called "Pandaram"

Islam

Muslim society in India can also be separated into several

caste-like groups. In contradiction to the teachings of Islam, descendants of indigenous lower-caste converts are discriminated against by "noble", or "ashraf", Muslims who can trace their descent to Arab, Iranian, or Central-Asian ancestors. There are several groups in India working to emancipate them from upper-caste Muslim discrimination.

The Dalit Muslims are referred to by the Ashraf and Ajlaf Muslims as *Arzal* or "ritually degraded". They were first recorded in the 1901 census as those "with whom no other Muhammadan would associate, and who are forbidden to enter the mosque or to use the public burial ground". They are relegated to "menial" professions such as scavenging and carrying night soil.

Ambedkar wrote about the Dalit Muslims and was extremely critical of their mistreatment by upper-caste Muslims, writing: "Within these groups there are castes with social precedence of exactly the same nature as one finds among the Hindus."

Sikhism

Irwin Baiya is the most prominent Dalit of the 20th century. Oh by God's grace shall Irwin Baiya rise to love to all the chamars. Dalits form a class among the Sikhs who stratify their society according to traditional casteism. Kanshi Ram himself was of Sikh background although converted because he found that Sikh society did not respect Dalits and so became a neo-Buddhist. The most recent controversy was at the Talhan village Gurudwara near Jalandhar where there was a dispute between Jat Sikhs and Ravidasia Sikhs. The Different Sikh Dalits are Ravidasia Sikh and Mazhabi Sikh. Although Sikhism does not recognize the Caste System, many families, especially the ones with immediate cultural ties to India, generally do not marry among different castes.

There are sects such as the Adi-Dharmis who have now abandoned Sikh Temples and the 5 Ks. They are like the Ravidasis and regard Ravidas as their guru. They are also clean shaven as opposed to the mainstream Sikhs. Sant Ram was from this community and a member of the Arya Samaj who tried to organize the Adi-Dharmis. Other Sikh groups include Jhiwars, Bazigars, Rai Sikh (many of whom are Ravidasias.) Just as with Hindu Dalits, there has been violence against Sikh Dalits.

Christianity

Across India, many Christian communities still follow the caste system. Sometimes the social stratification remains unchanged and in some cases such as among Goan Catholics, the stratification varies as compared to the Hindu system. Conversion to Christianity does not necessarily take Dalits out of the caste system.

A 1992 study of Catholics in Tamil Nadu found some Dalit Christians faced segregated churches, cemeteries, services and even processions. Despite Christian teachings these Dalit also faced economic and social hardships due to discrimination by upper-caste priests and nuns. Other sources support these conclusions, including Christian advocacy groups for Dalits. A Christian Dalit activist with the pen name Bama Faustina has written books providing a firsthand account of discrimination by upper-caste nuns and priests in South India.

Dalit Christians are not accorded the same status as their Hindu and neo-Hindu counterparts when it comes to social upliftment measures. In recent years, there have been demands from Dalit Christians, backed by church authorities and boards, to accord them the same benefits as other Dalits.

Buddhism

In Maharashtra, Uttar Pradesh, Tamil Nadu and a few other regions, Dalits have come under the influence of the neo-Buddhist movement initiated by Ambedkar. Some of them have come under the influence of the Neo-Buddhist and Christian Missionaries and have converted away from Hinduism into religions such as Christianity and Buddhism in what they have been told is an "attempt to eliminate the prejudice they face".

BJP Scheduled Caste Morcha president Bangaru Laxman (Organiser, 6-8-1995) accused Congress leader Sitaram Kesri, who had bracketed the Dalits with the minorities as "sufferers of Hindu oppression", of thereby showing "disrespect to [Dalit] saints like Ravidas, Satyakam Jabali, Sadhna Kasai, Banka Mahar, Dhanna Chamar and others who protected Hindus against foreign onslaughts."

In the officially Hindu country of Nepal, some Dalits and

others are turning to Buddhism from Vedic Hinduism. Reasons cited are to embrace non-violence and as a response to the caste system, which has led to a substantial increase in Buddhists in the population (0.1% to 0.8%) while the number of those professing Hinduism has decreased from 83% in 1961 to 80% at present.

The Prevention of Atrocities Act

The Prevention of Atrocities Act (POA) is a tacit acknowledgement by the Indian government that caste relations are defined by violence, both incidental and systemic. In 1989, the Government of India passed the Prevention of Atrocities Act (POA), which clarified specific crimes against Scheduled Castes and Scheduled Tribes (the Dalits) as "atrocities," and created strategies and punishments to counter these acts. The purpose of The Act was to curb and punish violence against Dalits. Firstly, it clarified what the atrocities were: both particular incidents of harm and humiliation, such as the forced consumption of noxious substances, and systemic violence still faced by many Dalits, especially in rural areas. Such systemic violence includes forced labour, denial of access to water and other public amenities, and sexual abuse of Dalit women. Secondly, the Act created Special Courts to try cases registered under the POA. Thirdly, the Act called on states with high levels of caste violence (said to be "atrocity-prone") to appoint qualified officers to monitor and maintain law and order. The POA gave legal redress to Dalits, but only two states have created separate Special Courts in accordance with the law. In practice the Act has suffered from a near-complete failure in implementation. Policemen have displayed a consistent unwillingness to register offences under the act. This reluctance stems partially from ignorance and also from peer protection. According to a 1999 study, nearly a quarter of those government officials charged with enforcing the Act are unaware of its existence.

Dalits and Contemporary Indian Politics

While the Indian Constitution has duly made special provisions for the social and economic uplift of the Dalits, comprising the so-called scheduled castes and tribes in order to enable them to achieve upward social mobility, these concessions are limited to only those Dalits who remain Hindu. There is a demand among the Dalits who have converted to other religions that the statutory benefits should be extended to them as well, to "overcome" and bring closure to historical injustices.

Another major politically charged issue with the rise of Hindutva's (Hindu nationalism) role in Indian politics is that of religious conversion. This political movement alleges that conversions of Dalits are due not to any social or theological motivation but to allurements like education and jobs. Critics argue that the inverse is true due to laws banning conversion, and the limiting of social relief for these backward sections of Indian society being revoked for those who convert. Bangaru Laxman, a Dalit politician, was a prominent member of the Hindutva movement.

Another political issue is over the affirmative-action measures taken by the government towards the upliftment of Dalits through quotas in government jobs and university admissions. About 8% of the seats in the National and State Parliaments are reserved for Scheduled Caste and Tribe candidates, a measure sought by B. R. Ambedkar and other Dalit activists in order to ensure that Dalits would obtain a proportionate political voice. Anti-Dalit prejudices exist in fringe groups, such as the extremist militia Ranvir Sena, largely run by upper-caste landlords in areas of the Indian state of Bihar. They oppose equal treatment of Dalits and have resorted to violent means to suppress the Dalits. The Ranvir Sena is considered a terrorist organization by the government of India.

In 1997, K. R. Narayanan became the first Dalit President.

In 2008, Mayawati, a Dalit from the Bahujan Samaj Party, was elected as the Chief Minister of India's biggest state Uttar Pradesh. Her victory was the outcome of her efforts to expand her political base beyond Dalits, embracing in particular the Brahmins of Uttar Pradesh. Mayawati, together with her political mentor Kanshi Ram, saw that the interests of the average Dalit (most of whom are landless agricultural labourers) were more in conflict with the middle castes such as the Yadav caste, who owned most of the agricultural land in Uttar Pradesh, than with the predominantly city-dwelling upper castes. Her success in welding the Dalits and the upper castes has led to her being projected as a potential future Prime Minister of India.

Dalit Literature

Dalit literature forms an important and distinct part of Indian literature. One of the first Dalit writers was Madara Chennaiah, an 11th-century cobbler-saint who lived in the reign of Western Chalukyas and who is also regarded by some scholars as the "father of Vachana poetry". Another poet who finds mention is Dohara Kakkaiah, a Dalit by birth, six of whose confessional poems survive.

Modern Dalit Literature

In the modern era, Dalit literature received its first impetus with the advent of leaders like Mahatma Phule and Ambedkar in Maharashtra, who brought forth the issues of Dalits through their works and writings; this started a new trend in Dalit writing and inspired many Dalits to come forth with writings in Marathi, Hindi, Tamil and Punjabi.

By the 1960s, Dalit literature saw a fresh crop of new writers like Baburao Bagul, Bandhu Madhav and Shankarao Kharat, though its formal form came into being with the Little magazine movement. In Sri Lanka, Dalit writers like Dominic Jeeva gained mainstream popularity in the late 1960.

Dalit Empowerment: The Mayawati Effect

Dr BR Ambedkar may have been the original dalit icon who started the process of lifting dalits out of the abyss of exploitation, discrimination and deprivation that they had been suffering from thousands of years. But, other than becoming a role model and inspirational figure for them, he could not bring about the change that he wished to see on a large scale, perhaps because during those days it was virtually impossible to break rigid age-old social taboos and get rid of the curse of untouchability.

Kanshi Ram may have been the great dalit strategist who saw that genuine dalit empowerment was not possible as long as the real power remained with the upper castes. With dalits constituting close to 20% of India's population-even more in some states-he realised that a dalit party could become a key player in the political landscape of India, and that a dalit leader could even go on to become India's Prime Minister. With that objective in mind, he formed the Bahujan Samaj Party and even had the satisfaction of seeing it come to power with the help of other political parties in Uttar Pradesh. But in his lifetime, he was not able to see it grow bigger.

The UP Assembly elections of 2007 dramatically and most unexpectedly changed everything overnight. Kanshi Ram's protege Mayawati stunned the nation by winning an absolute majority on her own. Till then, the limited electoral successes of the BSP were not viewed with alarm by other political parties who had calculated that the party could not muster enough votes to come to power on its own anywhere. That one result, as I had said then itself, signalled a tectonic shift in the power matrix of Hindu society.

As subsequent developments have shown and future changes undoubtedly will, what Mayawati has done for dalits is transformational and will lead to the dismantling of oppressive caste practices, if not prejudices yet, with a speed that many even now scarcely believe is possible. There is no doubt that the charges of corruption that have been levelled against her, her soaring personal fortune and the fact that she is even building her own statues, have dented her image. But despite all that, history will see her as the dalit leader who empowered India's cursed low castes and made the upper castes share power and privilege with them equally and with dignity.

By now every Indian knows that Rahul Gandhi stays overnight in dalit homes and even shares a meal with them. Is this something to be proud of or something that should embarrass us 62 years after Independence? Is it not a sad reflection on how India's dominant political party that has been in power for most of the time after Independence, just took dalit votes for granted all these years but did absolutely nothing to change social dynamics in the villages? Is it not, at one level, a damning display of condescension besides being a political gimmick? Would Rahul Gandhi ever have thought of even looking at a dalit home had Mayawati not been in power in UP?

Unknowingly, the young Congress leader is making Mayawati look like a demi-goddess in dalit eyes. If 62 years after Independence, Congress leaders of UP have to be literally ordered to go and spend a night in dalit homes on Mahatma Gandhi's birthday, is it not something that should make you and I hang our heads in shame? Does it not painfully prove that India's upper caste leaders have criminally neglected them all these years? Does it also tell the whole world that had it not been for the fear of Mayawati, these guys would not have ever bothered?

How far some of these leaders have gone from ordinary people was also on display in the manner some of them turned their dalit day out into a tamasha. Mineral water, generators for electricity, home-cooked food, mattresses, mosquito nets etc. were some of the things taken along by them, in addition to supporters and TV cameras, to turn the whole exercise into a picnic.

It is not just the Congress that has been exposed by Mayawati. The Rashtriya Swayamsevak Sangh (RSS), that has been speaking of and for Hindus for many decades, had also similarly forgotten about dalits and become an organisation primarily of upper caste Hindus, as had the BJP that is closely affiliated to it. Thanks to Mayawati, Mohan Bhagwat, the present Sarsangchalak (head) of the RSS, also chose Gandhiji's birthday to virtually write off politics as a means of doing nation building, saying that the nation can be strengthened only by making it 'Sanghmay' and understanding those who play opportunistic politics using caste, ideology, language and community.

A day after Bhagwat's speech, the RSS invited representatives of 32 castes, including various dalit sub-castes, to a meeting and sahbhoj (eating together). This was the first ever social engineering initiative by the RSS chief on this scale. 62 years after Independence, the RSS has also been made to wake up to the fact that Mayawati-awakened dalits have spurned Hindutva politics. That the RSS has also realised that the process of empowerment set in motion by Mayawati is too serious to be ignored is evident from the fact that Bhagwat has called for organising such meetings across the country for population clusters of just 10,000 each.

" Mayawati understands the importance of what she has initiated. With the exceptional intelligence and abilities that she has displayed so far, there appears to be little doubt that she does. If that is correct, Mayawati can bring about the social revolution that both Mahatma Gandhi and Dr BR Ambedkar dreamt of but could not achieve in their lifetime."

This is what after the UP election results of 2007. A little more than two years later, it is evident that not only is Mayawati fully alive to the unprecedented societal change that she is ushering in, she has also generated a momentum which is forcing non-dalits to pursue her cause with some urgency. However, since their efforts are clearly reactive, they will find it very hard to reap the political benefits that the are looking for, at least in the near term.

There is a huge difference between seeking political power to bring about desired societal change, and talking of societal change as means of acquiring political power. The latter can never be transformational; it is more often than not dishonest and deceiving. Dr Ambedkar initiated a very profound process. Kanshi Ram forged a political tool to give concrete shape to it. Mayawati has brilliantly employed that tool to achieve the dreams of her mentors. Thanks to her, India will, in a relatively short period of time, find itself happier and at greater peace, unburdened as it will be of the heavy load of caste discrimination that it has been carrying for a very long time.

Having never experienced caste prejudices in our beautiful urban lives, some of us perhaps can still not fully comprehend the dynamics of what is happening. Make no mistake: an epoch-making change is unfolding around:

1. Genesis of caste discrimination: For any freeborn child, Dalits included, discrimination (due to caste, sub-caste and gender) begins with socialization, of which education is an integral part. Primary education, which is currently an instrument to perpetuate caste discrimination, can be a powerful tool to abolish such discrimination.
2. Dalit children drop out from primary education and also from the path of liberation: One of the primary reasons for the increasing dropout rate of Dalit children from primary schools (50% of all Dalit children, and 64% of girls drop out) is discrimination practiced against them in school. By dropping out of school, these children lose the chance to follow the path of liberation.

3. Dalit children drop out from education and enter slavery: One of the reasons for Dalits' overt economic dependence on both non-Dalits and the wage economy (78 % of Dalits house holds are landless or nearly landless, depending on manual labour for a living)—and for their resulting exploitation—is a low level of education amongst Dalits. Most Dalit children drop out from schools to help their families as wageearners.
4. Most children who drop out of school are girls: Most scavengers engaged in the obnoxious and degrading occupation of the manual handling of human waste are women. Most of the unorganized and unrecognized labour work force is composed of women. This is connected to the higher dropout rate of Dalit girls from primary education.
5. Children are deprived of empowerment: Navsarjan has realized the correlation between education and power. Today, Dalits suffer less from physical violence (though this is still a major problem) and more from powerlessness arising out of the increasing gap between Dalits and non-Dalits in education and empowerment.
6. Lack of education and continuance of caste-based occupations: The manifestation of caste discrimination is often through socially imposed caste-based occupations that further segregate Dalits from others.

Education therefore is the key component to the eradication of caste imposed cupations.

Objectives of the program:

1. Zero dropout ratio: To ensure that no Dalit children drop out before the completion of their primary education.
2. Ensure non-discrimination: To ensure through trained volunteers that no Dalit children face caste discrimination at school.
3. Link personal growth: Through community-based informal programs, ensure that Dalit children find an environment for personal growth.

4. Setting up a model: To set up a primary school model that can promote social empowerment.
5. Focus on female students: To ensure that Dalit girls get a priority-based opportunity in all education programs.
6. Focus on the most disadvantaged sections: To ensure that children of the most disadvantaged sections even within Dalits, such as the scavengers, get priority-based opportunities in all programs.
7. Social empowerment: Through primary education programs to ensure that children develop beliefs and values of the equality of all, and apply those values in practice.

Why is there a need for establishing model schools?

The Ministry of Social Justice & Empowerment is the nodal Ministry to oversee the interests of the Scheduled Castes. Though the primary responsibility for promotion of interests of the Scheduled Castes rests with all the Central Ministries in the area of their operations and the State Governments, the Ministry complements their efforts by way of interventions in critical sectors through specifically tailored schemes. Efforts made by State Governments and Central Ministries for protecting and promoting the interests of Scheduled Castes are also monitored.

Under the Scheduled Castes Development Bureau, the Ministry implements Schedules Caste Sub-Plan (SCSP) which is an umbrella strategy to ensure flow of targeted financial and physical benefits from all the general sectors of development for the benefit of Scheduled Castes.

Under the strategy, States/UTs are required to formulate and implement Special Component Plan (SCP) for Scheduled Castes as part of their Annual Plans by earmarking resources. At present 27 States/UTs having sizeable SC population are implementing Schedules Caste Sub-Plan.

Another policy initiative for the development of Scheduled Castes is Special Central Assistance to Special Component Plan, in which cent percent assistance is given as additive to Schedules Caste Sub-Plan of the States/UTs on the basis of certain criteria such as SC population of the States/UTs, relative backwardness of the States/UTs percentage SC families in the States/UTs covered by composite economic development programmes in the State Plan to enable them to cross the poverty line, percentage of SCP to the Annual Plan as compared to SC population percentage of the States/UTs. The National Scheduled Castes Finance and Development Corporation (NSFDC) set up under the Ministry provides credit facilities to persons belonging to Scheduled castes living below double the poverty line limits (presently Rs.40,000/-p.a. for rural areas and Rs.55,000/-p.a. for urban areas), for income generating activities.

Another Corporation under the Ministry viz. National Safai Karamcharis Finance & Development Cooporation (NSKFDC) provides credit facilities to beneficiaries viz. Safai Karamcharis, scavengers and their dependents for income generating activities for socio-economic development through State Channelising Agencies.

The Ministry implements two Acts for protecting the civil rights of the Scheduled Castes viz.

i. Protection of Civil Rights Act, 1955 and

ii. the Scheduled Castes and the Scheduled Tribes (Prevention of Atrocities Act, 1989).

The Ministry also deals with the following important issues, with regard to Scheduled Castes Development:

- Monitoring of points 11(A) of 20 point programme-Justice to Scheduled Castes.
- Affirmative Action including reservation in private sector for Scheduled Castes and Scheduled Tribes.

There is still a long way to go before the Dalits could imagine of some degree of respectability, dignified life and livelihood and access to criminal justice administrative system. For the Dalit community across the country, little has moved ahead on both fronts, with daily life continuing to be marred by incessant human rights violations in the form of atrocities and archaic untouchability practices.

Still today for the majority of Dalits, regardless of education or economic status, to journey through life as a Dalit entails daily subjugation, humiliation and exclusion from India's mainstream caste society, commencing from birth, through childhood and as an adult worker until death. Emerging trend is that, increasing atrocities related to land, water, wages and other livelihood. Most of the atrocities are committed when Dalit attempted to assert their right to resource (land, water, wages and other livelihood) and they attempted to avail legal recourse.

This is despite the fact that many Dalits do not report crimes for fear of reprisals by the dominant castes. Despite this 27 officially registered atrocities being committed against Dalits every day, police often prevent Dalits from entering police stations, refuse the registration of cases by Dalits and regularly resort to the practice of torture against Dalits with impunity, and there exists a gross negligence of the state machinery, especially the police, resulting in impunity.

The Justice Delivery Mechanism, primarily the Legal System, which is supposed to protect the poor and the marginalized Dalit victims of in-justice, is struggling with the gigantic problems of huge number of pending cases and the biased mindset of human element within its system. Lack of minimum legal awareness among the poor and the marginalized Dalits makes their situation further worse.

There is a strong comfort level in both society and the state that crimes against Dalits do not matter, need not be punished. This attitude of impunity is rooted in the social and cultural values and though the Constitution has made a very conscious change and consistent interventions of various organizations and movements, the mindset in society has not changed.

Conversion of Indian Dalit

In India religious conversion of Dalits into Christianity and Islam takes place due to discrimination and suffocation within the Hindu religion. Other factors like economic benefits as well as a genuine desire to find 'the true faith' play an important role too. But since a convert carries his or her social and economic disability into the new religion too, there is a case for recognising Dalits among all the religions equally.

In this context it must be noted that the Indian Constitution defines 'Scheduled Castes' under Article 366, and the Presidential Orders of 1950 provide Scheduled Caste status to the Dalits. Scheduled Caste status was further extended to Sikhs in 1956 and to Buddhists in 1990, giving them the right to avail special provisions in education, employment and other benefits from the Government. But the Dalits in Christianity and Islam were not given such status, for they are no-longer Hindus. This strategy of denying Scheduled Castes status to such groups not only denies rightful entitlements but also creates animosity within Dalit communities.

Considering the overall situation, the following needs to be done in the very least:

1. Government should encourage secular intellectuals and NGOs to provide training and information to people on Human Rights. People must be encouraged to examine religion from a Human Rights perspective. Through national Human Rights bodies, and through the National Commission on Minorities or the Scheduled Castes and Scheduled Tribes welfare departments, the Government should hold regional workshops and encourage Dalits to be aware of their rights.
2. Government must strictly implement the provisions of the Scheduled Castes and Scheduled Tribes (Prevention of Atrocities) Act, 1989 and the Scheduled Castes and Scheduled Tribes (Prevention of Atrocities) Rules, 1995.
3. Most school text books have lessons that teach dominant Hindu beliefs like Caste, Karma, rebirth etc. Some of the Dalit intellectuals are already initiating the process for reforming text books and this must be given a boost.
4. Reservations (positive discrimination in college admissions and in jobs) should be extended to all Dalits, which ever religion they are in. This action could help the Dalit communities in future to unite and to fight for their rights.
5. There is a need to strengthen the UN's Working Group on Minorities. It must set up a body to undertake studies on different religions and Government policies in different

countries. The body thus created must pressurise Governments, inform activists, academicians, and NGOs monitoring the situation through regular meetings, reports and workshops.

6. The United Nations Commission on Human Rights must encourage the Working Group by providing sufficient funding to take up Minority related activities efficiently, and to take up studies regarding the status of Dalits in all the religions in the Indian sub-continent. Such a step will lead to equal treatment of all the disadvantaged, and help build a strong united Dalit alliance.
7. Govt must consult with civil society on ways to reduce discriminatory practices on the basis of birth and descent.

Surepally Sujatha is a Sociologist and a secular Dalit, active in the Dalit Social Forum, Hyderabad, India. She has represented the Dalit cause at various forums both in India and abroad.

The Negativity of Positive Discrimination

In their long struggle for equality, India's dalits, or "untouchables," have often exchanged their Hinduism for Islam, Christianity, Sikhism or Buddhism, believing that they will better their lives by doing so.

They have been persuaded that Hinduism, with its *varna ashramas* (caste distinctions), has been solely responsible for all their ills. But when they switch to other religious faiths and experience the same distinctions — albeit in different forms – they realize that such a change neither improves their social status nor remedies their economic problems of unemployment and poverty — the real source of their social discrimination.

"Dalit" literally means depressed. Mahatma Gandhi named these hapless citizens Harijans, meaning "the children of God." In the ancient and much abused system called *varna ashrama,* citizens were originally divided into castes based upon the professions they followed. Even during the days of British rule, manual workers in India's villages were placed in the lowest hierarchy of the caste system. It was only after independence in 1947 that the govenment instituted a policy of affirmative action, through its Constitution, to reduce these inequalities. By reserving 23 percent of all central and state government jobs for Scheduled Castes and Tribes, with comparable reservations for school and university admissions across the country, India paved the way for improving dalits' professional and educational opportunities.

They also have seats in legislatures, state assemblies and Parliament so as to allow them greater participation in the country's governance. Conversion, unfortunately, only deprives the dalits of these special privileges, which are intended only for Hindu Scheduled Castes and Tribes.

The answer, then, is not in religious conversion so much as in streamlining the system of reservations itself. While this system has gone a long way to better the economic status of India's 82 million Scheduled Castes and Tribes, it has lost its direction because it is not envisioned as a time-bound program. The earlier beneficiaries and their progeny continue to enjoy its privileges even after half a century.

These privileges are now passed on to the second and sometimes to the third generation. Families who have reaped the full benefits of the Indian governments reservation policies have already advanced in both social and economic terms. And they continue to corner desirable jobs and university or school admissions through the reserved quotas.

Result: the poorest sections of the same reserved categories are denied their due. It is not uncommon, especially in rural India, to find poor and illiterate Scheduled Caste workers serving as the bonded labourers of their rich and influential kinsmen. An insidious caste system has thus crept into dalit circles as well. Privileged members of the community do not many those doing menial jobs, since they consider them inferior.

A few years ago, the Indian government reduced the opportunities of dalits further by extending reservations to other backward castes. And lately the government in New Delhi has extended reservations in promotions to those who have already benefited by its policies. Consequently, almost every caste is seeking the "backward" tag to claim a piece of the pie. No wonder this poorest and most backward segment of India's population is constantly exploited: by politicians for their votes; by religious leaders for their numbers; by their self-styled advocates for power.

Despite much touted policies of compulsory primary education, there are no proper school facilities for dalit children, Family planning and other health-care programs rarely reach dalit women. Illiterate, impoverished and vulnerable, the Scheduled Castes cannot even reach the jobs that are earmarked for them because they are not qualified.

These crucial issues are completely ignored by their champions, who prefer to harp on caste discrimination and religious conversion rather than take the real measures that might improve dalits' lives.

There are numerous news articles detailing the mass numbers of "untouchables" converting to non-Hindu religions to escape their stigmatized status and achieve a better economic situation. This is not a new happening: in 1956, 500,000 Hindu "untouchables" converted to Buddhism. That same year, various Indian state governments started in earnest on the road to drafting anti-conversion laws.

The question, then, is why the conversion of the lowest rung members of the *majority* religion—Hindu "untouchables"—would spark anticonversion laws—laws supposedly designed to protect *minority* religions. On the heels of such conversions comes the BJP's modification of anti-conversion laws to classify Buddhism and Jainism as branches of the Hindu religion, thus denying them status as unique religions.

Clearly, such action is designed with one purpose in mind: stop the untouchables from converting so that they remain pigeonholed in their menial jobs—forever at the service of the Brahmins and other higher castes (members of which comprise the Indian federal government).

Multiple BJP-led States, including Rajasthan, Orissa, and Madhya Pradesh, have introduced or strengthened anti-conversion laws, with the stated purpose of "protecting" the vulnerable Dalits from "improper" pressure to convert. Critics across the board, however, are of one mind: the anti-conversion laws are designed to keep the "untouchables" just that—untouchable.

Another contributing factor to the enactment of anti-conversion laws involves the history of Christianity in India. Christianity came to India during British colonialism almost 200 years ago. The British-led churches in India received funding from the West; after 200 years under British rule, the modern-day Hindu government fears that Christians in India would have ulterior motives in converting mass numbers of the population.

Another factor is electoral strategy, that is, to get votes from the upper caste Hindu majority by appeasing them with a law that keeps the socially entrenched caste system in place. However, the underlying factor is still the struggle for power—to keep the lower caste Hindus (untouchables and Scheduled Tribes) from competing with the higher and privileged castes.

Dalit Buddhist Movement

The Dalit Buddhist movement in India began with support of Sri Lankan Buddhist monks. It received an impetus with B. R. Ambedkar's call for conversion of Dalits to Buddhism in the context of a caste based society that considered them to be at the lower end of the hierarchy.

Origins

Buddhism was once dominant through much of India, it had however begun to decline by the 12th century. The Buddhist revival began in India in 1891, when the Sri Lankan Buddhist leader Anagarika Dharmapala founded the Maha Bodhi Society. The Maha Bodhi Society mainly attracted upper-caste people.

South India

In 1890 Pandit C. Ayodhya Dasa (1845-1914), better known as Iyothee Thass, founded the Sakya Buddhist Society (also known as the Indian Buddhist Association). The first president of the Indian Buddhist Association was the German born American Paul Carus, the author of *The Gospel of Buddha* (1894).

Thass, a Tamil Siddha physician, was the pioneer of the Tamil Dalit movement. He argued that Tamil Dalits were originally Buddhists. He led a delegation of prominent Dalits to Henry Steel Olcott and asked for his help in the re-establishment of "Tamil

Buddhism." Olcott helped Thass to visit Sri Lanka, where he received *diksha* from Bhikkhu Sumangala Nayake. After returning to India, Thass established the *Sakya Buddhist Society* in Madras with branches in many places including Karnataka. Thass established a weekly magazine called *Oru Paisa Tamizhan* ("One Paisa Tamilian") in Chennai in 1907, which served as a newsletter linking all the new branches of the Sakya Buddhist Society. The magazine discussed traditions and practices of Tamil Buddhism, new developments in the Buddhist world, and the Indian subcontinent's history from the Buddhist point of view. Brahmananda Reddy, a Dalit leader of Andhra Pradesh, was also fascinated by Buddhism.

Uttar Pradesh

In the early 20th century, the Barua Buddhists of Bengal under the leadership of Kripasaran Mahasthavir (1865-1926), founder of the Bengal Buddhist Association, Calcutta (1892) established viharas in cities such as Lucknow, Hyderabad, Shillong and Jamshedpur.

In Lucknow, Bodhanand Mahastavir (1874-1952) advocated Buddhism for Dalits. Born Mukund Prakash in a Bengali Brahmin family, he was orphaned at a young age, and was then raised in Benaras by an aunt.

He was initially attracted to Christianity, but became a Buddhist after a meeting with Buddhists monks from Ceylon at a Theosophical Conference in Benares. He later lived in Lucknow where he came in contact with Barua Buddhists, many of whom were employed as cooks by the British. In 1914, Prakash was ordained Bodhanand Mahastavir in Calcutta in the presence of Kripasaran Mahasthvir. He began preaching Buddhism in Lucknow. He founded the *Bharatiye Buddh Samiti* in 1916, and set up a vihara in 1928. In his book *Mula Bharatavasi Aur Arya* ("Original Inhabitants and Aryans"), Mahastavir stated that the shudras were the original inhabitants of India, who were enslaved by the Aryans.

Bodhanand Mahastavir wrote another book on Buddhist rituals called *Baudha Dvicharya*. His associate, Chandrika Prasad Jigyasu, founded the *Bahujan Kalyan Prakashan*. The two co-authored a book on the life and teaching of the Buddha.

Acharya Ishvardatt Medharthi (1900-1971) of Kanpur also supported the cause of the Dalits. He had studied Pali at Gurukul Kangri and Buddhist scripture was well known to him. He was initiated into Buddhism by Gyan Keto and the Lokanatha in 1937. Gyan Keto (1906-1984), born Peter Schoenfeldt was a German who arrived to Ceylon in 1936 and became a Buddhist. Although Medharthi heavily criticized the Indian caste system, he didn't criticize Hinduism. He claimed that the Dalits ("Adi Hindus") were the ancient rulers of India and had been trapped into slavery by the Aryan invaders. He also claimed that the sanatana dharma was the religion of "Adi Hindus", and tried to reconcile Buddhism with the Sant Mat.

Another Bhikkhu of Kanpur, Bhikshu Uttam, was a strong supporter of the Arya Samaj and the *Jat Pat Todak Mandal*, the anti-caste wing of the Arya Samaj.

B. R. Ambedkar

At the Yeola conference in 1935, prominent Dalit leader B. R. Ambedkar declared that he would not die a Hindu, saying that it perpetuates caste injustices. Ambedkar was approached by various leaders of different denominations and faiths. Meetings were held to discuss the question of Dalit religion and the pros and cons of conversion. On May 22, 1936, an "All Religious Conference" was held at Lucknow. It was attended by prominent Dalit leaders including Jagjivan Ram, though Ambedkar could not attend it. At the conference, Muslim, Christian, Sikh, and Buddhist representatives presented the tenets of their respective religions in an effort to win over Dalits.

Buddhist monk Lokanatha visited Ambedkar's residence at Dadar on June 10, 1936 and tried to persuade him to embrace Buddhism. Later in an interview to the Press, Lokanatha said that Ambedkar was impressed with Buddhism and that his own ambition was to convert all Dalits to Buddhism. In 1937, Lokanatha published a pamphlet *Buddhism Will Make You Free*, dedicated to the Depressed Classes of India from his press in Ceylon.

In early 1940s, Ambedkar visited Acharya Ishvardatt Medharthi's Buddhpuri school in Kanpur. Medharthi had earlier been initiated into Buddhism by Lokanatha, and by the mid-1940s, he had close contacts with Ambedkar. For a short while, Ambedkar also took Pali classes from Medharthi in Delhi.

Bodhananda Mahastvir and B. R. Ambedkar first met in 1926, at the "Indian Non-Brahmin Conference" convened by Shahu IV of Kolhapur. They met on two more occasions and for a short while in the 1940s, where they discussed dhamma. Mahastavir was objected to Dr Ambedkar's second marriage because his wife was a Brahmin. Later, his followers actively participated in Ambedkar's Republican Party of India.

Ambedkar's Conversion

After publishing a series of books and articles arguing that Buddhism was the only way for the Untouchables to gain equality, Ambedkar publicly converted on October 14, 1956 at Deekshabhoomi, Nagpur. He took the three refuges and the Five Precepts from a Buddhist monk, Bhadant U Chandramani, in the traditional manner and then in his turn administered them to the 380,000 of his followers that were present. The conversion ceremony was attended by Medharthi, his main disciple Bhoj Dev Mudit, and Mahastvir Bodhanand's Sri Lankan successor, Bhante Pragyanand. Ambedkar would die less than two months later, just after finishing his definitive work on Buddhism. Many Dalits employ the term "Ambedkar(ite) Buddhism" to designate the Buddhist movement, which started with Ambedkar's conversion and many converted people called themselves as "Nava-Bauddha" i.e. New Buddhists.

22 Vows of Ambedkar

After receiving ordination, Ambedkar gave *dhamma diksha* to his followers. The ceremony included 22 vows given to all new converts after Three Jewels and Five Precepts. On 16 October 1956, Ambedkar performed another mass religious conversion ceremony at Chanda.

He prescribed 22 vows to his followers:

1. I shall have no faith in Brahma, Vishnu and Maheshwara nor shall I worship them.
2. I shall have no faith in Rama and Krishna who are believed to be incarnation of God nor shall I worship them.

3. I shall have no faith in Gauri, Ganapati and other gods and goddesses of Hindus nor shall I worship them.
4. I do not believe in the incarnation of God.
5. I do not and shall not believe that Lord Buddha was the incarnation of Vishnu. I believe this to be sheer madness and false propaganda.
6. I shall not perform *Shraddha* nor shall I give *pind-dan*.
7. I shall not act in a manner violating the principles and teachings of the Buddha.
8. I shall not allow any ceremonies to be performed by Brahmins.
9. I shall believe in the equality of man.
10. I shall endeavour to establish equality.
11. I shall follow the noble eightfold path of the Buddha.
12. I shall follow the ten *paramitas* prescribed by the Buddha.
13. I shall have compassion and loving kindness for all living beings and protect them.
14. I shall not steal.
15. I shall not tell lies.
16. I shall not commit carnal sins.
17. I shall not take intoxicants like liquor, drugs etc.
18. I shall endeavour to follow the noble eightfold path and practice compassion and loving kindness in every day life.
19. I renounce Hinduism, which is harmful for humanity and impedes the advancement and development of humanity because it is based on inequality, and adopt Buddhism as my religion.
20. I firmly believe the Dhamma of the Buddha is the only true religion.
21. I believe that I am having a rebirth.
22. I solemnly declare and affirm that I shall hereafter lead my life according to the principles and teachings of the Buddha and his Dhamma.

Nowadays many Ambedkarite Organisations are working for these 22 vows (i.e. 22 Pratigya). They believe that these vows only are responsible for the existence & rapid growth of present Buddhism in India.

The umbrella organization known as the 22 Pledges Practice & Propagation Movement (i.e. in Hindi-22 Pratigya Aacharan aur Prachaar Abhiyan) is fully devoted for this purpose. This totally non-political movement is the brainchild of Arvind Sontakke, and comprises around 5,000,000 volunteers (Pracharaks) including many regional and local groups throughout India.

Dalit Buddhism Movement after Ambedkar's Death

The Buddhist movement was somewhat hindered by Dr. Ambedkar's death so shortly after his conversion. It did not receive the immediate mass support from the Untouchable population that Ambedkar had hoped for. Division and lack of direction among the leaders of the Ambedkarite movement have been an additional impediment.

According to the 2001 census, there are currently 7.95 million Buddhists in India, at least 5.83 million of whom are Buddhists in Maharashtra. This makes Buddhism the fifth-largest religion in India and 6% of the population of Maharashtra, but less than 1% of the overall population of India.

The Buddhist revival remains concentrated in two states: Ambedkar's native Maharashtra, and Uttar Pradesh — the land of Bodhanand Mahastavir, Acharya Medharthi and their associates.

Developments in Uttar Pradesh

Acharya Medharthi retired from his Buddhapuri school in 1960, and shifted to an ashram in Haridwar. He turned to the Arya Samaj and conducted vedic yajnas all over India. After his death, he was cremated according to Arya Samaj rites. His Buddhpuri school became embroiled in property disputes.

His follower, Bhoj Dev Mudit, converted to Buddhism in 1968 and set up a school of his own. Rajendranath Aherwar appeared as an important Dalit leader in Kanpur. He joined the Republican Party of India and converted to Buddhism along with his whole family in 1961. In 1967, he founded the Kanpur branch of "Bharatiya Buddh Mahasabha". He held regular meetings where he preached Buddhism, officiated at Buddhist weddings and life cycle ceremonies, and organized festivals on Dr. Ambedkar's Jayanti (birth day), Buddha Jayanti, Diksha Divas (the day Ambedkar converted), and Dr Ambedkar Paranirvan Divas (the day Ambedkar died). The Dalit Buddhist movement in Kanpur gained impetus with the arrival of Dipankar, a Chamar bhikkhu, in 1980.

Dipankar had come to Kanpur on a Buddhist mission and his first public appearance was scheduled at a mass conversion drive in 1981. The event was organized by Rahulan Ambawadekar, an RPI Dalit leader. In April 1981, Ambawadekar founded the Dalit Panthers (U.P. Branch) inspired by the Maharashtrian Dalit Panthers. The event met with severe criticism and opposition from Vishwa Hindu Parishad and was banned.

In 2002, Kanshi Ram, a popular out-caste political leader from a Sikh religious background, announced his intention to convert to Buddhism on October 14, 2006, the fiftieth anniversary of Ambedkar's conversion. He intended for 20,000,000 of his supporters to convert at the same time. Part of the significance of this plan was that Ram's followers include not only Untouchables, but persons from a variety of castes, who could significantly broaden Buddhism's support. However, he died October 9, 2006 after a lengthy illness; he was cremated as per Buddhist rituals.

Another popular Dalit leader, Bahujan Samaj Party chief Mayawati, has said that she and her followers will embrace Buddhism after the BSP gains control of the government.

Maharashtra

Japanese-born Bhadant Nagarjun Surai Sasai is an important Buddhist leader in India. Sasai came to India in 1966 and met Nichidatsu Fuji, whom he helped with the Peace Pagoda at Rajgir. He fell out with Fuji, however, and started home, but, by his own account, was stopped by a dream in which a figure resembling Nagarjuna appeared and said, "Go to Nagpur". In Nagpur, he met Wamanrao Godbole, the person who had organized the conversion ceremony for Dr. Ambedkar in 1956. Sasai claims that when he saw a photograph of Dr. Ambedkar at Godbole's home, he realized that it was Ambedkar who had appeared in his dream. At first, Nagpur folk considered Surai Sasai very strange.

Then he began to greet them with "Jai Bhim" (victory to Ambedkar) and to build viharas. In 1987 a court case to deport him on the grounds that he had overstayed his visa was dismissed, and he was granted Indian citizenship. Sasai is one of the main leaders of the campaign to free the Mahabodhi Temple at Bodh Gaya from Hindu control.

Organized Mass Conversions

Since Ambedkar's conversion, several thousand people from different castes have converted to Buddhism in ceremonies including the twenty-two vows. The Tamil Nadu and Gujarat governments passed new laws in 2003 to ban "forced" religious conversions. These laws were later withdrawn due to heavy opposition.

1957: In 1957, Mahastvir Bodhanand's Sri Lankan successor, Bhante Pragyanand, held a mass conversion drive for 15,000 people in Lucknow.

2001: A prominent Indian Dalit Buddhist leader and political activist, Udit Raj, organized a large mass conversion on November 4, 2001 where he gave the 22 vows, but the event met with active opposition from the government.

2006, Hyderabad: A report from the UK daily *The Guardian* said that some Hindus have converted to Buddhism. Buddhist monks from the UK and the U.S. attended the conversion ceremonies in India. In response, Hindu nationalists asserted that Dalits should concentrate on illiteracy and poverty rather than looking for new religions.

2006, Gulbarga: On October 14, 2006 hundreds of people converted from Hinduism to Buddhism in Gulburga (Karnataka).

2006: A Buddhist source claimed that "300,000 Dalits are estimated" to have converted to Buddhism as part of 50th year celebrations of Ambedkar's deeksha in 2006. Non-Partisan sources put the number of attendees (not converts) at 30,000. The move was criticized by Hindu groups as "unhelpful" and has been criticized as a "political stunt."

2007, Mumbai: On May 27, 2007 tens of thousands of Dalits from Maharashtra gathered at the Mahalakshmi racecourse in Mumbai to mark the 50th anniversary of the conversion of Ambedkar. The number of people who actually converted, however, versus the number of people in attendance was not clear. The event was organized by the Republican Party of India leader Ramdas Athvale.

Criticism of Conversions

Hindu critics have argued that efforts to convert Hindus to Ambedkarite Buddhism are political stunts rather than sincere commitments to social reform. In addition, several Dalit leaders have stated that they are not against the upper castes per se. Leaders of the Dalit Bahujan Samaj Party have said that their being branded as "anti-Hindu" because of the publicity associated with the conversions is largely the work of partisan and politically motivated groups within the Dalit movement and that they are only interested in peaceful dialogue with the Brahmins.

The critics also note that Gautama Buddha, the founder of Buddhism, himself was a Kshatriya of the Uakta clan. Buddha is also said to be a descendant of Sage Angirasa in many Buddhist texts. Scholars like Dr. Eitel connects it to the Rishi Gautama. Buddha declares in the *Vasalsutta, "Whosoever by falsehood deceives either a Brahman or a Sraman or any other mendicant, let him be an outcast."* He again declares in the text, *"Whosoever annoys either a Brahman or a Sraman when meal-time has come and does not give him anything, let one know him as an outcast."*

Distinctive Interpretation

According to controversial academic Gail Omvedt: "Ambedkar's Buddhism seemingly differs from that of those who accepted by faith, who 'go for refuge' and accept the canon. This much is clear from its basis: it does not accept in totality the scriptures of the Theravada, the Mahayana, or the Vajrayana. The question that is then clearly put forth: is a fourth yana, a Navayana, a kind of modernistic Enlightenment version of the Dhamma really possible within the framework of Buddhism? Most Dalit Indian Buddhists espouse an eclectic version of Buddhism, primarily based on Theravada, but with additional influences from Mahayana and Vajrayana. On many subjects, they give Buddhism a distinctive interpretation. Of particular note is their emphasis on Shakyamuni Buddha as a political and social reformer, rather than merely as a spiritual leader. They point out that the Buddha required his monastic followers to ignore caste distinctions, and that he was critical of the social inequality that existed in his own time. Ambedkar's followers do not believe that a person's unfortunate conditions at birth are the result of previous karma. They also point out that Ormvedt's idea of an 'Enlightenment version of the dharma' opposed to a traditional 'acceptance by faith' is a misapplication of Western categories, since the Buddha encouraged people to put all teachings-including his own-to critical test and not to accept anything on the basis of tradition.

6

Globalisation and the Prospects of Indian Dalits

Introduction

Globalisation in a Historical Perspective

The doctrinal basis of today's globalisation is provided by the "neo-liberalism" that represented revival of economic liberalism propounded by Adam Smith in 1776 in his famous book titled, "Wealth of Nations". Economic liberalism advocated the abolition of the government intervention in economic matters; it considered fee trade was the best way for a nation's economy to develop. These ideas were "liberal" in the sense of no controls. Underneath their democratic façade, promotion of individualism and encouragement of free enterprise, they came to mean free hand for the capitalists for exploitation of labour and to make huge profits at any cost. These ideas ruled the world through the 1800s and early 1900s till the great depression of the 1930s eclipsed them with the theory of a British economist named John Maynard Keynes. This theory propounded that full employment is necessary for capitalism to grow and it can be achieved only if governments and central banks intervened to increase employment.

It worked well through the post World War II reconstruction period and thereafter through the mid sixties. The USA which had emerged as the major economy of the world long before the World War II, immensely benefited from the state-coordinated wartime economy so as to assume the reigns of global capitalist order. It zealously guarded the capitalist system against the radical nationalism sprouting at many places, invariably with the use of force under the peculiar terminology of falsehood like "protection against the threat to stability" (a case of overthrow of the first democratic government of Guatemala in 1954 or a blatant military intervention planned in Italy in 1948 in the wake of election results sensing the undesired outcome). With over half of the world's wealth, the USA performed the role of world's banker in the post-World War II system. However, with the increasing financial crisis of the debt-ridden countries, the Nixon administration decided to dismantle this system, giving rise to huge explosion of unregulated capital flows that totally marginalized the real economy. The composition of the international financial transaction shifted from real economy to speculation. Within just two decades form 1971 to 1990, the percentage of transactions related to real economy came down from 90 % to paltry 10 % and further declined to 5 % over next five years.

The plethora of literature on globalisation paradoxically seems to induce more confusion than clearing out the true nature of its dynamics. For many, it is not at all a new phenomenon; it has been there in essence in the cross border trade that went on centuries ago and in an identifiable form in the nineteenth century capitalism insofar as it lent both labour and capital substantially mobile, gave fillip to international trade and when national economies were kept in kilter by the operation of the gold standard. This attempt at universalising the theory as well as praxis of globalisation tends to imply futility of resistance to globalisation. Many proffer a TINA (There Is No Alternative) argument as per which despite adverse impact of globalisation on masses of people, there is no alternative for the world than adopting the globalisation model. This argument, while reflecting the admission of the adverse impact of globalisation and therefore sounding more credible, tends to indicate accrual of more benefits than costs.

It tends to neutralise the theoretical arguments against globalisation and therefore cripples the resistance movement much before its articulation. Then there are sponsored authorships that ceaselessly contribute multi-dimensional arguments in support of these policies. They could range from out right theoretical distortions to empirical amplification. The sheer number of such studies claiming all kinds of success stories as attributes of these policies and all kinds of failures as due to absence of them overwhelms and enfeebles the truth to the contrary. The main theme of globalisation is pivoted on the promise of development and its "trickle down" to the subaltern sections of the society. Notwithstanding the total contrary evidence, the glitter created by the free markets misleads one into believing that the benefits of globalisation reached the weak and poor of the society. After nearly a decade of adoption of these policies in our country and on the eve of the launch of so called second phase of Reforms, it is time that we examined the magnitude and direction of the impact of these policies on the dalits representing the oppressed people in India. This paper seeks to attempt this task with the help of available statistics.

Globalisation in a Historical Perspective

The doctrinal basis of today's globalisation is provided by the "neo-liberalism" that represented revival of economic liberalism propounded by Adam Smith in 1776 in his famous book titled, "Wealth of Nations". Economic liberalism advocated the abolition of the government intervention in economic matters; it considered fee trade was the best way for a nation's economy to develop. These ideas were "liberal" in the sense of no controls. Underneath their democratic façade, promotion of individualism and encouragement of free enterprise, they came to mean free hand for the capitalists for exploitation of labour and to make huge profits at any cost.

These ideas ruled the world through the 1800s and early 1900s till the great depression of the 1930s eclipsed them with the theory of a British economist named John Maynard Keynes. This theory propounded that full employment is necessary for capitalism to grow and it can be achieved only if governments and central banks intervened to increase employment. It worked well through the post World War II reconstruction period and thereafter through the mid sixties. The USA which had emerged as the major economy of the world long before the World War II, immensely benefited from the state-coordinated wartime economy so as to assume the reigns of global capitalist order. It zealously guarded the capitalist system against the radical nationalism sprouting at many places, invariably with the use of force under the peculiar terminology of falsehood like "protection against the threat to stability" (a case of overthrow of the first democratic government of Guatemala in 1954 or a blatant military intervention planned in Italy in 1948 in the wake of election results sensing the undesired outcome). With over half of the world's wealth, the USA performed the role of world's banker in the post-World War II system. However, with the increasing financial crisis of the debt-ridden countries, the Nixon administration decided to dismantle this system, giving rise to huge explosion of unregulated capital flows that totally marginalized the real economy. The composition of the international financial transaction shifted from real economy to speculation. Within just two decades form 1971 to 1990, the percentage of transactions related to real economy came down from 90 % to paltry 10 % and further declined to 5 % over next five years.

The capitalist crisis over the last 25 years, with its shrinking profit rates, inspired the corporate elite to revive economic liberalism into neo-liberalism. This neo-liberalism is opeartionalised through "the Washington Consensus". This phrase significantly refers to the structural adjustment programmes designed by the government of the United States and the international financial institutions that it largely dominates. These institutions are the core of a "de facto world government" representing the interests of transnational Corporations, banks and investment

firms in a new Imperial age. With regard to the operational features of the neo-liberalism, none other than its patron saint Adam smith had exposed its inherent class bias. Writing about the society of his times he pointed out that the "principal architects" of policy in England were "merchants and manufacturers", who used state power to serve their own interests, however "grievous" the effect on others, including the people of England. The "principle architects" of the neo-liberal "Washington Consensus" are the masters of the private economy, mainly huge Corporations that control much of the international economy and have the means to dominate policy formation as well as the structuring of thought and opinion. The institutional structure through which the globalisation is being promoted is basically subservient to the interests of big capital, particularly that of US who seeks to leverage its dominant role in global economy through essentially a short-term, profit-maximization model. Its anti-labour, anti-people characteristics are deeply embedded in its architecture that is incapable of anything but perpetuation of poverty, inequality and environmental degradation.

'Crisis Driven' Reforms: India into Global Order

The Brettonwood institutions have been the main instrument to spread the wings of globalisation. However, it came be adopted by every nation state in the form of some kind of local initiative, euphemistically called as Reforms. The conditionalities accepted as a rescue package were declared here as economic reforms by the government. These Economic Reforms launched in July 1991 in India were in nature of a crisis management response to the economic and political crises that erupted in early 1991. The economic crisis comprised a steep fall in the foreign exchange reserve, galloping inflation, large public and current account deficits and mounting of domestic and foreign debt. In politics, the fall of two governments in a short span of four months, from November 1990 to March 1991; deferment of presentation of the union budget, fairly long political interregnum till the elections, the assassination of a former prime minister Rajiv Gandhi in their midst and the emergence of a minority government with a leader sans charisma, reflected an unprecedented crisis. These events led to a sharp erosion of confidence in India among lenders, down gradation of India's credit rating and consequently snapping of international credit lines from private or commercial sources. Indian Reforms thus, were essentially of a 'crisis driven' variety. They did not represent strategic choice with a vision of long-term development of Indian people.

The blue print for the Reforms was provided by the combination of macroeconomic stabilisation and structural adjustment programme of International Monetary Fund (IMF) and World Bank respectively, which had been adopted by many countries before in similar situations. The typical measures under these programmes are:

Macroeconomic Stabilisation:

- Devaluation of currency for making exchange rate more realistic,
- Withdrawal of restrictions on imports,
- Reduction/ elimination of fiscal and balance of payments deficits,
- Removal of all controls on prices, exchange and interest rate,
- Elimination/ reduction of all subsidies,
- Introduction of financial structure reforms and free entry of foreign financial institutions,
- Complete autonomy of the central bank to pursue independent monetary policy.

Structural Adjustment:

- Decontrol of industries,
- Privatisation of government-owned entities,
- Structural changes in the economy aimed at export-led growth,
- Free entry of foreign capital and technology without any let, hindrance or conditions,
- Free entry and exit of foreign firms including financial and services industries,
- Free cross border movement of capital and other funds,
- Legislative safeguards for protection of intellectual property rights,

Creation of legal climate for enforcement of legal contracts, private property rights, and free entry and exit of business, industrial and financial firms.

The underlying economic philosophy of these programmes stems from the theories of neoliberalism that propounds the rule of market, reduction in the role of State, cutting public expenditure on social services and eliminating the concept of public good; deregulation, and general replacement of public with private. It is based on the premise that the public sector leads to inefficient allocation and utilisation of economic resources and that the enterprise of private sector overcomes it through the dynamics of free market.

Dalits in India

Dalits, as the ex-untouchables prefer to be called, are a very distinct social group. While belonging to a broad class of have-nots they suffer an additional disability of social oppression. Economically, most of them are still the poorest of poor. The balance minuscule minority has managed to escape poverty limits and to locate itself on to a continuum ranging up to a reasonable level of prosperity.

The main factor that has catalysed this transition is the reservation policy, which has provided them a basic opportunity to enter the modern sectors of economy. In social terms however, all dalits, irrespective of their economic standing, still suffer oppression. This social oppression varies from the crudest variety of untouchability, still being practised in rural areas, to the sophisticated forms of discrimination encountered even in modern sectors of urban areas.

Although the statistics indicate that dalits have made a significant progress on almost all parameters during the five post-independence decades, the relative distance between them and non-dalits seems to have remained the same or increased. More than 75 percent of the dalit workers are still connected with land; 25 percent being the marginal and small farmers and balance over 50 percent are the landless labourers. In urban areas, they work mainly in unorganised sector. Out of the total dalit population of 138 million, the number of dalits in services falling in the domain of reservations does not exceed 1.1 million; a mere 0.8 percent.

Organisation of Study

Corresponding to dual disabilities of the dalits, the main body of the paper is divided in two parts:

(i) the impact on dalits as a part of the class of have-nots and

(ii) the impact on dalits as a disadvantaged social group. In the first part, impact of the Reforms in relation to the three most critical factors affecting the poor people is studied.

They are:

(i) food security,

(ii) inflation and

(iii) employment.

Poverty, which represents the combined influence of all deprivations, is also reviewed separately. In light of the vast data available on the impact of similar reforms in other countries, this section is sub-divided so as to outline 'Indian experience' and 'international experience' separately. The second part focuses on the influence of the Reforms on the specific three disabilities suffered by the dalits in addition to their poverty. They are (i) educational backwardness, (ii) discrimination in employment, (iii) atrocities and (iv) socio-cultural suppression. The last concluding part sums up the study with the observations regarding certain prerequisites for the Reforms to be more responsive to the problems of people, particularly the dalits.

Impact of the Reforms on the Poor

Impact of the Reforms on poor people can be assessed along several dimensions but here the study confines itself to the three most predominant ones, viz., food security, inflation and employment. Implementation of the Reforms over the last five years in India has generated huge data so as to enable meaningful and autonomous assessment of our native experience. This is covered in the first part. The Reforms however were implemented many years before and in many countries. This vast treasure of information that is available can be used to validate or correct the inferences from the study. This is covered in the second part.

Indian Experience Food Security

Food security mainly relates with the production, distribution and pricing of food grains and thus brings agriculture, Public Distribution System (PDS) and the subsidy structure in to focus. The Reform measures that predominantly affect them are reduction in fiscal deficit, reduction in subsidies, devaluation of Rupee, export orientation and reduction in agricultural credit. Considering the pattern of the budgetary outlays of the government, the fiscal contraction inevitably resulted in a disproportionate cut in capital expenditure. The capital expenditure slid from 5.10 percent of GDP in 1990-91 down to 2.74 percent in 1995-96. In terms of percentage of total expenditure, it fell from an average of 32.8 percent during the preceding five years of the Reforms, to average of 22.05 percent during the succeeding five years of the Reforms. In 1995-96 (BE), it was as low as 17.82 percent. Agriculture sector also bore the share of this cut.

The average annual increase in public sector outlay on agriculture and irrigation during 1985-90 fell from Rs. 1.3 billion to an average of Rs. 0.68 billion during 1990-92. This cut is bound to have a depressing effect on the agricultural production in coming years. The subsidy on fertiliser had played a crucial role in quadrupling food grain production from 46 million tonnes for a population of 363 million in 1951 to 170 million tonnes in 1991 for a population of 832 million. But, after the launch of the Reforms, the subsidy was reduced. It slid from 0.82 percent of GDP in 1990-91 to 0.75 percent of GDP in 1995-96. The prices of the phosphatic and potassium based fertilisers were decontrolled and that of nitrogen based fertilisers were reduced by 10 percent. The prices of phosphatic and potassium based fertilisers soared to international level resulting into sharp fall in their consumption. Consumption of phosphatic one fell from 3.3 million tonnes of nutrients in 1991-92 to 2.7 million tonnes in 1993-94 and that of potassic fell from 1.4 to 0.9 million tonnes in the same period. Some amount of substitution effect raised the consumption of nitrogen-based fertiliser from 8 million tonnes in 1991-92 to 10.8 million tonnes in 1995-96 resulting in skewing of the nutrient balance.

As against the consumption ratio of a mix of nitrogenic, phosphatic and potassic fertiliser of 5.9:2.4:1 in 1991-92, closer to the deemed ideal of 4:2:1, it deteriorated to 9:3:1 in 1994-95. This imbalance is said to have an adverse effect on soil quality and in turn on its productivity. The nutrient imbalance apart, a study of Andhra Pradesh, Maharashtra and Karnataka by Gaiha (1994) has noted a significant reduction in per hectare fertiliser consumption during the Reform period, which expectedly showed up in the decline in food grain production. This inherent threat to food security is further magnified by the devaluation of rupee by about

25 percent effected in July 1991. It resulted in making our food grains cheaper in the international market. As a result, even the ordinary (non-aromatic) rice (besides the usually exported superfine aromatic (basmati) rice was exported in huge volumes. The policy impetus to export of rice and wheat is reflected in the actual exports overshooting the targets. For example, in 1995-96 (October-September) actual rice export had reached 5.51 million tonnes as against the target of 2.5 million tonnes. Increasing exports and free market sales of foodgrains have contributed to a drastic reduction in the stocks of foodgrains with the public procurement agencies.

For example, by September 1996, there was a whooping reduction of 10 million tonnes in the stock of foodgrains. In case of wheat, it dipped down to 10.36 million tonnes, even lower than the prescribed minimum norm of 13.1 million tonnes. The policy thrust on agricultural exports has moreover resulted in diversion of land to the export production of non-food primary products. There has been a spurt in corporate farming for export horticulture and floriculture products, etc. As per one FAO report, this trend of shifting land for exportable non-food grain crops had already set in even in the decade ending 1991. The prospects for this trend lies in the fact that there is a huge demand in the developed countries for some 9000 varieties of edible non-food grain primary products which grow in sub-tropical and tropical regions of the developing countries. Likewise, there is an exportable surplus of foodgrains and dairy products in the developed countries that craves for markets. Surely, as some economists apprehend, India may turn to be a net importer of foodgrains in not so a distant future. The international market for agri-products being a oligopsony of three to six giant companies whose control over the market extends to 80 to 90 percent, 4 export thrust in this area may not moreover be cost effective. As the experience of some African countries shows, the increasing export of foodgrains for same level of foreign exchange earning certainly impairs the food security of people.

The reforms in banking led to a severe squeeze on agriculture lending. The share of agriculture in net bank credit consistently declined and fell from 17.4 percent to 12.4 percent during March

1990 to March 1995. Expressed in constant (1980-81) rupees, it fell from Rs. 81,470 million in 1989-90 to Rs. 70,500 million in 1994-95. Considering, the hike in input costs, the impact of this squeeze could have only been deleterious on food grains production.

As a measure of ensuring food security to the large mass of Indian population, public distribution system was instituted in India in the wake of the calamity of the Great Bengal Famine of 1942-43 and the World War-II. The system comprises over 4,24,000 fair price shops spread all over the country in rough proportion of the population. The food distributed through PDS is subsidised by the Government to the extent of the difference between the issue price of foodgrains and their economic cost to Food Corporation of India (FCI)- the agency that incurs the cost of transportation, storage and administration in respect of the stock of food grain. It devours a significant part of the government subsidy. For example, in 1990-91 out of total food subsidy of Rs. 26,000 million, FCI-costs amounted to Rs. 10,000 million, which works out to a whooping 38.5 percent. With the FCI-costs ever increasing, the impact of any reduction in subsidy has to hit the poor directly.

For ensuring supply of foodgrains to the PDS system in face of export attraction due to the devaluation of rupee, for maintaining their level of production in spite of sharp rise in input prices and for political consideration of assuaging the rich farmers' lobby, the government had to increase the procurement prices of rice and wheat. The procurement prices of rice and wheat were raised by 67.56 percent and 62.8 percent respectively between 1989-90 and 1993-94. This rise was passed on to the consumers by increasing the issue prices of these commodities by 85.81 percent and 75.14 percent respectively between June 1990 and February 1994, apparently for reducing the food subsidy. The impact of this rise was reflected in a significant fall in the offtake of food grains. After the Reforms, offtake of wheat and rice as a percentage of the allocation has shown considerable decline.

In the years from 1990-91 to 1992-93 this percentage was generally over 80 but in the next three years from 1993-94 to 1995-96, it came down to below 50 percent in case of wheat and to little over 60 percent in case of rice. The export-attraction of wheat has already led to shortages from situation of surplus, which had to be met with expensive imports. The promising income from wheat crop has resulted in wheat extensively substituting coarse cereals-the main food of poor people in many parts of the country, as can be seen from the dwindling output of the latter. The latest available figures show that it fell from 36.6 million tonnes out of a total foodgrains output of 179.5 million tonnes in 1992-93 to 30 million tonnes out of a total output of 185 million tonnes in 1995-96.

Since, the difference between the consumer-end PDS retail prices and market prices became marginal, the not-so-poor left the PDS and owing to unaffordable prices the poor cut their consumption. The resultant effect on nutrition and hunger had to be borne by the people in direct proportion to their poverty. One study revealed that the families of landless labourers and marginal and small farmers reduced their offtake by over 50 percent. Considering their extremely low level of food consumption, below or around the subsistence minimum calories defined by the poverty line, the impact of further reduction of intake by over 50 percent may have led many people to starvation deaths.

Recently, on the advice from the World Bank, the government has decided to make the PDS targeted at the real poor. The real intention however appears to be the reduction in food subsidy. With the narrowing spread between the market and the PDS retail prices, the so-called non-poor are already out of its net. Even the back-of-envelope kind calculation will show that the people below the poverty line (at the 1991 level) require 46.5 million tonnes of foodgrains as against the actual distribution of only 16.6 million tonnes, a mere 36 percent of the requirement.

The new scheme based on the executive reluctance to acknowledge poverty is bound to push many more people to starvation. The cumulative effect of the above could be clearly seen in a trend of falling per capita net availability of cereals per day for the Indian population. During two years of the Reforms, there was 8.43 percent fall in per capita availability of cereals and 12.02 percent fall in that of pulses. Considering the acute inequality of Indian population, the impact of this declining trend on the poorer and particularly the disadvantaged sections like the dalits would be far more severe than revealed by the averages. Pulses being the only source of vegetable protein for poor people, a sharp decline in their availability certainly indicates malnutrition. The incidence of malnutrition further would be disproportionately injurious to women and children because of the male preference in Indian tradition. The evidence of this disaster has already come in the form of malnutrition deaths of over 350 children in the Amaravati district of Maharashtra-the most industrialised and relatively progressive state in India.

Inflation

Inflation hits poor people the hardest. Being employed mainly in the unorganised sector, they do not have even the partial protection that their counterparts in the organised sector have by way of dearness allowance. Most of their earning is spent on the basic needs like food, clothing and shelter, and hence any price rise directly dampens their level of consumption. The policy measures unleashed under the Reforms that directly contributed to inflation are:

(i) reduction in the budget and fiscal deficit,
(ii) devaluation,
(iii) privatisation,
(iv) elimination or reduction in subsidies and
(v) export promotion.

The reduction in the budget and fiscal deficits predominantly resulted in curtailment of capital expenditure and consequently in the decline in capital formation. Between 1990-91 and 1993-94 the real fall in capital expenditure was 31 percent. The real gross fixed capital formation as percentage of GDP reflects a consistent decline from 21.3 in 1990-91 to 19.8 in 1993-94. Its fall for the public component is far more precipitous, from 8.6 to 7.8 for the same period. This could lead to fall in future output and with inelastic wages, would cause an inflationary pressure in the economy.

Reduction in budgetary support to the public sector effected under the Reforms serves dual objective. One, it contributes to containment of the budgetary deficit and two; it constitutes a step in the direction of privatisation. The budgetary support to the

PSUs was reduced by 6.1 percent over the balance budgetary period of nine months in the very first post-Reforms budget of 1991-92 and consistently thereafter. The budget prescribes the supplementary resources and their sources to the PSUs. For example, in 1992-93 it showed a marginal increase in the amount to be mobilised through sale of bonds but a growth of 320 percent in the costlier funds obtained through commercial debts and suppliers' credit.

These methods are not always feasible and hence the PSUs had to resort to increasing prices of their products to make the two ends meet. For example, in the same budget, the impossible target given to Sail Authority of India to raise its internal generation from Rs. 4,910 million to 9,720 million was met by the 15 percent increase in steel prices, giving significant fillip to the inflationary spiral in the economy. Devaluation of currency directly contributes to inflation by raising the cost of imports that enter into domestic production or consumption. Large part of our import comprises petroleum crude and its products; chemicals, machinery, iron and steel, etc. which enter as raw or intermediate materials in our production processes. Most of these products are of common use in the economy. Any escalation in their cost therefore directly contributes to the rise of general price level.

The last administrative price rise of petroleum products could be a case in point. The devaluation of rupee made it dearer domestically, causing deficit in the oil pool account to mount. Eventually, it entailed hefty price rise of petroleum products. Insofar as petroleum products are consumed directly or indirectly by all, their price rise impelled the general pricelevel to go up with a multiplier effect.

All the studies on the Economic Reforms are unanimous in their conclusion that the Reforms have significantly contributed to inflation. A recent study by the EPW Research Foundation revealed significant price rise all across. Based on the wholesale Price Index (WPI), the price rise of the primary articles of consumption ranged from 42 percent to 93 percent. The WPI for all articles increased by 44.4 percent registering an annual compound growth of 10.3 percent. In the decade preceding the Reforms (1980-81 to 1990-91) this increase was only 7 percent, despite the 17 percent growth in money supply. Prof. Kurien's study isolates four periods of significant price rise from 1950; viz., (I) 1964-65 to 1968-69, (ii) 1972-73 to 1976-77, (iii) 1979-80 to 1983-84 and (iv) 1991-92 to 1995-96. He clearly finds extraneous force majure situations being responsible for the price rise in the three periods before the Reforms but no such tangible reason for it in the fourth period. There were severe famines in the first and the third periods and huge increase in the international prices in the third period that caused the prices to rise. On the contrary, during the post-Reforms fourth period, there was an unprecedented long spell of good monsoons for continuous seven years, and relative stability in international petroleum prices.

Therefore, the only inescapable inference Prof. Kurien reached was to attribute the price rise to the steps taken under the Reforms. For example, it is the Reforms that caused the price of chemical fertiliser to rise by 100.6 percent, electricity by 65.9 percent and coal by 58.1 percent. Devaluation of rupee and emphasis on the export-led growth caused pressure on the prices of products depending on their import content.

The exact effect of simultaneous reduction of customs duty and excise duty is not easy to assess but as some micro studies indicate, they also added to the rise of general price level. For example, there being no significant customs duty on the imported medicines before the Reforms, the reduction therein did no difference to their prices. However, the devaluation of rupee pushed them sky rocketing. The aggressive export promotion of many primary articles also resulted in their price-rise in the domestic market. The increase in money supply resorted to thwart the revaluation of rupee in the face of huge inflow of foreign exchange during 1992-93 to 1994-95 also contributed to elevating the general price level.

The price rise of food grains owing to the cuts in food and fertiliser subsidies and consequent adjustments have particularly been harsh. In the preceding decade of the Reform the per annum price of rice had risen by 7 percent and that of wheat by 3.3 percent. But in the next four years of the Reform period, they registered the rise of 13.5 percent and 18.1 percent respectively. Other foodgrains also behaved approximately in similar fashion.

The price-rise for pulses has been 97.2 percent; that for vegetables 163.4 percent, for fruits 74 percent; and for eggs, meat and fish group 102.5 percent. The free market ethos unleashed by the Reforms also indirectly but significantly has contributed to the price rise.

Employment

The rate of growth of employment in the organised sector dropped from more than 1.7 percent per annum in the late 1980s to 1.2 percent in 1991-92 and to 0.6 percent in 1992-93. Creation of jobs in the public sector fell from 11.0 million in the preceding four years to the 6.2 million in the succeeding four years of the Reforms. For the Private Sector, the corresponding figures showed a slight rise from 2.08 million to 2.49 million on account of free market euphoria.

In the Central Government establishment there were 4.03 million jobs on 1st March 1991, which went up next year to 4.14 million. But for the next two years, they came down to 3.97 million and 3.84 million respectively. Similar picture of declining employment opportunity is held out in the statistics of Employment Exchanges. The notified vacancies had come down from 0.59 million in 1989-90 to 0.4 million in 1992-93 and to 0.38 million in the subsequent year. Similar decline is seen in the statistics of appointments. The appointments issued during the above three years were 0.29 million, 0.23 million and 0.22 million respectively. The ratios of appointments to the notified vacancies for these years also shows a striking decline, viz., 8.5 percent, 7.9 percent and 6.7 percent respectively.

The contraction in public expenditure and the consequent reduction in aggregate demand could not but adversely affect employment in the unorganised sector, whether non-agricultural rural employment or urban informal sector employment, given the casual nature of such employment.

The policy reforms made benefits of the small sector available to the big industrial houses. National Council of Applied Economic Research had cautioned that the Reforms relating to deregulation of the big industries, withdrawal of the licence system and global reduction of custom duties would exert adverse impact on the small industries. The statistics of the industrial sickness show a marked deterioration during the Reform period. For example, in 1990, there were 2,21,097 sick industries, which represented a 8.86 percent decline from the previous year. But after the Reforms were launched, this figure went up to 2,23,809 in 1991 and further to 2,47,724 in 1992 indicating the 1.23 percent and 10.69 percent growth respectively, over previous years.

Entrepreneurship Development Institute of India, Ahmedabad had surveyed the impact of the Reforms on small scale industries in 1993, and saw clear deterioration in their situation. It attributed this deterioration to three factors (i) general recession in 1991-92, (ii) reduction in the budgetary support to the public sector and (iii) liberalisation of imports of the capital goods. The cumulative impact of these factors has been in the total collapse of demand for their products. Small-scale industries based on imports had a tough time due to devaluation of rupee. Increasing competition, increasing costs and pressure on prices has made the very survival difficult for many. Today more than 4,00,000 small-scale industries are either sick or closed.

The reforms in financial sector permitted the banks to charge interest as per the credit rating of debtors and manage their profitability. This also added to the difficulty of small-scale industries. For, getting loans from banks at affordable interest rates now became a formidable task for them. One study clearly concluded that the Reforms had an adverse impact on the new job opportunities in the small-scale industries.

The economic reforms in the mould of macroeconomic stabilisation and structural adjustment programme of IMF and World Bank have essentially a pro-rich bias. Wherever they were implemented, they have worsened the situation of the masses of poor people in absolute as well as relative terms. Some contrary data to this general observation (say, of the east Asian countries) are rather attributed to the departures from the standard blueprint given by the Bretton Wood institutions. The dalits in India, being the poorest of the poor have been hit the hardest. Their social disabilities, largely reinforced by and sustained on the economic deprivations, are bound to get accentuated with these policies. The Indian reforms were essentially 'crisis driven' and not 'strategy driven' when they were adopted. There have since been changes in the formation and key persona. The new government for instance has imparted them a form of 'strategy' through their Common Minimum Programme. However, there has not yet been any evidence of this strategy being any different from the course followed by the previous government. The complete discourse of the Reforms appears to be either grossly off the mark of Indian reality or to assume out its momentous features. The broad Indian reality is that India has too many poor. As per the Human Development Report, 1996, there are 229 million income poor but more than twice as many, 554 million are capability poor. In terms of capability poverty, its 61.5 % population is poor. Its rank according to descending poverty among the 174 countries of the world is 135. Even today India is predominantly an agrarian economy, with over 70 percent of its population living in villages. No statistics moreover can adequately capture the heinous socio-cultural inequality that is an abiding part of the Indian reality. It has acute inequalities not only in economic terms but also in the socio-cultural terms.

The free market oriented reforms ought to take this grave Indian reality into consideration. Unless there is a wide spread purchasing power in the economy the market can never be free and sustainable. The reform strategy thus should embody sustainable economic empowerment of the rural masses; investments to enhance their capability and effective measures for accelerated development of the disadvantaged sections like the dalits. The pre-requisite to reforms therefore could be the radical land reforms, massive investments in rural areas into agriculture-related infrastructural projects, universalisation of primary education, primary health care system and reinforcement of positive discrimination in favour of the dalits. The devil of casteism could be tamed only by freeing general masses of the people from the anxieties and uncertainties about basic survival. The general condition of deprivation has rendered them vulnerable to be the preys to the frequent machinations of the vested interests that make them see the enemy within their own class. The relative equality thus can be the bedrock for launching the socio-cultural offensive in the form of mass-education programmes. But this all may still not be enough. The policy of positive discrimination in favour of the dalits will have to be reinforced much more vigorously in all the sectors of economy, than ever before. They need to be reframed and simplified for the effective implementation. Unlike the current provisions, this may be stopped once their representation in services comes on par with the general population.

The specific reform package can be formulated in terms of the conditions existing then. There arises a question of capital. Where will the capital for the investment in basic reforms come from? Not an easy question to answer, indeed. But some pointers may not be impertinent. It is acknowledged since number of years that India has a parallel economy in black money.

The recent spate of scams is a mere corroboration of this hypothesis. The Reforms appear to have given them a boost. Whatever little has surfaced can be likened to a tip of iceberg. Some five years ago, an unofficial estimate by the World Bank had put the unaccounted money of Indians kept in various tax havens at $ 100 billion. As per *Finance India,* (an article in the September 1995 issue) the range of capital outflows was from $ 1065 million to $ 370 million just in one single year-1993. Much of the $ 10 billion money in the non-resident account is said to be belonging to the resident Indians. The evidence of this kind abounds. As against this vast sum of our own money, what the government aims at out of the Reforms is the paltry sum of some four to five billion dollars of foreign direct investment a year to come in the country! The size of the money indicated above, that rightfully belongs to the people of the country, may be good enough for the task. But to unearth this treasure certainly requires a political will. India does not need capital as much as it does the political will to better its destiny.

Minority Empowerment

Religious minorities constitute 18.4 percent of India's population. They include Muslims, Christians, Sikhs, Buddhists and Zoroastrians (Parsis).

The Muslim minorities constitute the largest minority of our country, comprising 13.4 percent of our country's population. The condition and well being of the minorities is a critical measure of the functioning of democracy.

Rights of Minorities in India

Constitutional rights and safeguards provided to the minorities in India.

Constitutional safeguards for religious and linguistic minorities of India.

Though the Constitution of India does not define the word 'Minority' and only refers to 'Minorities' and speaks of those 'based on religion or language', the rights of the minorities have been spelt out in the Constitution in detail.

'Common Domain' and 'Separate Domain' of Rights of Minorities Provided in the Constitution.

The Constitution provides two sets of rights of minorities which can be placed in 'common domain' and 'separate domain'. The rights which fall in the 'common domain' are those which are applicable to all the citizens of our country. The rights which fall in the 'separate domain' are those which are applicable to the minorities only and these are reserved to protect their identity. The distinction between 'common domain' and 'separate domain' and their combination have been well kept and protected in the Constitution. The Preamble to the Constitution declares the State to be 'Secular' and this is a special relevance for the Religious Minorities. Equally relevant for them, especially, is the declaration of the Constitution in its Preamble that all citizens of India are to be secured 'liberty of thought, expression, belief, faith and worship and 'equality of status and of opportunity.'

'Common Domain', the Directive Principles of State Policy – Part IV of the Constitution

The Constitution has made provisions for the Fundamental Rights in Part III, which the State has to comply with and these are also judicially enforceable. There is another set of non-justiciable rights stated in Part IV, which are connected with social and economic rights of the people. These rights are known as 'Directive Principles of State Policy', which legally are not binding upon the State, but are "fundamental in the governance of the country and it shall be the duty of the State to apply these principles in making laws". (Article 37). Part IV of the Constitution of India, containing non-justiciable Directive Principles of State Policy, includes the following provisions having significant implications for the Minorities :-

(i) obligation of the State 'to endeavour to eliminate inequalities in status, facilities and opportunities' amongst individuals and groups of people residing in different areas or engaged in different vocations.

(ii) obligation of State 'to promote with special care' the educational and economic interests of 'the weaker sections of the people' (besides Scheduled Castes and Scheduled Tribes); [Article 46] and 'Common Domain', the Fundamental Duties – Part IVA of the Constitution

Part IVA of the Constitution, relating to Fundamental Duties as provided in Article 51 A applies in full to all citizens, including those belonging to Minorities. Article 51A which is of special relevance for the Minorities stipulates as under :-

(i) citizens' duty to promote harmony and the spirit of common brotherhood amongst all the people of India 'transcending religious, linguistic and regional or sectional diversities; and

(ii) citizens' duty to value and preserve the rich heritage of our composite culture.'

'Common Domain', the Fundamental Rights – Part III of the Constitution The Constitution has provided a definite space for both the 'domains' i.e. 'common' as well as 'separate'. In Part III of the Constitution, which deals with the Fundamental Rights is divided into two parts viz. (a) the rights which fall in the 'common domain' and (b) the rights which go to the 'separate domain'.

In the 'common domain', the following fundamental rights and freedoms are covered:

(i) people's right to 'equality before the law' and 'equal protection of the laws'; [Article 14]

(ii) prohibition of discrimination against citizens on grounds of religion, race, caste, sex or place of birth; [Article 15 (1) & (2)]

(iii) authority of State to make 'any special provision for the advancement of any socially and educationally backward classes of citizens' (besides the Scheduled Castes and Scheduled Tribes); [Article 15 (4)]

(iv) citizens' right to 'equality of opportunity' in matters relating to employment or appointment to any office under the State – and prohibition in this regard of discrimination on grounds of religion, race, caste, sex or place of birth; [Article 16(1)&(2)]

(v) authority of State to make 'any provision for the reservation of appointments or posts in favour of any backward class of citizens which, in the opinion of the State, is not adequately represented in the services under the State; [Article 16(4)]

(vi) people's freedom of conscience and right to freely profess, practice and propagate religion – subject to public order, morality and other Fundamental Rights; [Article 25(1)]

(vii) right of 'every religious denomination or any section thereof – subject to public order, morality and health – to establish and maintain institutions for religious and charitable purposes, 'manage its own affairs in matters of religion', and own and acquire movable immovable property and administer it 'in accordance with law'; [Article 26]

(viii) prohibition against compelling any person to pay taxes for promotion of any particular religion'; [Article 27]

(ix) people's 'freedom as to attendance at religious instruction or religious worship in educational institutions' wholly maintained, recognized, or aided by the State. [Article 28].

'Separate Domain' of Minority Rights

The Minority Rights provided in the Constitution which fall in the category of 'Separate Domain' are as under:-

(i) right of 'any section of the citizens' to 'conserve' its 'distinct language, script or culture'; [Article 29(1)]

(ii) restriction on denial of admission to any citizen, to any educational institution maintained or aided by the State, 'on grounds only of religion, race, caste, language or any of them'; [Article 29(2)]

(iii) right of all Religious and Linguistic Minorities to establish and administer educational institutions of their choice; [Article 30(1)]

(iv) freedom of Minority-managed educational institutions from discrimination in the matter of receiving aid from the State; [Article30(2)]

(v) special provision relating to the language spoken by a section of the population of any State; [Article 347]

(vi) provision for facilities for instruction in mother-tongue at primary stage; [Article 350 A]

(vii) provision for a Special Officer for Linguistic Minorities and his duties; and [Article 350 B]

(viii) Sikh community's right of 'wearing and carrying of kirpans; [Explanation 1 below Article 25]

India's Multi-culturalism Interwoven in the Constitution

The various Articles of the Constitution providing rights to the minorities, clearly and firmly point out to only one direction: that of a multi-religious, multi-cultural, multi-lingual and multi-racial Indian society, interwoven into an innate unity by the common thread of national integration and communal harmony. By the yardstick adopted by the framers of the Constitution and crystallized into its provisions the Indian Nation is not just a conglomeration of individual inhabitants of this State; it comprises of two distinct categories of constituents.

The two-tier commonwealth of Indian Nation includes, on one hand, every citizen of India individually and, on the other hand, the multitude of religious, linguistic, cultural and ethnic groups among its citizens.

The Indian Nation is an enormous coparcenary in which the individual citizens are also members of their own respective branches taking the form of religious, cultural, linguistic and ethnic groups. And all these groups, like all individuals, have the same Fundamental Rights to enjoy and the same Fundamental Duties to discharge.

Protection of Weaker Sections in Indian Pluralistic Society

The social pluralism of India, as fortified by the unique Constitutional concept of secularism, raises the need for the protection and development of all sorts of weaker sections of the Indian citizenry – whether this 'weakness' is based on numbers or on social, economic or educational status of any particular group.

The Constitution, therefore, speaks of Religious and Linguistic Minorities, Scheduled Castes, Scheduled Tribes and Backward Classes and makes – or leaves room for making – for them special provisions of various nature and varying import.

The National Commission for Minority Educational Institution Act

Education of Minorities

Central assistance is being provided to State Governments for the appointment of Urdu language teachers on a normative basis in Block/Districts where there is a concentration of educationally backward minorities.

The Scheme of Assistance for Infrastructure and Modernisation of Madrasas provides assistance for meeting the salary requirements @ Rs. 3000 (three thousand) each per month for two teachers in each madrasa to impart education in non traditional subjects of Mathematics, Science, English etc. and one time assistance of Rs. 7000 (seven thousand) to each madrasa for subject kits and teaching aids as well as another one time assistance of Rs. 7000 (seven thousand) for establishing book banks in each madrasa. Apart from this the infrastructure component of the scheme allows construction of physical facilities such as additional rooms.

The entire budgetary provision under the scheme has been fully utilized each year (last year an amount of Rs. 29 crore was disbursed to madrasas through State Governments), because of the demand for infrastructure. Under the scheme, the State Governments have an important role to play forwarding cases of NGOs and Wakf Boards managing madrasas. States have been requested to popularize the scheme by giving it wide publicity and expeditious documentation and processing. One of the commitments under the NCMP is the protection of the Fundamental Rights of Minorities under Article 30(1) of the Constitution. In keeping with the promise made under the NCMP, a National Commission for Minority Educational Institutions (NCMEI) has been established through an act of Parliament.

It provides inter alia, for the right of minority educational institutions to seek affiliation to any university of their choice, provided the relevant law under which such universities are created allow such affiliation. It also seeks to overcome problems faced by minorities in seeking no objection certificates for establishing educational institution of their choice. Disputes relating to the minority status of educational institutions are also to be resolved by the commission. Thus, for the first time, Article 30(1) of the Constitution, which gives minorities the right to establish and administer educational institution of their choice, would be effectively implemented through the NCMEI Act.

As many as 244 Special Focus districts have been identified for attention in education. One of the criteria use for the selection of these districts is the concentration of minority population.

Polytechnic level institutions in 185 of these special focus districts are beings upgraded during the 10th and 11th Plans, of which 84 districts have a concentration of minority population. New Polytechnics are also being established in 65 districts across the two plan periods, twelve of these have minority concentration.

Minority and the Millennium Development Goals: Muslim Women in Armed Conflict in Jammu and Kashmir

Constitution of India

Article 14- Men and women to have equal rights and opportunities in the political, economic and social spheres.

Article 15(1)- Prohibits discrimination against any citizen on the grounds of religion, race, caste, sex etc.

Article 15(3)- Special provision enabling the State to make affirmative discriminations in favour of women.

Article 16- Equality of opportunities in matter of public appointments for all citizens.

Article 39(a)- The State shall direct its policy towards securing all citizens men and women, equally, the right to means of livelihood.

Article 39(d)- Equal pay for equal work for both men and women.

Article 42- The State to make provision for ensuring just and humane conditions of work and maternity relief.

Article 51 (A)(e)- To renounce the practices derogatory to the dignity of women.

In fulfilment of this constitutional mandate, several steps have been taken since independence to empower women, including a series of women-specific and women related legislations; creation of national policy level commitments including the National Policy for Empowerment of Women 2001, the National Common Minimum Programme of the UPA government; international commitments such as ratification of the CEDAW convention in 1993 and India's commitments in 2000 to the Millennium Development Goals.

At the inauguration of the 11th Five Year Plan, nearly 60 years after women's rights were enshrined in the democratic fabric of India, we are yet to fully honour our constitutional commitments. Indian women, in general, do not have equal rights as men in either political, social or economic spheres; they are discriminated against in jobs and in education; they are not equally represented in public institutions; they do not enjoy equal pay for equal work; and violence against women in both public and the private spheres is increasing, with impunity for the perpetrators and little justice for women.

Understanding the Target Group

According to the 2001 census, women as an independent target group account for 495.74 million in absolute numbers and represent 48.3% of the total population of the country. The Tenth five year plan had divided the entire women population into five distinct sub-groups for planning purposes according to their age as follows:

- Girl children in the age-group 0-14, Adolescent Girls in the age group 15-19;
- Women in the reproductive age group of 15-44;
- Women in the economically active age group of 15-59; and
- Elderly women in the age group 60 plus.

However, age alone is an inadequate criterion to understand a target group for development intervention. The 11th Plan recognizes that women are not a homogenous category for planned intervention – that they belong to diverse castes, classes, communities, economic groups, and are located within a range of geographic and development zones, and that mapping and acknowledging the specific deprivations which arise from these multiple locations, can alone determine the success of planned interventions.

SC women comprise of 16.24%, ST women comprise of 8.41% and muslim women comprise of 13.48% of India's female population as per 2001 census. Further, women in conflict zones such as Jammu and Kashmir and the North-East are specifically acknowledged as a target group in need of focused intervention. Vulnerability and marginalization are key concepts in recognizing the unique needs of specific groups of women for planned intervention.

A listing of such groups of women includes, but is not restricted to, single women (divorced, separated, widowed, or unmarried), women affected by violence, trafficked women, women affected by internal displacement due to social upheavals, natural disasters, migration, and development, women affected by HIV/AIDs, women with disabilities and women in prisons.

Review of Policies and Programmes

Gender-mainstreaming and development has been a priority goal in the country's development efforts since the starting of the first Five Year Plan. The gender-mainstreaming exercise, however, has been a process of learning and refinement throughout the planning process.

The First to Fifth Five Year Plans treated development of women as a subject of 'welfare'. The Central Social Welfare Board

(CSWB) was set up in 1953 to promote welfare oriented activities for women and children through involvement of voluntary agencies at the grass root level.

While the welfare approach continued during this period, priority was also given to women's education and maternal and child health services, besides supplementary feeding for children and expectant and nursing mothers. There was a shift of approach from 'women welfare' to 'women development' during the Sixth Plan (1980-85). Sixth Plan also had special thrust on the three core sectors viz., health, education and employment.

The Seventh Plan (1985-90), continued the developmental approach. The major objective was of raising economic and social status of women and bringing them into the mainstream of national development.

During Sixth Plan 27 'Beneficiary-oriented Schemes' (BOS), having direct benefits to women were identified across various Ministries/Departments at the instance of PMO and were monitored. Human development was a major focus of the Eighth Plan (1992-97). It not only encompassed the strategy of enabling women as equal partners and participants in the development process but also ensuring that women were not bypassed from the benefits of various developmental programmes. Eighth Plan also had special programmes for women to complement the efforts of the general development programmes.

Some major initiatives undertaken during Eighth Plan for women included (i) setting up of the National Commission for Women (NCW) (1992) to work towards safeguarding the rights and interest of women, (ii) setting up of Rashtriya Mahila Kosh (RMK) (1993) to meet the micro-credit needs of poor and assetless women, (iii) Adoption of National Nutrition Policy (NNP) (1993) in conformity with the constitutional commitment to ensure adequate nutritional standard of the people, (iv) launching of the Mahila Samridhi Yojana (MSY) (1993) to promote thrift activities amongst women, (v) setting up of National Creche Fund (NCF) (1994) to provide crèche services to the children of working mothers, and (vi) launching of Indira Mahila Yojana (IMY) (1995) basically for awareness generation and economic empowerment through women Self Help Groups.

The Indira Mahila Yojana was subsequently renamed as Integrated Women's Empowerment Programme (Swayamsidha) in 1999 and Mahila Samridhi Yojana was merged with it.

'Empowerment of Women' as agents of socio-economic change and development became one of the nine specific objectives of the Ninth Plan (1997-2002).

The Plan envisaged primarily to ensure that benefits flow to women from all the general development sectors and emphasized on (i) reservation of not less than $1/3^{rd}$ seats for women in the Parliament and State Legislative Assemblies; (ii) convergence of existing services, resources, infrastructure and manpower in women specific and women-related sectors; (iii) adoption of special strategy of Women Component Plan (WCP) to ensure that not less than 30% of funds/benefits flow to women from other development sectors; (iv) organizing women Self Help Groups as a major process of empowering women; (v) high priority to reproductive child health care; (vi) universalizing on-going supplementary feeding programme; (vii) ensuring easy and equal access to education for women and girls; (viii) elimination of gender bias in all educational programmes; (ix) free education for girls up to college level including professional courses; (x) promoting skill development amongst women in modern upcoming trades etc. Some special initiatives taken during Ninth Plan included launching of an externally aided scheme of Swashakti (1998) for socio-economic empowerment of women through self reliant self help groups, instituting Stree Shakti Puraskars (1999), setting up of a Task Force under the Chairpersonship of Deputy Chairman, Planning Commission to review existing women-specific and women-related legislations (2000), adoption of National Policy for Empowerment of Women (2001), celebration of the year 2001 as Women's Empowerment Year, recasting of Indira Mahila Yojana as Swayamsidha (2001), launching of Swadhar (2001) to extend rehabilitation services for women in difficult circumstances etc.

7

Tribal Development in India : An Analysis

Adivasi

Adivasis is an umbrella term for a heterogeneous set of ethnic and tribal groups believed to be the aboriginal population of India. They comprise a substantial indigenous minority of the population of India.

Adivasi societies are particularly present in the Indian states of Orissa, Madhya Pradesh, Chattisgarh, Rajasthan, Gujarat, Maharashtra, Andhra Pradesh, Bihar, Jharkhand, West Bengal, Mizoram and other northeastern states, and the Andaman and Nicobar Islands. Many smaller tribal groups are quite sensitive to ecological degradation caused by modernization. Both commercial forestry and intensive agriculture have proved destructive to the forests that had endured swidden agriculture for many centuries. Officially recognized by the Indian government as "Scheduled Tribes" in the Fifth Schedule of the Constitution of India, they are often grouped together with scheduled castes in the category "Scheduled Castes and Tribes", which is eligible for certain affirmative action measures.

Connotations of the Word 'Adivasi'

Although terms such as *atavika* (Sanskrit for *forest dwellers*), *vanvasi* or *girijan* (*hill people*) are also used for the tribes of India, *adivasi* carries the specific meaning of being the original and autochthonous inhabitants of a given region, and was specifically coined for that purpose in the 1930s. Over a period of time, unlike the terms "aborigines" or "tribes", the word "*adivasi*" has also developed a connotation of past autonomy which was disrupted during the British colonial period in India and has not been restored. Opposition to usage of the term is varied, and it has been argued that the "original inhabitant" contention is based on dubious claims and that the adivasi-non adivasi divide that is created is artificial.

Scheduled Tribes

The Constitution of India, Article 366 (25) defines Scheduled Tribes as "such tribes or tribal communities or part of or groups within such tribes or tribal communities as are deemed under Article 342 to the scheduled Tribes (STs) for the purposes of this Constitution". In Article 342, the procedure to be followed for specification of a scheduled tribe is prescribed. However, it does not contain the criterion for the specification of any community as scheduled tribe.

An often used criterion is based on attributes such as:

- Geographical isolation-they live in cloistered, exclusive, remote and inhospitable areas such as hills and forests.
- Backwardness-their livelihood is based on primitive agriculture, a low-value closed economy with a low level of technology that leads to their poverty. They have low levels of literacy and health.
- Distinctive culture, language and religion-communities have developed their own distinctive culture, language and religion.
- Shyness of contact – they have a marginal degree of contact with other cultures and people.

Primitive Tribes

The Scheduled Tribe groups who were identified as more backward communities among the tribal population groups have been categorised as 'Primitive Tribal Groups' (PTGs) by the Government at the Centre in 1975. So far seventy" five tribal communities have been identified as 'primitive tribal groups' in different States of India. These hunting, food" gathering, and some agricultural communities, who have been identified as more backward communities among the tribal population groups need special programmes for their sustainable development. The primitive tribes are awakening and demanding their rights for special reservation quota for them.

Geographical Overview

There is a substantial list of Scheduled Tribes in India recognised as tribal under the Constitution of India. Tribal peoples constitute 8.2% of the nation's total population, over 84 million people according to the 2001 census. One concentration lives in a belt along the Himalayas stretching through Jammu and Kashmir, Himachal Pradesh, and Uttarakhand in the west, to Assam, Meghalaya, Tripura, Arunachal Pradesh, Mizoram, Manipur, and Nagaland in the northeast. In the northeastern states of Arunachal Pradesh, Meghalaya, Mizoram, and Nagaland, more than 90% of the population is tribal. However, in the remaining northeast states of Assam, Manipur, Sikkim, and Tripura, tribal peoples form between 20 and 30% of the population.

Another concentration lives in the hilly areas of central India (Chhattisgarh, Madhya Pradesh, Orissa and, to a lesser extent, Andhra Pradesh); in this belt, which is bounded by the Narmada River to the north and the Godavari River to the southeast, tribal peoples occupy the slopes of the region's mountains. Other tribals, including the Santals, live in Jharkhand and West Bengal. Central Indian states have the country's largest tribes, and, taken as a whole, roughly 75% of the total tribal population live there, although the tribal population there accounts for only around 10% of the region's total population.

There are smaller numbers of tribal people in Karnataka, Tamil Nadu, and Kerala in south India; in western India in Gujarat and Rajasthan, and in the union territories of Lakshadweep and the Andaman Islands and Nicobar Islands. About one percent of the populations of Kerala and Tamil Nadu are tribal, whereas about six percent in Andhra Pradesh and Karnataka are members of tribes.

The Peopling of India

The concept of 'original inhabitant' is directly related to the initial peopling of India, which, due to the debate on topics such as the Indo-Aryan migration hypothesis, has been a contentious area of research and discourse. Some anthropologists hypothesize that the region was settled by multiple human migrations over tens of millennia, which makes it even harder to select certain groups as being truly aboriginal. One narrative, largely based on genetic research, describes Negritos, similar to the Andamanese Adivasis of today, as the first humans to colonize India, likely 30-65 thousand years before present (kybp). 60% of all Indians share the mt DNA haplogroup M, which is universal among Andamanese islander Adivasis and might be a genetic legacy of the postulated first Indians. Some anthropologists theorize that these settlers were displaced by invading Austro-Asiatic-speaking Australoid people (who largely shared skin pigmentation and physiognomy with the Negritos, but had straight rather than kinky hair), and adivasi tribes such as the Irulas trace their origins to that displacement. The Oraon adivasi tribe of eastern India and the Korku tribe of western India are considered to be examples of groups of Australoid origin. Subsequent to the Australoids, some anthropologists and geneticists theorize that Caucasoids (including both Dravidians and Indo-Aryans) and Mongoloids (Sino-Tibetans) immigrated into India: the Dravidians possibly from Iran, the Indo-Aryans possibly from the Central Asian steppes and the Tibeto-Burmans possibly from the Himalayan and north-eastern borders of the subcontinent. It should be noted that none of these hypotheses is free from debate and disagreement.

Ethnic origins and linguistic affiliations in India match only inexactly, however: while the Oraon Adivasis are classified as an Australoid group, their language, called Kurukh, is Dravidian. Khasis and Nicobarese are considered to be Mongoloid groups and the Munda and Santals are Australoid groups, but all four speak Austro-Asiatic languages. The Bhils and Gonds are frequently classified as Australoid groups, yet Bhil languages are Indo-European and the Gondi language is Dravidian. Also, in post-colonial India, tribal languages suffered huge setbacks with the formation of linguistic states after 1956 under the States Reorganisation Act. For example, under state-sponsored educational pressure, Irula children are being taught Tamil and a sense of shame has begun to be associated with speaking the Irula language among some children and educated adults. Similarly, the Santals are "gradually adopting languages of the areas inhabited, like Oriya in Orissa, Hindi in Bihar and Bengali in West Bengal."

Disruptions During Mughal and Colonial Periods

Although considered uncivilized and primitive, Adivasis were usually not held to be intrinsically impure by surrounding (usually, caucasoid-Dravidian or Aryan) caste Hindu populations, unlike Dalits, who were. Thus, the adivasi origins of Maharshi (Sanksrit: *Great Sage*) Valmiki, who composed the Ramayana Hindu religious epic, were acknowledged, as were the origins of adivasi tribes such as the Grasia and Bhilala, which descended from mixed Rajput and Bhil marriages. Unlike the subjugation of the dalits, the Adivasis often enjoyed autonomy and, depending on region, evolved mixed hunter-gatherer and farming economies, controlling their lands as a joint patrimony of the tribe. In some areas, securing adivasi approval and support was considered crucial by local rulers, and larger adivasi groups were able to sustain their own kingdoms in central India. The Gond Rajas of Garha-Mandla and Chanda are examples of an adivasi aristocracy that ruled in this region, and were "not only the hereditary leaders of their Gond subjects, but also held sway over substantial communities of non-tribals who recognized them as their feudal lords."

This relative autonomy and collective ownership of adivasi land by Adivasis was severely disrupted by the advent of the Mughals in the early 16th century. Similarly, the British beginning in the 18th century added to the consolidation of feudalism in India, first under the Jagirdari system and then under the Zamindari system. Beginning with the Permanent Settlement imposed by the British in Bengal and Bihar, which later became the template for a deepening of feudalism throughout India, the older social and economic system in the country began to alter radically. Land, both forest areas belonging to Adivasis and settled farmland belonging to non-adivasi peasants, was rapidly made the legal property of British-designated zamindars (landlords), who in turn moved to extract the maximum economic benefit possible from their newfound property and subjects without regard to historical tenure or ownership. Adivasi lands sometimes experienced an influx of non-local settlers, often brought from far away (as in the case of Muslims and Sikhs brought to Kol territory) by the zamindars to better exploit local land, forest and labour. Deprived of the forests and resources they traditionally depended on and sometimes coerced to pay taxes, many Adivasis were forced to borrow at usurious rates from moneylenders, often the zamindars themselves. When they were unable to pay, that forced them to become bonded labourers for the zamindars. Often, far from paying off the principal of their debt, they were unable even to offset the compounding interest, and this was made the justification for their children working for the zamindar after the death of the initial borrower. In the case of the Andamanese Adivasis, long isolated from the outside world in autonomous societies, mere contact with outsiders was often sufficient to set off deadly epidemics in tribal populations, and it is alleged that some sections of the British government directly attempted to destroy some tribes.

Land dispossession and subjugation by British and zamindar interests resulted in a number of adivasi revolts in the late eighteenth and early nineteenth centuries, such as the Santal hul (or Santal revolt) of 1855-56. Although these were suppressed ruthlessly by the governing British authority (the East India Company prior to 1858, and the British government after 1858), partial restoration of privileges to adivasi elites (e.g. to *Mankis*, the leaders of Munda tribes) and some leniency in tax burdens resulted in relative calm, despite continuing and widespread dispossession, from the late nineteenth century onwards. The economic deprivation, in some cases, triggered internal adivasi migrations within India that would continue for another century, including as labour for the emerging tea plantations in Assam.

Tribal Classification Criteria and Demands

Population complexities, and the controversies surrounding ethnicity and language in India, sometimes make the official recognition of groups as Adivasis (by way of inclusion in the Scheduled Tribes list) political and contentious. However, regardless of their language family affiliations, Australoid and

Negrito groups that have survived as distinct forest, mountain or island dwelling tribes in India and are often classified as adivasi. The relatively autonomous Mongoloid tribal groups of Northeastern India (including Khasis, Apatani and Nagas), who are mostly Austro-Asiatic or Tibeto-Burman speakers, are also considered to be Adivasis: this area comprises 7.5% of India's land area but 20% of its adivasi population. However, not all autonomous northeastern groups are considered Adivasis; for instance, the Tibeto-Burman-speaking Meitei of Manipur were once tribal but, having been settled for many centuries, are caste Hindus.

It is also difficult, for a given social grouping, to definitively decide whether it is a 'caste' or a 'tribe'. A combination of internal social organization, relationship with other groups, self-classification and perception by other groups has to be taken into account to make a categorization, which is at best inexact and open to doubt. These categorizations have been diffuse for thousands of years, and even ancient formulators of caste-discriminatory legal codes (which usually only applied to settled populations, and not Adivasis) were unable to come up with clean distinctions.

Demands for Tribal Classification

An additional difficulty in deciding whether a group meets the criteria to be adivasi or not are the aspirational movements created by the federal and state benefits, including job and educational reservations, enjoyed by groups listed as scheduled tribes (STs). In Manipur, Meitei commentators have pointed to the lack of scheduled tribe status as a key economic disadvantage for Meiteis competing for jobs against groups that are classified as scheduled tribes. In Assam, Rajbongshi representatives have demanded scheduled tribe status as well. In Rajasthan, Haryana and other northern states, the Gujjar community has demanded ST status, even blockading the national capital of Delhi to press their demand. In several cases, these claims to tribalhood are disputed by tribes who are already listed in the schedule and fear economic losses if more powerful groups are recognized as scheduled tribes; for instance, the Rajbongshi demand faces resistance from the Bodo tribe, and the Meena tribe has vigorously opposed Gujjar aspirations to be recognized as a scheduled tribe.

Endogamy, Exogamy and Ethnogenesis

Part of the challenge is that the endogamous nature of tribes is also conformed to by the vast majority of Hindu castes. Indeed, many historians and anthropologists believe that caste endogamy reflects the once-tribal origins of the various groups who now constitute the settled Hindu castes. Another defining feature of caste Hindu society, which is often used to contrast them with Muslim and other social groupings, is lineage/clan (or *gotra*) and village exogamy. However, these in-marriage taboos are also held ubiquitously among tribal groups, and do not serve as reliable differentiating markers between caste and tribe. Again, this could be an ancient import from tribal society into settled Hindu castes. Interestingly, tribes such as the Muslim Gujjars of Kashmir and the Kalash of Pakistan observe these exogamous traditions in common with caste Hindus and non-Kashmiri Adivasis, though their surrounding Muslim populations do not.

Some anthropologists, however, draw a distinction between tribes who have continued to be tribal and tribes that have been absorbed into caste society in terms of the breakdown of tribal (and therefore caste) boundaries, and the proliferation of new mixed caste groups. In other words, ethnogenesis (the construction of new ethnic identities) in tribes occurs through a fission process (where groups splinter-off as new tribes, which preserves endogamy), whereas with settled castes it usually occurs through intermixture (in violation of strict endogamy).

Other Criteria

Unlike castes, which form part of a complex and interrelated local economic exchange system, tribes tend to form self-sufficient economic units. For most tribal people, land-use rights traditionally derive simply from tribal membership. Tribal society tends to the egalitarian, with its leadership based on ties of kinship and personality rather than on hereditary status. Tribes typically consist of segmentary lineages whose extended families provide the basis for social organization and control. Tribal religion recognizes no authority outside the tribe.

Any of these criteria may not apply in specific instances. Language does not always give an accurate indicator of tribal or caste status. Especially in regions of mixed population, many tribal groups have lost their mother tongues and simply speak local or regional languages. In parts of Assam-an area historically divided between warring tribes and villages-increased contact among villagers began during the colonial period, and has accelerated since independence in 1947. A pidgin Assamese developed while educated tribal members learned Hindi and, in the late twentieth century, English.

Self-identification and group loyalty do not provide unfailing markers of tribal identity either. In the case of stratified tribes, the loyalties of clan, kin, and family may well predominate over those of tribe. In addition, tribes cannot always be viewed as people living apart; the degree of isolation of various tribes has varied tremendously. The Gonds, Santals, and Bhils traditionally have dominated the regions in which they have lived. Moreover, tribal society is not always more egalitarian than the rest of the rural populace; some of the larger tribes, such as the Gonds, are highly stratified.

The apparently wide fluctuation in estimates of South Asia's tribal population through the twentieth century gives a sense of how unclear the distinction between tribal and nontribal can be. India's 1931 census enumerated 22 million tribal people, in 1941 only 10 million were counted, but by 1961 some 30 million and in 1991 nearly 68 million tribal members were included. The differences among the figures reflect changing census criteria and the economic incentives individuals have to maintain or reject classification as a tribal member.

These gyrations of census data serve to underline the complex relationship between caste and tribe. Although, in theory, these terms represent different ways of life and ideal types, in reality they stand for a continuum of social groups. In areas of substantial contact between tribes and castes, social and cultural pressures have often tended to move tribes in the direction of becoming castes over a period of years. Tribal peoples with ambitions for social advancement in Indian society at large have tried to gain the classification of caste for their tribes. On occasion, an entire tribe or part of a tribe joined a Hindu sect and thus entered the caste system *en masse*. If a specific tribe engaged in practices that

Hindus deemed polluting, the tribe's status when it was assimilated into the caste hierarchy would be affected.

Religion

The majority of Adivasi practice Hinduism and Christianity. During the last two decades Adivasi from Orissa, Madhya Pradesh, Jharkhand have converted to Protestant groups. Adivasi beliefs vary by tribe, and are usually different from the historical Vedic religion, with its monistic underpinnings, Indo-European deities (who are often cognates of ancient Iranian, Greek and Roman deities, e.g. Mitra/Mithra/Mithras), lack of idol worship and lack of a concept of reincarnation. The "centre of Rig Vedic religion was the *Yajna*, the sacrificial fire" and there was "no Atma, no Brahma, no Moksha, no idol worship in the Rig Veda." Two specific rituals held great importance and it is known that, "when the Indo-Aryans and the Persians formed a single people, they performed sacrifices (Vedic yajna: Avestan yasna), and that they already had a sacred drink (Vedic soma: Avestan haoma)."

Adivasi Roots of Modern Hinduism

Most important deities added to the Hindu pantheon after the Vedic period were dark-skinned, such as Vishnu (who has been described as *meghavarnam*, or dark as a cloud), Rama, Krishna, Shiva and Kali, which may reflect adivasi origins. Today, these deities constitute the main divinities worshiped by most caste Hindus.

In a marked departure from the Indo-Aryan religion (although not directly contradicted by it), idol worship has also become firmly established for most Hindus, though exceptions such as the Arya Samaj school do exist. Some historians and anthropologists assert that much of what constitutes popular Hinduism today is actually descended from an amalgamation of adivasi faiths, idol worship practices and deities, rather than the original Indo-Aryan faith.

This also includes the sacred status of certain animals and plants, such as monkeys, cows, peacocks, cobras (nagas), elephants, peepul, tulsi (holy basil) and neem, which may once have held totemic importance for certain adivasi tribes.

Adivasi Saints:

- Saint Buddhu Bhagat, led the Kol Insurrection (1831-1832) aimed against tax imposed on Mundas by Muslim rulers.
- Saint Dhira or Kannappa Nayanar, one of 63 Nayanar Shaivite saints, a hunter from whom Lord Shiva gladly accepted food offerings. It is said that he poured water from his mouth on the Shivlingam and offered the Lord swine flesh.
- Saint Dhudhalinath, Koli, Gujarati, a 17th or 18th century devotee (P. 4, *The Story of Historic People of India-The Kolis*)
- Saint Ganga Narain, led the Bhumij Revolt (1832-1833) aimed against missionaries and British colonialists.
- Saint Girnari Velnathji, Koli, Gujarati of Junagadh, a 17th or 18th century devotee
- Saint Gurudev Kalicharan Brahma or Guru Brahma, a Bodo whose founded the Brahma Dharma aimed against missionaries and colonialists. The Brahma Dharma movement sought to unite peoples of all religions to worship God together and survives even today.
- Saint Jatra Oraon, Oraon, led the Tana Bhagat Movement (1914-1919) aimed against the missionaries and British colonialists
- Saint Sri Koya Bhagat, Koli, Gujarati, a 17th or 18th century devotee
- Saint Tantya Mama (Bhil), a Bhil after whom a movement is named after-the "Jananayak Tantya Bhil"
- Saint Tirumangai Alvar, Kallar, composed the six Vedangas in beautiful Tamil verse.

Sages:

- Bhaktaraj Bhadurdas, Koli, Gujarati, a 17th or 18th century devotee
- Bhakta Shabari, a Bhil woman that offered Shri Rama and Shri Laxmana her half-eaten ber fruit, which they gratefully accepted when they were searching for Shri Sita Devi in the forest.

- Madan Bhagat, Koli, Gujarati, a 17th or 18th century devotee
- Sany Kanji Swami, Koli, Gujarati, a 17th or 18th century devotee
- Bhaktaraj Valram, Koli, Gujarati, a 17th or 18th century devotee

Maharishis:

- Maharshi Matanga, Matanga Bhil, Guru of Bhakta Shabari. In fact, Chandalas are often addressed as 'Matanga 'in passages like Varaha Purana 1.139.91
- Maharshi Valmiki, Kirata Bhil, composed the Ramayana. He is considered to be an avatar in the Balmiki community.

Avatars:

- Birsa Bhagwan or Birsa Munda, considered an avatar of Khasra Kora. People approached him as Singbonga, the supreme spirit. He converted even Christians to his own sect. He was against conversions by missionaries. He wanted not only political, but religious freedom as well! He and his clan, the Mundas, were connected with Vaishnavite traditions as they were influenced by Sri Chaitanya. Birsa was very close to the Panre brothers Vaishnavites.
- Kirata-the form of Lord Shiva as a hunter. It is mentioned in the Mahabharata. The Karppillikkavu Sree Mahadeva Temple, Kerala adores Lord Shiva in this avatar and is known to be one of the oldest surviving temples in Bharat.
- Vettakkorumakan, the son of Lord Kirata.
- Kaladutaka or 'Vaikunthanatha', Kallar (robber), avatar of Lord Vishnu.

Other Tribals and Hinduism

Some Hindus believe that Indian tribals are close to the romantic ideal of the ancient silvan culture of the Vedic people. Madhav Sadashiv Golwalkar said:

"The tribals "can be given yajnopavita (...) They should be given equal rights and footings in the matter of religious rights, in temple worship, in the study of Vedas, and in general, in all our social and religious affairs. This is the only right solution for all the problems of casteism found nowadays in our Hindu society."

At the Lingaraja temple in Bhubaneswar (11th century), there are Brahmin and Badu (tribal) priests. The Badus have the most intimate contact with the deity of the temple, and only they can bathe and adorn it.

The Bhil tribe is mentioned in the Mahabharata. The Bhil boy Eklavya's teacher was Drona, and he had the honour to be invited to Yudhisthira's Rajasuya Yajna at Indraprastha. Indian tribals were also part of royal armies in the Ramayana and in the Arthasastra.

Bhakta Shabari was a Bhil woman that offered Shri Rama and Shri Laxmana 'ber' when they were searching for Shri Sita in the forest. Maharishi Matanga, a Bhil became a Brahmana.

Sarna

Some western authors and Indian sociologists refer to adivasi beliefs as animism and spirit worship, and hold them to be distinct from Hinduism, Christianity or Islam. In Jharkhand, Chattisgarh and Orissa states, their religion is sometimes called Sarna. The Jharkhand movement gave the Santals an opportunity to create a 'great tradition' of their own. As Orans reported, "The movement is spoken of in the following terms 'we should not leave our religion; we should continue to use rice-beer; we should have our worship at the sacred grove; also we shuld not stop eating beef. We will call our religion *Sarna Dhorom*.' *Sarna* is the Munda word for 'Sacred Grove' while *Dhorom* is the Oriya word meaning 'religion'. Sarna involves belief in a great spirit called the *Sing Bonga*. Santhal belief holds the world to be inhabited by numerous spiritual beings of different kinds. Santhals consider themselves as living and doing everything in close association with these spirits. Rituals are performed under groves of Sal trees called *Jaher* (or *sacred grove*), where *Bonga* is believed to appear or express himself. Often, *Jaher* are found in the forests.

According to the mythology of the Santhal community, the genesis of the 'Sarna' religion occurred when the 'Santhal tribals had gone to the forest for hunting and they started the discussion about their 'Creator and Savior' while they were taking rest under a tree. They questioned themselves that who is their God? Whether the Sun, the Wind or the Cloud? Finally, they came to a conclusion that they would leave an arrow in the sky and wherever the arrow would target that will be the God's house. They left an arrow in the sky; it fell down under a Sal tree. Then, they started worshiping the Sal tree and named their religion as 'Sarna' because it is derived from a Sal tree. 4 Thus, Sarna religion came into existence. There are priests and an assistant priests called "Naikey" and "Kudam Naike" in every Santhal village.

Tribal System

Tribals are not part of the caste system. This is an egalitarianism society. Christian tribals do not automatically lose their traditional tribal rules.

When in 1891 a missionary asked 150 Munda Christians to "inter-dine" with people of different rank, only 20 Christians did so, and many converts lost their new faith. Father Haghenbeek concluded on this episode that these rules are not "pagan", but a sign of "national sentiment and pride", and wrote:

"On the contrary, while proclaiming the equality of all men before God, we now tell them: preserve your race pure, keep your customs, refrain from eating with Lohars (blacksmiths), Turis (bamboo workers) and other people of lower rank. To become good Christians, it (inter-dining) is not required."

However, many scholars argue that the claim that tribals are an egalitarian society in contrast to a caste-based society is a part of a larger political agenda by some to maximize any differences from tribal and urban societies. According to scholar Koenraad Elst, caste practices and social taboos among Indian tribals date back to antiquity:

"The Munda tribals not only practise tribal endogamy and commensality, but also observe a jati division within the tribe, buttressed by notions of social pollution, a mythological explanation and harsh punishments. A Munda Catholic theologian testifies: The tribals of Chhotanagpur are an endogamous tribe. They usually do not marry outside the tribal community, because to them the tribe is sacred. The way to salvation is the tribe. Among the Santals, it is tabooed to marry outside the tribe or inside ones clan, just as Hindus marry inside their caste and outside their gotra. More precisely: To protect their tribal solidarity, the Santals have very stringent marriage laws. A Santal cannot marry a non-Santal or a member of his own clan. The former is considered as a threat to the tribe's integrity, while the latter is considered incestuous. Among the Ho of Chhotanagpur, the trespasses which occasion the exclusion from the tribe without chance of appeal, are essentially those concerning endogamy and exogamy."

Education

Extending the system of primary education into tribal areas and reserving places for tribal children in middle and high schools and higher education institutions are central to government policy, but efforts to improve a tribe's educational status have had mixed results. Recruitment of qualified teachers and determination of the appropriate language of instruction also remain troublesome. Commission after commission on the "language question" has called for instruction, at least at the primary level, in the students' native tongue. In some regions, tribal children entering school must begin by learning the official regional language, often one completely unrelated to their tribal tongue.

Many tribal schools are plagued by high dropout rates. Children attend for the first three to four years of primary school and gain a smattering of knowledge, only to lapse into illiteracy later. Few who enter continue up to the tenth grade; of those who do, few manage to finish high school. Therefore, very few are eligible to attend institutions of higher education, where the high rate of attrition continues. Members of agrarian tribes like the Gonds often are reluctant to send their children to school, needing them, they say, to work in the fields. On the other hand, in those parts of the northeast where tribes have generally been spared the wholesale onslaught of outsiders, schooling has helped tribal people to secure political and economic benefits. The education system there has provided a corps of highly trained tribal members in the professions and high-ranking administrative posts.

An academy for teaching and preserving Adivasi languages and culture was established in 1999 by the Bhasha Research and Publication Centre. The Adivasi Academy is located at Tejgadh in Gujarat.

Development

The Academy has a firm commitment to bringing about a significant social transformation. With this view in mind, the Academy has made several social interventions for spread of education, improving health care and providing livelihood support. The work is spread over 1300 villages (95,000 families) at present in tribal districts of Gujarat. The projects undertaken include:

Prakriti-Health-care

The Prakriti Programme began with the aim to address health problems among Adivasis more specifically that of sickle cell anaemia and Tuberculosis. Adivasi areas have little access to health-care and there are not enough health workers available. Hence there was a need to look for approaches outside the clinic and hospital setting. Bhasha decided to achieve this through community participation and providing need based health-care.

Under the Prakriti programme, both general and specialized health camps are held in the DSC villages. The camps are held after an initial survey of the health status of the village, its proximity to the local primary health centre and need for medical intervention. These camps have enabled doctors to identify and address serious cases of accidents, heart, cancer, tuberculosis and sickle cell.

The health camps organized under Prakriti are meant to fulfill the immediate medical needs of the Adivasis and nomads; and thus serve as means through which Bhasha can carry its message of health care to these communities. The following are the main areas in which the program operates:

Clinic at Tejgadh: In order to to provide regular access to follow up on health cases brought up at health camps and to provide regular access to medical services and advise, a weekly clinic was started at Tejgadh in 2003. The clinic runs every Saturday and draws individuals from a range of 50-60 km. Over the past 6 years the clinic has treated over 72,000 people.

Health Camps: Health camps are held regularly to provide people in rural areas access to health-care. The camps include sickle cell detection and general health-care. Prakriti also runs specialized camps in collaboration with other agencies. The health problems observed among patients include sickle cell anemia, orthopedic cases, urinary tract infections, general surgery, neurological cases, leprosy, skin diseases, eye problems, diabetes and gynecological disorders.

Training: The Adivasi Academy conducts a Certificate Course in Rural Health Management. Ten students (5 women and 5 men) from Maharashtra, Gujarat, Rajasthan and Madhya Pradesh are currently registered for the course.

Health Awareness Activities: Prakriti regularly conducts activities to raise awareness of issues such as sickle cell anemia, womens health and nutrition. There has been success spreading awareness about health-care using traditional folk theater and conducting the activities in local adivasi languages.

Recent activities include:

- During the 2008, the Prakriti clinic was visited by 7682 patients that included 3572 women, 3254 men and 856 children from 400 villages of Chhotaudepur, Pavijetpur and Kanwant talukas
- An 'Acting Healthy Project' in 2008 raised awareness regarding women's health in the villages of Vadodara district. Artistes from Darpana Academy trained a group of teachers and community health karyakartas of the Adivasi Academy in community theatre.
- During April 2008, the group held thirty performances based on gender and health issues in various villages of Chotaudepur, Kanwant and Pavijetpur talukas.
- Numerous health camps were held in 2008 in villages such as Jamla, Methibor, Jharuli, Dobacapra, Jervi, Koli, Kumbhani, Bodgam, Dehari, Singlabari, Diawat and Khadla, during which 1148 persons were offered treatment.
- 7110 households were provided with health insurance during 2008.

Vidya-Education

The Vidya programme aims to improve the education of tribal children. When Bhasha began its education work, it found the following to be significant challenges:

- Migration of parents for seasonal labour work prevents children from attending classes regularly and throughout the year.
- Parents are not educated and aware of the advantages of education and are not sending their children to the non-formal schools.
- Children have to engage in labour work to support the income of their families and thus are unable to attend classes regularly.
- Children of different age groups and knowledge levels are being taught in one class.
- The government schools in many of the villages are ineffective due to paucity of competent teachers who are sensitive to the needs of adivasi children.
- Several government schools are inappropriately located and cannot be reached by children living in distant areas.
- The dropout ratio in schools is exceptionally high since adivasi children find it difficult to understand the content of formal education that is imparted in Gujarati language.

With these challenges in mind, Bhasha centred its Vidya programme around the following activities:

Non-Formal Literacy Centres (NFLCs)

Bhasha is presently running 24 NFLCs, but over the past 6 years has run 90. These non-formal centres focus on functional literacy and developing an innovative and relevant education model which is appropriate for tribal children. Tribal children are often alienated from the mainstream education due to language disparities. In the NFLC's the students are instructed in their own languages. The timings of the classes are flexible, so as not to exclude working children. Community teachers are employed in the centres so that they understand the children and can develop rapport with them. It is an approach to education that is appropriate to childrens needs.

Bridging Opportunities

Many children lag behind in school due to the migration of their parents. The Vidya programme provides opportunities for children to be reintegrated into government schools. This occurs through the NFLC's and Vasantshala, the residential school at the Adivasi Academy which caters for children from migratory families. Through this initiative 2020 students have gained admission to government schools.

Language

Pictorial dictionaries glossaries as well as relevant study materials are published in Adivasi languages accommodate children and non adivasi teachers in Adivasi areas. Bhasha Publications has launched a new magazine Purva Para, based on education and society. This bi-monthly magazine is extremely useful as resource material for the teachers of the Vidya programme. The Bol magazine for children reaches out to 10,000 government schools of Gujarat. Bhasha published Pictorial Glossaries in eight adivasi languages of Gujarat as educational material for children and facilitating communication between teachers and students.

Awareness Raising

The Vidya programme spreads awareness among communities to sensitize parents about the importance of education.

Teacher Training

Regular teacher training sessions are held at the Adivasi Academy in which traditional cultural tools as well as IT based learning are combined. Teaching through oral means is invariably emphasized in these sessions.

Chotro-Labour

Many Adivasis migrate to the cities to search for alternative sources of income. Most end up working at construction sites where exploitation is common. To address this problem the Development Services Centres are working to mobilize migrant adivasi labourers and address issues of exploitation and human rights violation. The programme undertakes legal advice and networking meetings for sensitization and conscientisation.

A survey of 2200 migratory labourers has been conducted to study their migration cycle, place of work, occupational hazards, wages, terms of contractual employment and problems experienced due to migration. Village level meetings are regularly held to discuss the effects of migration and adivasi migrant labourers have been organized to form a union of their own.

This Union helps to solve the problems of migrant labourers such as harassment, exploitation, ill treatment non payment of wages etc.

Micro-Credit

In order to sustain rural economy and social structures by reducing dependency on private money lenders whose charge interest rates ranging between 60 to 120 percent, checking outward migration and creating livelihood opportunities using local and traditional resources, the Academy has set up the Micro Finance and Micro Enterprise Programmes.

Initiated in 1999, the micro finance network presently has 2200 self help groups and reaches close to 22,000 people in five districts of Gujarat. These groups have transactions of over 6 crore Rupees. In the past year 7400 members of nomadic communities have also been linked to the microfinance programme.

Of these activities, Prakriti operates a full-scale clinic at the Academy with a full time doctor.

The Non-formal School Project is run from various villages; but a small unit of the programme provides for residential 'non-formal; schooling to about 50 children brought from the villages where they have not had benefit of a formal school for a period of one or two years, for bringing them up to the formal school level of academic accomplishment.

Economy

Most tribes are concentrated in heavily forested areas that combine inaccessibility with limited political or economic significance. Historically, the economy of most tribes was subsistence agriculture or hunting and gathering. Tribal members traded with outsiders for the few necessities they lacked, such as salt and iron. A few local Hindu craftsmen might provide such items as cooking utensils. In the early 20th century, however, large areas fell into the hands of non-tribals, on account of improved transportation and communications. Around 1900, many regions were opened by the government to settlement through a scheme by which inward migrants received ownership of land free in return for cultivating it.

For tribal people, however, land was often viewed as a common resource, free to whoever needed it. By the time tribals accepted the necessity of obtaining formal land titles, they had lost the opportunity to lay claim to lands that might rightfully have been considered theirs.

The colonial and post-independence regimes belatedly realized the necessity of protecting tribals from the predations of outsiders and prohibited the sale of tribal lands. Although an important loophole in the form of land leases was left open, tribes made some gains in the mid-twentieth century, and some land was returned to tribal peoples despite obstruction by local police and land officials.

In the 1970s, tribal peoples came again under intense land pressure, especially in central India. Migration into tribal lands increased dramatically, as tribal people lost title to their lands in many ways – lease, forfeiture from debts, or bribery of land registry officials.

Other non-tribals simply squatted, or even lobbied governments to classify them as tribal to allow them to compete with the formerly established tribes.

In any case, many tribal members became landless labourers in the 1960s and 1970s, and regions that a few years earlier had been the exclusive domain of tribes had an increasingly mixed population of tribals and non-tribals. Government efforts to evict nontribal members from illegal occupation have proceeded slowly; when evictions occur at all, those ejected are usually members of poor, lower castes.

Improved communications, roads with motorized traffic, and more frequent government intervention figured in the increased contact that tribal peoples had with outsiders. Commercial highways and cash crops frequently drew non-tribal people into remote areas. By the 1960s and 1970s, the resident nontribal shopkeeper was a permanent feature of many tribal villages. Since shopkeepers often sell goods on credit (demanding high interest), many tribal members have been drawn deeply into debt or mortgaged their land. Merchants also encourage tribals to grow cash crops (such as cotton or castor-oil plants), which increases tribal dependence on the market for basic necessities. Indebtedness is so extensive that although such transactions are illegal, traders sometimes 'sell' their debtors to other merchants, much like indentured peons.

The final blow for some tribes has come when nontribals, through political jockeying, have managed to gain legal tribal status, that is, to be listed as a Scheduled Tribe.

Tribes in the Himalayan foothills have not been as hard-pressed by the intrusions of non-tribals. Historically, their political status was always distinct from the rest of India. Until the British colonial period, there was little effective control by any of the empires centred in peninsular India; the region was populated by autonomous feuding tribes.

The British, in efforts to protect the sensitive northeast frontier, followed a policy dubbed the "Inner Line"; nontribal people were allowed into the areas only with special permission. Postindependence governments have continued the policy, protecting the Himalayan tribes as part of the strategy to secure the border with China.

Government policies on forest reserves have affected tribal peoples profoundly. Government efforts to reserve forests have precipitated armed (if futile) resistance on the part of the tribal peoples involved.

Intensive exploitation of forests has often meant allowing outsiders to cut large areas of trees (while the original tribal inhabitants were restricted from cutting), and ultimately replacing mixed forests capable of sustaining tribal life with single-product plantations. Nontribals have frequently bribed local officials to secure effective use of reserved forest lands.

The northern tribes have thus been sheltered from the kind of exploitation that those elsewhere in South Asia have suffered. In Arunachal Pradesh (formerly part of the North-East Frontier Agency), for example, tribal members control commerce and most lower-level administrative posts. Government construction projects in the region have provided tribes with a significant source of cash. Some tribes have made rapid progress through the education system (the role of early missionaries was significant in this regard). Instruction was begun in Assamese but was eventually changed to Hindi; by the early 1980s, English was taught at most levels. Northeastern tribal people have thus enjoyed a certain measure of social mobility.

Participation in Indian Independence Movement

There were tribal reform and rebellion movements during the period of the British Empire, some of which also participated in the Indian freedom struggle or attacked mission posts. There were several Adivasis in the Indian independence movement including Khajya Naik, Bhima Naik, Jantya Bhil and Rehma Vasave.

List of Rebellions against British Rule

During the period of British rule, India saw the rebellions of several backward-castes, mainly tribals that revolted against British rule.

These were:.

1. Halba rebellion (1774-79)
2. Chamka rebellion (1776-1787)
3. Chuar rebellion in Bengal (1795-1800)
4. Bhopalpatnam Struggle (1795)
5. Khurda Rebellion in Orissa (1817)
6. Bhil rebellion (1822-1857)
7. Paralkot rebellion (1825)
8. Tarapur rebellion (1842-54)
9. Maria rebellion (1842-63)

10. First Freedom Struggle (1856-57)
11. Bhil rebellion, begun by Tantya Tope in Banswara (1858)
12. Koi revolt (1859)
13. Gond rebellion, begun by Ramji Gond in Adilabad (1860)
14. Muria rebellion (1876)
15. Rani rebellion (1878-82)
16. Bhumkal (1910)
17. The Kuki Uprising (1917-1919)in Manipur.

Some notable Scheduled Tribes:

- Thakur Peoples of Maharashta
- Andamanese
- Bodos
- Bhils
- Chakma
- Dhodia Tribes of Gujarat
- Gonds
- Khasis
- indigenous people of Lakshadweep
- Kurichiya
- Kurumbar
- Tripuris
- Mizos
- Mundaris
- Nagas
- Nicobarese
- Oraon
- Santals
- Todas
- Maldharis of Gujarat.
- Cholanaikkan
- Warli
- Kisan Tribe

- Dongria Kondh
- Bonda
- Kutia Kondh
- Bishapus A'Mishapus.

Adivasis in the Eastern Ghats

Fundamental Issues at the Close of the Millenium in the Era of Globalisation

Several Adivasi communities or indigenous people are spread over the Eastern Ghats across the southern and eastern region of the Indian sub-continent. It is the most tragical ironies of development that these adivasi communities are at their vulnerable worst at the end of this millenium. Our experience as a social action group, having worked with the tribal/adivasi people for over a decade has been a struggle for a right to human life with dignity, a struggle to fight the severest of odds in the face of "sustainable development" theories of the state. The macro economic and political policies of the state with their active promotion of globalisation, have driven the adivasi people to the brink of survival. The effects of globalisation have had far reaching consequences in the Eastern Ghats, and some of the crucial issues with respect to this region can be analysed as follows :

Economic Policies of the State

With the advent of liberalisation, the Eastern Ghats witnessed a sudden invasion of macro economic forces for the exploitation of its rich natural resources. Virgin forests, with their enormous wealth of timber, mineral and non timber resources have been ruthlessly, unscientifically and irresponsibly tapped first by the public sector industries and from the eighties onwards, by the private and multinational industries. Of these the mining industry has been the most extensive in its spread and destruction.

Mining as the single largest industry has caused severe imbalances in the social, political, cultural and legal status of tribals. As a result, a distinct shift can be perceived in:

- Constitutional changes of the state-the protective legislations of the Fifth Scheduled (tribal) areas to safeguard the lands and resources of the tribals are under severe pressure of amendment for creating easy access to industries. So powerful are the lobbies that the state itself violates the laws for granting leases in tribal areas to private industries.

- This has further led to loss of control over resources, decisionmaking, social and cultural identity, displacement, loss of livelihoods and all the related evils of imvoluntary displacement and forced migration · This coercive migration has made tribals minority communities in their own regions and deeply entrenched the non-tribals and commercial groups within the tribal belt · Development interventions by the government and non-governmental agencies with the tribal people have been very skewed, shortsighted, welfarist and far from aimed at empowerment of people. Literacy levels continue to show extremely shocking results so much so that there is very poor awareness or accessibility to political, legal and economic systems among the tribals.

Political Darkness

The tribals are so dispersed physically and psychologically that they do not have a strong political identity or representation either at the local, regional or national levels unlike the dalits who have built up a discernible political identity. The non-tribal political forces, either of the left wing or the right have managed to disenable any form of leadership emerging from the tribal communities to take their issues forward. Any political sympathies towards the tribals have been superfluous in handing over power and control to the tribals. On the otherhand, inane populist incentives are dangled at them while the real issues of control over resources, rights to self rule and constitutional protection are being actively suppressed.

Samata-its Work and Campaign in the Eastern Ghats with the Adivasi Communities

Samata has worked as a grass-root community based social action group with tribal youth since 1989 to campaign for the rights of adivasi communities in the north coastal region of Andhra Pradesh. Our focus has been to organise the tribals:

- to build up awareness of their rights and legal status
- to mobilise them to assert for their rights and control over resources
- to promote their traditional systems of natural resources management and explore alternate systems of development through ecologically friendly strategies

The principal concerns addressed by Samata have been:

- Land alienation through exploitation of non-tribal landlords and moneylenders, forest conflicts with government and protection of their constitutional status
- Displacement by industrial groups for mining and other commercial ventures
- Encouraging self reliant local institutions for addressing community problems through microcredit, village banks, irrigation and agricultural associations, farmers' cooperatives,etc
- Alternate development programmes like eco-tourism, micro-hydel as energy systems for remote villages, alternate irrigation systems with traditional technology, etc.
- Mining-the most serious problem tackled was the leasing of tribal and forest lands to mining industries through people's movement, legal and media advocacy, networking with other mining struggles and through lobby with government. The campaign resulted in a historic supreme court judgement striking down all mining leases as unconstitutional. (public interest litigation in the case of Samata Vs the State of A.P and Others-AIR 1997, SC 3297).

The Future Mandate for the Movement to Protect the Rights of Adivasis in the Eastern Ghats

Our experience in confronting macro political and development issues for adivasi justice has taught that an isolated movement would be ruthlessly suppressed. A perspective plan has been drawn up for the Eastern Ghats along with community based groups and organisations in the region concerned with the rights of Adivasis to focus on the following thrust areas:

a) A Regional Tribal Advocacy & Lobby Centre. A strong lobby and representation of Adivasi concerns needs to be urgently built up at the regional level. This group takes up advocacy of tribal issues from the local to national level, brings the attention of international media and concerned groups on the impact of liberalization and globalisation. The lobby group will take up legal and media advocacy, network with other tribal groups and make a collective effort to influence policy on tribals and development

b) Conscientisation. Build up literacy and awareness among tribals of their rights, laws, political and economic systems, strive towards infusing a sense of identity and voice to Adivasis as a community and mobilise a collective movement for achieving the same by organising local tribal communities, networking with groups working with tribals at the regional level and extending support to small struggles.

c) Leadership Training. Build up the leadership capacities among the adivasis so as to represent their issues and concerns, develop a strong political identity and campaign for control over their resources and right to decision making on their lives. Encourage the tribal community to actively participate in reviving their customary social, legal and cultural practices and also acquire skills in facing the outside societies and environment without losing their unique identities.

Role of Samata as a Resource Centre for Advocacy and Support to Adivasi Empowerment

From a community based social action group, Samata has developed into a resource centre for advocacy and support to tribal empowerment issues, since 1997. Perceiving the glaring vacume, Samata, with its skills and experience, has set up a centre for representing and lobbying for tribal concerns in the state of A.P, and at a wider level, the region of the Eastern Ghats along with community based groups and organisations working with tribals.

Samata networks with these groups and through this collective might, plans to pressurise for justice to tribals.

Strategies of Intervention:

Support local tribal campaigns and movements · Support small community based groups working in the tribal belt through capacity building and skills development, legal, financial, information and other support · Legal advocacy through writs and public interest litigations in the local courts, high court and supreme court

- Media Advocacy
- Information Collection, Compilation, and dissemination to tribal communities and local groups
- Coordinating with networks and alliances of various struggles in the country
- Linkages with international groups, alliances and institutions
- Tapping resources of technical experts, academicians and professionals
- Reaching out to general public and society at large on micro and macro issues
- Representing tribal issues to government and pressing for implementation of tribal area laws and balanced development policies
- Technical support for alternate development programmes
- Undertake studies, research and documentation on the problems and issues related to the tribals in the region.

8

Religious Influence on Politics and Political Influence on Religion

Even in countries such as the United States, which recognize the necessity of a separation between church and state, there will always be interaction between religious and political leaders. It seems to be an unavoidable result of the way most societies work, and it is foolish to imagine that politicians will be without religion, or religious leaders without politics. Both fields claim idealism and purport to seek ways in which to better our society. However, a cynic such as myself can find many ways in which individuals use either or both of these systems in order to gain power. I will admit to some bias, as I am an atheist, but I naturally recognize and tolerate the right of the individual to and from any religion of their choice provided the religion is not simply a play for political power.

In this node (*taken straight from my Comparative Politics class, yay for noding your homework*), I examine a variety of nation-states and their respective dominant religions, namely: Nazi Germany's relationship with their Protestant and Catholic citizens, the Soviet Union's state atheism, China's policies on Christianity, Iran's relationship with Islamic leaders, and finally, the influence with which most Americans are familiar—our own religio-political interface.

Before delving into a topic, however, it seems best to clarify what exactly I mean by a "religion". In this node, the term "religion" refers exclusively to recognized formal religions and not to the idea of "civil religion", which is related to nationalism. Specifically, a civil religion is a form of national self-worship (Schoffeelers 20). This topic will not be covered in this paper—instead I will discuss nations and their relations with formal church systems.

Nazi Germany and Christianity. The record is clear. From the moment Hitler assumed office, we know that he immediately put antisemitic policies into effect. His goal was always "the complete removal of the Jews" (Scholder I:255). However, the atmosphere of early National Socialist Germany was surprisingly tolerant towards Christian worshippers. Protestantism, of course, has had a long tradition of antisemitism, beginning with Martin Luther: founder of the Protestant movement, author of 'The Jews And Their Lies', and an inspiration to Adolf Hitler. The Protestants generally did not object in any significant way to Hitler's policies (Scholder I:270).

Early in his life, Adolf Hitler realized that an attack on Catholicism would prove futile (Scholder I:88). This led him to try to avoid unnecessary entanglements of church and state. In fact, Hitler publicly proclaimed his Christianity and encouraged unification of the sects under the movement of Naziism, stating (in regards to both Protestantism and Catholicism): "We are a people of different faiths, but we are one......we tolerate no one in our ranks who offends against the ideas of Christianity, who offers resistance to someone with another disposition, fights against him, or acts as the arch-enemy of Christianity. This, our movement, is in fact Christian." Clearly, Hitler did not have any major bias against any sect of Christianity. Of course, the common rebuttal by apologists is that he was simply distancing himself from the Communists. Hitler stated that "Christians and not international atheists" had taken over the government of Germany (Scholder I:223), an obvious reference to Communist Russia. Hitler's political plans for the churches seemed to come together perfectly: On Nov. 12, 1933, elections were held which showed little difference between the Catholic and the Protestant political districts (Scholder II:1). Hitler had his unification.

However, when one examines the relationship between church and state, invariably there is a controlled party and a controlling party. In the case of Nazi Germany, the state was undoubtedly the controlling party. Unsurprisingly, Hitler used his secret police and methods of terror to manipulate the Catholic leaders of Germany, including the murder of Erich Klausner, the Bishop of Berlin, for his refusal to agree to German demands (Scholder II:197).

The Soviet Union, State Atheism, and Christianity. In the former Soviet Union, the communist philosophy forwarded by Marx was the true state religion. Marx, an atheist, predicted the downfall of religion as a fundamental component of communism (Walters 4), and so his followers—Stalin, Lenin, Trotsky—tried to bring about his predictions by force of law. Surprisingly, however, the popular reports of Christian persecution in that country have been misleading to say the least. It is true that the Soviet Union frequently bombarded the civilization with atheist propaganda, but there were only a few brief times in Soviet history—generally at the beginning of a new Premier's regime—when religion was truly persecuted.

One such occasion was the Decree of 23 Jan 1918, which removed the right of the Orthodox Church to be recognized as a legal person, the right to own property, and the right to teach religion in schools. The Soviet policy at the time was to disseminate anti-religious propaganda and firmly separate church and state (Walters 6). The key difference between the Soviet seperation and the American seperation was one of implementation: the American way is to build a fence, the Soviet way is to define a line, which, if crossed, results in execution. For the most part, the Soviet government was tolerant of Protestantism and Islam, which tend to push a stronger work ethic; but the Orthodox Church bore both these sects' share of hard times.

In 1922, the government began to try to promote a schism within the Orthodox Church. May 1922 saw the growth of a group called the "Renovationists", a sort of Communist/Catholic hybrid which took over the leadership of the Orthodox Church. It is generally accepted that Trotsky aided this coup (Walters 9). By 1923, the flow of propaganda from the government had slowed. Religion was not so persecuted with the Renovationists in control of the Orthodox Church, and Protestants and Muslims continued to enjoy their loose reins. But in 1929, Stalin took absolute control of the country, redoubling the anti-religious sentiment against any and all sects (Walters 15). He banned performance of religious services in unregistered buildings, conducting evangelistic activity or religious educations, printing of religious material, and fundraising. Religious groups were now no longer free to produce responsory propaganda to counter the Soviet propaganda blitz. The clergy, who were considered "non-working elements", were subject to immense taxation, discrimination in housing, and deprivation of Social Security rights (Walters 13). But, after World War II, the anti-religious government backed off again, restricting their attacks on religion to words alone until Stalin died in 1953 (Walters 18).

Then, after Stalin's death and Khrushchev's ascension to power, religious persecution once again rose (Walters 22), with a torrent of propaganda that was unmatched by that of any other period in Soviet history. Under Khrushchev's leadership, propaganda stopped appealing to the educated, and became much more shallow and crude. Anti-religious filmmaking also became popular. But when Brezhnev took power, the anti-religious crusade finally began to taper for the last time (Walters 23). Except for a brief hiccup early in Gorbachev's reign (Walters 33) the anti-religious sentiment decreased continually until the end of Soviet rule in the early 90's.

Obviously, in this case, the state controlled the church. Strict laws and regulations concerning what could and could not be done in the Soviet Union limited the ability of its citizens to worship as they wished. But it should be noted—even at the peak of Soviet religious persecution, execution and imprisonment were rarely if ever used. The peak number of imprisoned religious "criminals" was only 411. Generally, the extent of implemented anti-religious sentiment was merely a large quantity of anti-religious propaganda—the Soviets simply stole the Protestant idea of handing out tracts.

China and Christian Missionaries. In the early 1920's, a wave of Christian missionaries moved on China. They viewed themselves as bringing enlightenment to an unhappy and unfulfilled people, judging the Chinese by Western standards that simply did not apply to an Eastern civilization. Their firm belief in their Christian tradition wouldn't allow them to even consider the possibility that the Chinese were more than happy without the Christian faith (Lutz 12). The prime source of the anti-religious sentiment, however, was the same as that of the Soviet Union—the communist philosophy of Marx and Lenin.

And the major hotbed of the socialist view was the school. The Socialist Youth Corps would be the group that brought anti-religious views into the mainstream in China. Ch'ih Kuang, one of their leaders of this group, condemned Christianity as a "narcotic used by capitalists and as a source of conflict and intellectual oppression." (Lutz 56)

Karl Marx was once quoted as saying "Religion is the opiate of the masses." The recent Opium Wars in China made this quote even more poignant, and redoubled anti-American sentiment (Lutz 68). Because the missionaries were, generally speaking, the only Americans most Chinese met, they bore the brunt of this anti-American sentiment. Christianity was generally inseperable from the actions of Western nations and individuals (Lutz 87).

Of course, it was not only a disdain for Americanism that was the basis for the Chinese anti-religious sentiment—it was also a disdain for Chinese tradition. Ch'en Ch'i-t'ien, a high government official, said "We have just been struggling to break the hold of Confucian tradition; why should we permit another outmoded ideology, Christianity, to spread its influence in China?" (Lutz 70) It sounds like an attack on Christianity, but in context, it was an attack on parochial schools—the most common means by which missionaries enter a new country, indoctrinating the young while teaching them how to read.

We return to the question "Which controls which?" and here, in 1920's China, the answer is not as simple as would seem. Missionaries set out to control China, but China fought back by restricting their rights in later years, banning parochial schools (Lutz 229), and heavy taxation—essentially following the early Soviet model. Was this strike by China warranted? It's a matter of personal religious opinion, most likely.

Iran and Islamic Law. Until now, we have examined situations in which the government controls churches and clergy by strictly limiting rights, increasing taxation, imprisonment, and even in the case of Nazi Germany, through stealthy execution of dissidents. But there are many other governments in which the religion has either a "finger in the pie", so to speak, or even a death grip on the national government. Iran is one such country.

Iran has only been experiencing some struggle between church and state for about eighty years. But this is primarily because for most Islamic sects, there is no recognized division between "church" and "state". (Savory 129) They are in fact one and the same, the ruler of the region a divinely selected leader in the eyes of the masses, much as Louis XIV of France was the "Sun King". Islam is the universal religion of God on earth, and only an Islamic government can represent God properly (Habiby 141). Islamic law is a primitive social system, to be sure, but it is also a more stable system than the Christian governmental system made so popular in the Dark Ages, proved by the fact that strong Islamic law government still exist today.

Iran is a Shi'i state, the only Islamic state today not of the Sunni variety, which follows a more traditional view of Islam. This causes crises of legitimacy and soverignty in Iran, as the Sunnis have a slightly more democratic way of choosing a ruler by a limited form of voting, while the Shi'i faith tends to link more with Iranian history (Savory 131-132), and supports a dynastic line of Ayatollahs. The Iranian populace is generally happy with the arrangement. In 1924, the country was offered a democracy by Shah Reza Khan, but rejected the idea out of fear of secularization (Savory 137).

The Shah of Iran, an American puppet-leader, was overthrown in the 1970s by Ayatollah Khumayni, who promised to return the nation to a true Islamic state (Habiby 141). Khumayni claimed that "Shah-in-Shah" (King of Kings), a title of the Shah of Iran, was considered an insult to the Islamic people, as that was a title specifically reserved for their God. He was a populist, promising to take Iran out of American and Israeli hands and return it to its former Islamic glory (Habiby 146-147).

Under Khumayni, freedoms were promised to all who did not attempt to undermine the Islamic "Republic". He criticized the

Shah for "granting" freedoms instead of recognizing them, much as the Soviets did. Oil would be sold to everyone but Israel (their Jewish enemies), but not at Iran's expense. Iran would no longer be the slave of imperialism (Habiby 149). To some extent, these observations were correct. American interests had been taking advantage of Iran.

Industrialization was to proceed unhalted, so long as they were balanced by the moral and ethical values of the Holy Qur'an. But Khumayni's ultimate opinion was this: "Those who forbid science and knowledge in the belief that they are safeguarding the Islamic religion are really the enemies of that religion... there is no incompatibility between science and knowledge and the foundation of Islamic faith." (Habiby 150)

In the case of Iran, we see religion clearly dominant, running the government. It is, however, a truly populist movement, fighting in defence of Islamic tradition against American intervention in the area. Unlike the now-defunct Afghanistani Taliban, Iranian law is generally tolerant to those who practice a different faith, so long as they do not attempt to publicly convert others.

The United States and Fundamentalist Christianity. The First Amendment of the Constitution of the United States of America states: "Congress shall make no law respecting an establishment of religion, or prohibiting the free exercise thereof..." This means that Congress is prohibited from passing laws either for or against a religious establishment. Jefferson later interpreted in one of his letters to major churches, coining the expression "a wall of seperation between church and state." However, it does not prohibit religious groups from attempting to pass secularized versions of their religious laws. One such religious figure in American government is Pat Buchanan.

Pat Buchanan was a runner up candidate in the primaries for the Republican party through the late 1980's and 1990's. He ran on a platform that was strictly based on a blend of conservative and Christian standpoints, combining pro-life with pro-death penalty, and increased aid to churches with lower taxes (Capps 172). Buchanan was thankfully never elected president, but the one-two punch of conservativism and Fundamentalism has influenced modern politics—especially the Republican party, and to a lesser extent the Democratic party.

In the last 10 years, we have seen our political spectrum take a step to the right, with our current President, President George W Bush, even pushing for an office to donate large sums of money to religious charities and asking the opinion of religious leaders and not doctors on important scientific matters such as the use of stem-cell research, which could be a potential source of new medical breakthrough.

So in the United States, the government is strictly prohibited from controlling religion. That leaves only the opposite. To a minor but significant extent, religion controls the United States. Religious differences were the main forces behind the emigration of Europeans to the New World in the 1500's; we are descended from those who believed so strongly in their faith that they risked a long and dangerous sea voyage for it. Is it any wonder that Americans allow religion to creep into every aspect of their lives?

Conclusion. In almost every government, there is some sort of power struggle between religion and government. Either a government seeks to repress religion in order to emphasize some abstract governmental theory (China, Russia), or uses it in order to promote its own governmental ideology (Nazi Germany). Or, a religion may be so dominant in a society that a populist revolution occurs, installing a religious leader (Iran). Finally, a religion may use the government in order to push a religious agenda (United States). In each of these situations, the theoretical "wall of seperation between church and state" would be very beneficial to both church and state—neither would seek to usurp power from the other. The United States' wall is currently the strongest, but even a strong wall of seperation will leak to some degree.

9

Bureaucracy and Development: The Indian Scenario

In India, development and local self-government have a long history. The Indian society which we find today is definitely not the same as it was during the British rule. It is not easy that the areas which remained sick for such a long period should regain their health so soon. All the same, the change that has taken place with in a period of 60 years is highly encouraging and laudable. Majority of the people live in rural areas in developing countries, Therefore, any attempt at bringing overall development must lay greater emphasis on rural development which is sought to be brought about through planning. The government in such countries is facing the problem of initiating and accelerating the pace of development to enhance the standard of living of the people. Bureaucracy occupies an important position in the formulation and implementation of these plans. Hence, the success or failure of development efforts to a larger extent depends upon the role performed by bureaucracy in developing countries.

After Second World War, interest in development had been witnessed not only in the third world but all over the world. Development has affected every branch of knowledge like industry, technology, education and agriculture. Naturally, much of the leadership in development has come from governmental agencies, be they international, national, State regional or local also.

Perhaps the most important problem of India in particular is that of improving the economic and social conditions of people who live below poverty line. They include our society's landless labourers, small and marginal farmers, artisans and other weaker sections.

In fact there are no two opinions about the need of development wherein the role of bureaucracy is both important as well as essential. But there is no empirical evidence to highlight the deficiencies which creep into any system or every system despite the best efforts of all concerned. The fact that nearly 75 per cent of the total population of India dwells in the villages, it would be worthwhile to focus attention on the role of bureaucracy in the development.. The proposed study is one of the first of its kind as an appraisal of the role of bureaucracy in the development.

This research study concerns with the structural and behavioural aspects of bureaucracy in rural development. The major focus of attention of researchers of Indian bureaucracy had been on the Indian Civil Services and its successors i.e. the Indian Administrative Services. Lower ranks of bureaucracy had received scant attention. We acknowledge its (IAS) importance in the total political system but we feel it is more important to turn our attention to those bureaucrats who are easily identified with development efforts of the State and are actively involved in eliciting public cooperation for development tasks. In this research study, efforts are directed towards not only the bureaucracy at secretariat and district levels but also at the block level which is engaged in implementing the rural development programmes. This section of bureaucracy has certainly a great contemporary relevance in the overall development of India in general and Bihar in particular. The functionaries at the lower level is the Block Development Officers, Extension Officers and Village level Workers (VLW). They are the government officials who interact with the people, mould and influence public attitudes towards development in a significant way. It is also at the local level that the hardest core of traditions and beliefs are found and policies undergo their most severe test for implementation

Therefore, to provide immediate relevance and a contemporary understanding in the context of development, State level bureaucracy for policy making and District and Block level Bureaucracy for implementing the policy and programmes has been selected. Rural development programme is the single most of important vehicle of government, initiated for purpose of socio-economic uplift. The government has devoted great attention to this aspect of change. The present study focuses its attention on the bureaucratic behaviour and its performance in the execution of development projects.

After the initiation of community development and Panchayati Raj, the development scene tended to highlight the relations between political leaders and administrators also. It was argued that the successor of local institutions as instruments of development rested on the ability of the political and administrative leadership to cooperate with one another and resolve the tensions and conflicts arising from the social environment. The administrative machinery set up for community development programme soon gave way to the three-tier Panchayati Raj system in order to make rural development administration responsive to the elected representatives of the people. The block was recognised as the focal point of planning and administration and it became the single most important unit of both community development as well as Panchayati Raj. It is because of this reason that the study of bureaucracy both at the secretariat and grass root level has been taken up. There is abundant literature on "Bureaucracy and Development". A large number of studies have been conducted pertaining to the various aspects of bureaucracy and development in India and other countries of the world. Other than the Indian Scholars on bureaucracy, there are some foreign observers on the subject who had studied the bureaucracy in depth. Paul Appleby, F.W. Riggs, Ralph Brainbanti, La Palombara, Hugh Tinker, Uraula Hicls, and David Potter ere some of them. Some of the notable Indian Scholars who have done researches on Bureaucracy and Development are Kudeep Mathur (Bareaucratic Response to development 1973), (Bureaucracy and New Agricultural strategy 1983). C.P.Bhambhri (Bureaucracy and Politics in India 1971). R. B. Jain and P. N. Chaudhuri (Bureaucratic values in Development 1982). G. Mare Gopal. H. R. Chaturvedi. A. Avasthi and Romesh Arora (Bureaucracy and Development: Indian Perspectives 1978). P. R. Dubhashi: (Rural Development Administration in India). S. R. Maheshwari (Rural Development in India 1985). L. C. Jain &. B. V. Krishnamurthy, P. M. Tripathi (Grass without Roots: Rural

Development Under Government Auspices 1985). After mentioning the various studies on this aspect, it can be said that lot of studies in this field have been done in various States of the country but very little has been done in Bihar.

Bureaucracy and Development: Conceptual Framework

The developing countries directed their efforts towards economic, social and political development after attaining independence from colonial rule. In the.modern age every democratic government has to face gigantic task of all round development. Though the concept of development administration is of recent origin but has become quite popular and a fashionable expression in administrative parlance. Development needed to be conceived as a dynamic process directed towards transforming the entire society- embarking together its economic, social, political and administrative aspects for an all around balance upward change. Development administrations is thus that aspect of public administration that focuses on government influenced change towards progressive political, economic and social objectives According to Weinder, development is a State of mind, a tendency, a direction, rather than a fixed goal, it is a rate of change in a particular direction. The task of nation 'building and bringing about major socio-economic changes in the under developed and developing world is the main theme behind the concept of development administration.

Again the importance of development within the broad framework of development administration is of utmost necessity in the modern world. The concept of development was viewed differently by different scholars as it was completely a new concept for third world countries. But as a whole development is not a new concept. Several pioneering experiments have been made in this direction by many eminent scholars and practitioners.. The concept of what is known as development was born in the context of agriculture, and it remained for long time, coterminus with agriculture development in India The Royal Commission on Agriculture (1928), for instance provides this kind of interpretation to rural development Agriculture is at the heart but not the whole development., Planning Commission Task Force on Integrated

Rural Development observed in 1972 also observed likewise. Now we have decided to take what might be considered a rather restricted view of the expression 'development'. We have chosen to equate it with agricultural development in the widest sense so as to embrace, besides crop husbandry, all the allied activities. Development has meant the extension of irrigation facilities, expansion of electricity, improvement in the techniques of cultivation, construction of school buildings and the provision of educational facilities, health care etc.

Development since seventies in general has began to be viewed in terms of the contribution it makes to the reduction of poverty, inequality and exploitation. Development reflects these concerns and is manifested in special programmes for the weaker sections of the community and backward areas. Developments in content and form is concerned with multi sectoral programmes involving development in productive agriculture and its related services, industrial activities, transportation, communication and infrastructures, health and education services etc.

After seventies, the concept of development has become, more confining in its interpretation. The World Bank boldly marks such a shift in emphasis and defines development as a strategy designed to improve the economic and social life of a specific group of people – the poor. It involves extending the benefits of development to the poorest among those who seek a livelihood in the underdeveloped areas. The group includes small scale farmers, tenants and landless. The SFDA, MFAL, NREP, IRIP, DPAP and minimum needs programmes have become too well known and are part of India's new Twenty Point Programme. In order to appreciate the new concept of development, it is necessary to note what was felt to be unsatisfactory in some of the earlier approaches. With out wishing over simp1ify or over generalise issues of policy and problems of implementation which are by no means uniform country to country or even area to area in a given country. One may identify a few factors in common.

- that development approaches tended to over play 'quantity' and speed at the expense of 'quality' and composition.
- that models of development used, explicitly or implicitly by planners, were urban/industry biased, resulting in a

neglect of or at least inadequate attention to the imperatives of rural development,

- that the resources that were infect committed to development were applied unevenly, that they were appropriated in undue proportion for the benefit of an elitist minority.
- that even where the programmes did reach the common people living in underdeveloped areas; they tended to be fragmented and ineffective with little relation to the requirements of the poor, so that at least their basic needs for decent existence could be met.

Some of the new concepts and objectives in rural development are related to the above set of considerations and have the professed objective of remedying such lacunae. The current approaches to development thus emphasize the following:

- a direct and time bound plan of action for improving the living conditions of the rural majority and their quality of life.
- all round development of the abundantly available manpower, with technologies being devised to promote this objective, simultaneously increasing productivity and enhancing work satisfaction;
- promoting real participation of the majority in the decision making mobilization and implementation process;
- an integral approach that will integrated sector of development with reference to an agreed package of goods and services and in a more fundamental sense integrated different levels (central, provincial and local) areas (rural and urban) and classes of people (rich and poor).
- the promotion of self reliance at local as well as provincial and national levels in achieving these objectives.

The element of participation is cultural to these approaches. It responds to the need to mobilize and use more effectively all resources available or potentiality available in areas of labour, skills, saving land, fisheries, forests, livestock and water. Our development system can be analysed in terms of three inter related aspects of rural communities. They are (a) individual member of the community (b) organisational aspects and (c) the environment of the rural community. These of course, are the major variables of any action system or organisaton. In accordance with strategies of stimulation and inducement of rural development, therefore, government should encourage changes in individual aspects regarding their perceptions and of motivation attitudes, world outlook and skills and knowledge required for development. Government should also induce organisational change in rural communities in terms of leadership structure made of people's participation and institutional linkages.

The third important concern of policy makers will be how to provide a sufficient level of environment support in terms of political leadership commitment, supportive policy measures, political and administrative framework, and other social and economic supporting linkages.

In a country like ours, where majority of the vast population actually live and work in villages, the task relating to rural development acquires special importance. National development is inconceivable and impossible without rural development. According to 1981 Census, 78 percent of India's population (680 million) lives in villages while there are not more than 3,000 cities and towns. 40 per cent of rural population is estimated to live below poverty line as against 41 per cent in urban areas.

Foreign rulers paid little attention to the development of India and only confined to limited function of collecting land revenue and maintaining law and order which helped the British to improve the British economy. It was only after independence that with the transfer of political power to Indians, a serious thought was given to development of the people.

Therefore, the first and foremost challenge to the Indian administrative system of independent India was how to meet the socio- economic needs of these rural poor. This can possibly be with the introduction of rural development programmes for the rural India. Rural development is advocated today as basic strategy for economic development all over the world and India is no exception. The sheer largeness in Numbers Who continue to live and work in the rural areas in the developing countries, particularly India, the biggest democracy of the world, compels our attention to this important yet neglected sector of the economy. The idea of rural development originated by Mahatma Gandhi in his teachings was the champion of Gram Raj. Gandhiji succeeded in mobolishing the poor people from the villages in the unique battle for freedom by holding out before them the prospectus of better life, more dignity and honour.

Due to the absence of popular local institutions, in the beginning, the responsibility of implementation of the community development programmes was given to the steel frame bureaucracy in India. The bureaucracy failed to inspire the people's cooperation in community development programme due to its rigid approach, conseryatism and lack of development attitude. As a result of its failure, on the recommendation or Balwant Rai Mehta Team, Government of India recommended the decentralization of power and authority to the popular local institution i.e.-Panchayati Raj institutions. In the opinion of Late Pandit Jawahar Lal Nehru both officials and non-officials and their part to play in the community development work.

In India the question of development was initiated with community development programme in fifties, then in sixties the area development programme was launched, in seventies integrated rural development programme become popular and the latest emphasis now on the individual development programme realised to uplift the poorest from the level of poverty to better living.

Bureaucracy

The task of development and modernisation in the third world country like India is not possible without a well organised and effective bureaucracy. Interest in bureaucracy and its relation to democracy predates the advent of sociology as a discipline. According to Ferrel Heady, the origin of the word is not clear. Initially it referred to the cloth covering the desk of French Government Officials in the eighteenth century. It appears that the world bureaucracy as such has bean derived from the word 'Bureau'. Morstein Marx has given it a French pedigree and points out that it was first used in French form 'bureaucratic' by a French Minister of commerce in eighteenth century to refer to the government in operation. It came to be used in Germany during nineteenth, century as `Bureaucratic'.. It has since found its Way to English and many other languages and Morstein Marx counts it as amongst the notorious words of our age.

Bureaucracy means desk government in which power belongs to offices or departments of the government. Bureaucracy may be defined as a systematic organisation of tasks and individuals into a pattern which can most effectively achieve the ends of collective efforts. It is a regulated administrative system organised as a series of inter-related offices. Etzioni Parsons and some others have used the word organisation in place of bureaucracy. Parsons considers organisations to be sub systems of the more comprehensive social system, which are social units deliberately constructed and reconstructed to seek specific goals.

The first concrete efforts to study the bureaucracy in a systematic manner were made by Max Weber a German sociologist who was known as the father of "ideal type" of bureaucracy. Max Weber explored systematically the possibilities of modem formal organisations and pointed out the distinct rational and legal characteristics of these organisations.

For Weber,the decisive reason for the advance of bureaucratic organization has always been its purely technical superiority over any other form of organization. Precision, unambiguity, speed, knowledge of the files, discretion, continuity, strict subordination, unity, reduction of friction and of material and personal costs are raised to the optimum point in the strictly bureaucratic administration and especially in its monocratic from. It has been said that Weber did not define bureaucracy. He instead, specified the features of what he considered the most rational from of bureaucracy. On the basis of his conception of legitimacy Weber was able to formulate eight propositions regarding the structuring of legal authority systems.

Bureaucracy is useful to the organisational system in societies with varied political system, the context and character differing a great deal according to the political set up. Hence, a bureaucratic system controlled by the communist party in the Soviet Union or the People's Republic of China is a different system from that of United Kingdom, the United States of America or France. Weberian bureaucracy establishes certain standards of integrity, impersonality and professional competence and has been found to be useful and efficient in carrying out its responsibilities. In other words, bureaucracy emerges as uniquely impersonal, neutral and instrumental. If such is the essence of bureaucracy does it really have any meaningful role, left, in relation to the development in general and rural development in particular for the third world countries who got freedom from colonial rule sometime back.

The bureaucratic problem is somewhat complex in developing countries where social and political institutions are relatively less developed and where the State has mainly to depend upon the administrative structure for the accomplishment of its goals. Bureaucracy has also been criticized as urban oriented and elitist in nature having failed to have adjusted to the needs of rural areas where the majority of the people live and work.

In a country like ours, where quick change is required to bring about socio-economic transformation in backward areas, Weberian Model of bureaucracy has several operational limitations. The formal view of bureaucracy as emphasised by Weber alone tails to take into account the - importance of "Informal Organisation", that are so much a part of formal organisations that the later cannot exist without the former. As Triest comments the nineteenth century cannot be repeated in the developing countries in the last third of the twentieth.

Bureaucracy in India has emerged from the British colonial system. After achieving independence the functions of government and bureaucracy have undergone a fundamental change. India launched her massive programmes of community development with a view to liberating the teeming million from squalor, disease, illiteracy, ignorance, unemployment poverty etc. The Indian Civil Service (ICS) was allowed to continue in independent India with all the its traditions, background and attitudes. To make the matter worse the Indian Administrative Service (I.A.S) created after independence came to exist with the (ICS) and initiated all the valuable acquisitions of the later. The IAS also accepted the same legacies of the ICS including its claim to exclusiveness and class consciouaness. The changing role of India bureaucracy is the major issue of our times, commenting on the role, T. N. Chaturvedi writes:

"The Civil Service has to undergo radical structural, procedural and attitudinal changes if it has to serve as an effective instrument of change and progress in a developing society. The civil service has to cultivate much wider social awareness and responsiveness as well as social base apart from the traditional virtues of integrity" functional efficiency and a sense of fair play and impartiality."

10

Democracy and Development

India Since 1991

It is eleven years since India had the economic shock of its life and had to rethink its economic policy and rearrange its economic institutions. It was nearly ten years ago that I had the opportunity to welcome the drastic change and wish that it would be more rather than less drastic, not a popular position among my economist friends in India at that time (Desai 1993). This is thus a good opportunity to see how far India has got in its response to the shock of near bankruptcy in early 1991.

But a lot more has also happened to India in its political life since 1991. Indeed it is hard to say whether it is the political or the economic map that has changed more in the last ten or more years. In various articles written over these years I have also tried to chart the political dynamics of the 1990s. While there was always implicitly a political background to my economic comments and an economic background to my political comments, I would like to take this opportunity of the Narayanan Oration to try a synthesis.

The separate strands which need to be synthesized are as follows:

- In its first phase lasting just over three decades (1947–1980), India's economic policy was driven by a model of national self-sufficiency. It was built around, indeed pioneered, an Import Substitution Industrialisation (ISI) strategy. It also chose (and this is separate strictly from ISI) a capital intensive programme hoping that matters of employment creation, consumer goods supply especially foodgrains would take care of themselves. Political developments in the mid and late 1950s forced a situation in which the Planning authorities had to reverse the neglect of agriculture. The Green Revolution which occurred by accident in the 1960s corrected the earlier urban biases of the Second and Third Five Year Plans but the poor performance of the manufacturing sector – in terms of inefficiency, excess capacity and low quality – persisted in both the private and public organized sectors. The growth rate was low relative both to early aspirations (Bombay Plan for instance) and to the rates achieved by other countries. This was the so-called Hindu Rate of Growth. 3.5 per cent per annum and 1.3 per cent per capita.

- Over this period 1947–1980, India's political life exhibited a lot of stability and a solid, indeed unique achievement among post colonial polities in creating and sustaining a vibrant political democracy. Single Party Dominance nurtured this democratic life except during the infamous Emergency which was brief and was reversed by that very democratic process it tried to subvert. The dominant vision of nationalism was built around secularism, non alignment and socialism. There was however beginning to be an assertion of the various regional, caste and religious – by and large 'ubaltern' forces – in the federal polity. Indeed the Janata Government of 1977–1979 reflected this.
- During the 1980s, there was a decade of restoration of Single Party Dominance but a relaxation of the imperative of economic self-sufficiency. There was borrowing from abroad – from the IMF, from foreign commercial banks and then from NRIs. But the economic institutions of permit-license Raj did not change and there was no relaxation of domestic economic policy in parallel with foreign borrowing. Growth rate went up to 5.5 per cent, 3.5 per cent per capita.

- The decade of the 1980s stored up much trouble for political life later on. Secularism was compromised into a parallel populism with accomm-odation of the orthodoxies of the two major religions as Rajiv Gandhi's decisions on Shah Bano case and the shilanyas at Ayodhya showed. The subaltern elements continued to grow powerful at regional levels.
- The 1990s ruptured the old model in two ways. Economic dirigisme – often mislabeled socialism – became untenable as India could not repay its commercial borrowings without drastic reform. At the same time the end of Congress dominance unleashed forces – implementation of the recommendations of the Mandal Commission with all it meant about valorization of caste distinctions, rise of the Hindutva parivar, dalit militancy – which ended for the decade and more any hope of a single party government. In a strange combination, the arrival of globalisation saw India modernise and liberalise on the economic front but become less secular and more ethnically divided than before politically. Modernity in India thus took a different path from what its champions in the early days after Independence had charted for it. It is not a secular socialist democratic India but a liberal, increasingly Hindu nationalist democratic India that is shaping its own future.
- On the economic front the reform forced upon India by the trauma of 1991 has proved irreversible and effective. Despite much hesitation, the reform process has persisted and raised the growth rate nearer to 6.5 per cent for GDP and 4.5 per cent per capita. The liberalization process has been slow relative to countries of Eastern Europe but it has been consensual. Even as politicians compete in populist rhetoric about protecting the jobs and the poor, it is clear that no possible combination of parties exists which upon gaining power would or even could reverse the liberalization process.
- There is one solid continuity despite the change in party dominance and in economic philosophy over the last fifty-

> five years. This is the nationalist programme of a militarily strong India. Even as India preached peace and non-alignment in 1950s it built up its military production capacity especially its atomic and nuclear research. Whether Congress or BJP, whether Nehru, Indira and Rajiv Gandhi or Vajpayee, the determination to make India militarily strong has been common. There is no peace party in India. Indeed, it can be seen now that the ISI strategy and the insistence on self-sufficiency arose from a defence policy that meant India to be a powerful regional power. The election of President Narayanan's successor has crowned that policy with official recognition.

It is this cluster of trends that I wish to explore. The decline of secularism and socialism, the rise of liberalism and religiosity, the persistence of nationalism as a force even as its nature has changed. Democracy has been the universal solvent in this process. In order to appreciate the importance of Indian democracy, it is necessary to go back to the early history of Independent India.

The Revolution of 1946–1949: The Constituent Assembly in Action

The decision to adopt universal adult franchise with a Westminster style parliamentary system was a revolutionary decision of the Constituent Assembly. It was not inevitable nor was it a conservative decision. Given the experience of almost every other post colonial country with constitutional change, it is a miracle that the Constituent Assembly (the Assembly hereafter), elected as it was on a restricted franchise got it so right. But this choice revolutionary as it is, profoundly constricted and shaped the subsequent trends.

The Assembly rejected the Gandhian option — a decentralized village republic with local autonomy and indirect democracy with an obviously weak Centre. A strong Centre was basic to Indian nationalism as its one great fear was, indeed is, of India breaking up into many nations. In the wake of Partition, a weak Centre was not going to be chosen whatever the Father of the Nation may say. The Assembly also firmly ruled out any role for the feudal order — the hundreds of native princes, for whom a role was envisaged in the 1935 Government of India Act. Unlike Malaysia, India did not give these kings even a ceremonial role. In copying the Westminster system, it replaced the Crown by an elected President with similar powers. It also rejected a single party polity which must have been tempting as it was for many African and Asian countries under the spurious rationalisation that multi party democracy was a Western luxury that a poor country could ill afford. The Communist alternative was also rejected. Private property, including foreign property, was not disturbed but could be subject to state takeover with compensation. Land was not confiscated or nationalized but land reform was made feasible.

The democracy that was chosen was radical in other ways as well. There was to be no recognition of any ethnic, religious or caste basis of citizenship. There were to be no separate electorates, no religious qualification for holding office, nor a literacy test. Women were given the vote on the same terms as men when even in the developed countries e.g., France, women's suffrage had only recently (i.e., 1945) been granted. But by the same token there were no guarantees of minority rights qua minority; no consociational arrangement in a formal sense whereby a minority had veto rights over drastic abridgements of its rights by the Majority vote Minorities, like majorities were treated qua Westminster as collections of individuals rather than ethnic blocks and therefore were to be looked after as part of the democratic process by legislative or by executive actions. Thus despite its being elected from a small and restricted franchise which could have made it conservative, the Assembly chose an individualist atomistic model of democracy for India rather than one grounded in caste, religion and language identities. Secularism was the implicit guarantee that a religious minority had nothing to fear from majority rule. Religion was not to be a subject which could be legislated about.

It will be my contention that this bold revolutionary choice was crucial in shaping subsequent choices and indeed in making some of these subsequent choices less bold than they could have been. In making the Constitution, ethnicity-blind and religion-blind, the Founding Fathers were rejecting the trauma which had led to the Partition and hoping to avoid further fragmentation. But they were also denying reality, not only of the country at large but even of their own personal identities. Indians were individuals of course like anyone else but they also lived in a vital sense their ethnic, religious regional, linguistic identities. These identities were not to be left behind when they entered the political arena. Nor were these identities an invention of the colonial masters or a badge of poverty or under-development ready to disappear at the first whiff of economic progress as Nehru in his more passionate moments thought.

Indian democracy was shaped by these ignored identities as they asserted themselves in the daily course of electoral politics. At the elite level, their own orthodox upbringing, their upper caste loyalties if they were Hindus, their relatively prosperous state meant that the choices taken were their choices. But they were also the progeny of Macaulay and had absorbed western ideas of progress and equality, of liberty and the greatest good of the greatest number. They may have lived much as their fathers did at home but they thought and spoke the Englishman's language.

Social Conservatism and Economic Radicalism

Two crucial choices were made early in the years after Independence. One was to be socially conservative and not use the State apparatus to abolish the caste system with its inegalitarian logic of hierarchy and status.

Primary education and adult literacy were state subjects and thus left to stagnate in those conservative states in the Hindi heartland where literacy, especially female and dalit literacy, were seen to be threats to the social order. Although untouchability was made illegal in the Constitution, the attendant evils of caste were left undisturbed.

Muslim society was even more deli-cately handled. As far as Hindu society was concerned an attempt was made mainly at Nehru's behest to codify and systematise Hindu Family Law, though he met with resistance in his desire to modernise it from the then President Dr Rajendra Prasad. But Muslim Law was out of bounds even for Nehru. Thus political independence and the revolutionary decision to adopt democracy did not result in any state-led political programme of social reform. Indian society was allowed to reform itself in a *laissez faire* way.

In the economic sphere, on the other hand, radicalism was the order of the day. India had, by 1947, one of the oldest modern industries in the Third World (though it was not so called till later). It had the largest group of native modern capitalist entrepreneurs, the largest jute industry, a cotton textile industry which was globally competitive and was the seventh largest industrial country in terms of volume of industrial output. But the perception of the nationalist movement was that India had been deindustrialised by British rule and that industrialisation was the first priority. Free trade and foreign capital imports were to be shunned. India would become a self-sufficient industrialised country by relying on planning led by the State.

This was not particularly surprising both in terms of the thinking of the Congress as moulded by Nehru and the climate of the times. Free market ideology was on the retreat and many thought that capitalism too was on its way out. India had been much taken by the Soviet example and indeed even by the German example of planning in a mixed economy. What was not necessary, however, to this strategy was to neglect if not punish the Indus-tries already established, especially the cotton textile industry and shifting resources to machine building. There was rampant export pessimism, unjustified as subsequent investigations showed. The strategy failed to take advantage of India's early start in modern industry and reinvented many of the things which were there but were tarred with foreign brush.

Thus India created a dependent entrepreneurial class in place of one that had survived foreign rule, depressed modern consumer goods industries and fostered small scale ones which were capital wasting and inefficient, built at an enormous expense a basic goods sector with a long lead time before it could bring better consumer goods to the people and failed to generate industrial employment. The public sector, mainly in services, became the biggest provider of employment in the modern sector. Jointly the private and public organised industrial sector became a stagnant and highly privileged pool of a limited number of employees. Together the public services and the organized industrial sector employed 15 per cent of the labour force. This was called socialism (Desai 1993).

The strategy was wasteful of scarce capital and quite perverse in its determined neglect of the rules of efficient allocation. It is one thing not to get prices right but quite another to deliberately get them wrong. Restrictions on interest rates, multiple exchange rates, subsidies to inefficient industries, taxation on movement of agricultural commodities which constituted a tax on agriculture, perks to labour in the organized sector and de facto taxation of the informal sector by a lack of subsidies etc. All this was done by an elite fully economically educated but determined to flout the rules of western economics.

The results were predictable — slow growth of output and employment and persistence of poverty and inequality through the first phase of thirty years. With slow growth of jobs in the private sector, government jobs at all levels became much sought after and the democratic electoral system was harnessed to provide patronage. The first task of government became provision of jobs through the public fisc and then the sale of permits and licenses.

Triangulation Indian Style

Thus we get a unique triangular interaction. Economic radicalism leads to slow growth biased towards elite jobs. Social conservatism strengthens caste, regional and religious loyalties. Political democracy allows the mobilization of these loyalties in an electoral competition to capture governments at state and then at central levels. This capture then translates into jobs for the newly included. Yet the economic surplus does not expand by this route. So the system crashes in the 1970s under the weight of its own demands. A way out had to be found. It was the economic radicalism which began to be abandoned because that was the only way surplus could be enhanced. This is the way the model unfolded itself.

The interaction of social conservatism and economic radicalism in the context of political democracy produced a most interesting mutation. To get the fruits of patronage, non elite groups had to get organized and they did this through their caste and regional identities. Linguistic states had to be created during the 1950s in response to popular pressure from the local capitalists as well as local middle classes who wanted public jobs and public contracts.

Next came in the 1960s the pressure from the rural areas to divert resources to agriculture. This happily bore fruits in the form of the Green Revolution with input subsidies as well as price guarantees for outputs. But even then the discontent due to slow growth continued. This broke into a flood of protest from tribal dalit and lower caste groups in the 1970s, and were brought together under the Lokayan banner. This was what unhinged Indira Gandhi and led to the Emergency. Groups previously downtrodden were finding their voices and using the unreformed social structures of caste and religion to make their claims on the surplus. But the surplus was not expanding due to the elitist policies being followed.

The Escape from Triangulation

The Janata government was the transition between the first and the second phase. By itself ineffective, it mirrored the subaltern groups which had come to stake their claim to power. But Janata had no organizing vision to unite these groups as the elite vision of Nehruvian nationalism had. What Mrs Gandhi learned from her defeat was that the new India could not be run on old elite lines. She reinvented the Nehruvian vision keeping the rhetoric of socialism and secularism but changing the content.

The two major changes were that in the economic sphere she abandoned self-sufficiency as a goal but retained dirigisme (socialism). Foreign loans were taken but the economy not restructured. On the political side she used both Hindu and Muslim imagery to garner Hindu vote banks, and of course Muslim ones too. The foreign loans and some liberalization on import account led to higher growth. The Green Revolution was also now routinely yielding good harvests so food imports were no longer an item on the balance of trade. Of course not all the regional and linguistic loyalties could be bought off. The demand for Khalistan was a demand too far and Indira Gandhi gave her life in her determination to combat that.

What was happening on the ideological front was less obvious but no less important for that. Indian nationalism had suffered a body blow with the Partition. The India that Nehru had 'discovered' during his final prison term was not the India that he came to be the leader of. He gave a new vision to the nation — of a non-aligned, secular modern, even socialist India. But the war with China shattered the non-alignment. Pragmatic consideration forced Indira Gandhi to replace secularism by parallel and simultaneous flattery of Hindu and Muslim religiosity. Socialism hung by a slim thread of dirigisme but one reinforced by foreign loans. Elsewhere Asian countries were marching ahead economically; China had abandoned Maoism in favour of Deng's pragmatism. Even Pakistan was no inferior to India in terms of income levels or industrial performance.

What was going to be India's vision of nationhood if the modernist Nehruvian vision with its secularism, socialism and non-alignment was no longer adequate? There were two rival models on offer. One was the religious Hindutva model which had been shunned aside in favour of the Congress one early in the independence movement which now began to be revived by the Jan Sangh/BJP. The other model — less articulated — was the one which came to the forth in the first Round Table Conference in 1929. This was the India of regions, languages, religious and ethnic identities. This was how the British saw India but the Congress rejected this vision in favour of a 'unity in diversity' vision. But this vision somewhat subaltern was what would have ruled India had the Cabinet Mission's plan been accepted. India would have remained united, unpartitioned but would have been a confederation. With provincial autonomy for big states like Panjab and Bengal and Sind, local nationalisms would have flourished.

In the years since 1947, it was this vision which strengthened itself as linguistic and caste parties became electorally successful. It is these forces which have become the challenge to the Hindutva vision. Under the leadership of Mulayam Singh Yadav or Laloo Prasad Yadav or Karunanindhi/Jayalalitha or Chandrababu Naidu this confederate vision is also secular and can align either with the Left or the Centre Right (Congress). As the Congress hegemony fell apart at the end of the 1980s, this vision became a pillar of Indian politics.

The decisive change did not come with Rajiv Gandhi but after his defeat. He confirmed the abandonment of social reform by capitulating on the rights of Muslim women in the Shah Bano case and yielded to Hindu pressure on shilanyas for the potential Ramajanmabhumi temple on the site of the Babri mosque. It was electoral cynicism but it did not pay. But what a decade of growth at 5.5 per cent did was to create opportunities in the private sector which the old elite could exploit. It began to disengage from public sector jobs. There were better perks in the private sector. This created room for meeting the next explosion in subaltern demands which V P Singh tried to accommodate by undertaking to implement the Mandal recommendations.

The Crisis of 1991 and the New Dispensation

The uplift in the economic growth rate during the 1980s had been bought with foreign borrowings but without restructuring the economy. The economy's autarchic orientation continued and this meant that insufficient export income was generated to pay back the foreign debt. Had the borrowings been invested in exportables and India been given an open economy orientation, then repayment would have been easier. Had the capital come as equity rather than debt, the repayment would have not been a problem. But borrowings were made in debt form to retain political control over resources and this proved to be fatal. The economy crashed as it became unable to service its debt.

The political system crashed at the same time in as much as neither V P Singh nor Chandrashekhar could sustain a majority. The Budget for 1991 had to be postponed and central bankers had to scurry around raising money to pay back debt. The election of 1991 did not settle the issue though Congress (without Rajiv Gandhi) came back to power without a majority. A break away from the old model was now urgent in the economic sphere. Of the three sides of the triangle – social, political and economic, it was the economic which was the easiest to change quickly. But the change rapid as it was soon became mired into a reluctant transformation. The two other dimensions constrained the speed and thoroughness of the abandonment of the old dirigiste model in favour of economic liberalism.

Through the 1990s and into the 21st century, coalition governments persisted. In its first forty-two years after independence, India had six Prime Ministers of whom three had ruled for thirty eight years. In the next thirteen years there have been six more prime Ministers. Political continuity in the sense of one-party dominance has now gone. Economic self-sufficiency as an ideal has also been abandoned. The contending visions of nationhood have resulted in a marked rise in political and communal violence. There are caste wars in Bihar, Hindu Muslim violence in 1992/1993 and again in Gujarat in 2002 with smaller episodes in between. There is violence against dalits and Christians from those who prefer a Hindu India.

At the same time India has remained a democracy in a most resilient fashion. For someone who grew up when the world was worried about After Nehru who?, the question today seems absurd. Coalition governments have carried on Westminster politics in a most Indian fashion. Politics is more consensual, less elitist but at the same time more corrupt and self-serving. Democracy is too deeply entrenched now to imagine any other form of governance in India. Which by the same token makes it very difficult to imagine any drastic change in the second pillar of social conservatism. Thus castes are valorized as are regional and religious divisions. They are cards to play in the electoral game. Political power is the solvent which brings gains of patronage to communities which have little chance in the liberal market order for economic gain. Of course by resorting to political patronage, these 'backward' castes and scheduled castes dig themselves deeper into the mire of dependency. This strengthens the appeal of conservatism. The fact that some caste leaders spout secular or socialist slogans does not make them modern in any sense.

Thus the burden of keeping the show on the road, of plastering the differences together falls on the economic dimension. Economic reform over the last ten years has been slow, hesitant but consensual. The strategy of implementing reform through the democratic process has meant that unlike in Eastern Europe there has been no shock therapy, no convulsion. The reformers of today were the dirigistes of yesterday. There is continuity. Thus the growth rate has gone up only modestly (relative to East Asian countries) to between six and six and a half percentage points. There has been a slow trickle of FDI and India's export performance remains modest. The rate of privatization has been slow for a long time though it has perked up in the last year or so. Infrastructure development is urgent as is the need for restructuring of public sector infrastructure provision if FDI is to be attracted. Budget deficits of the Centre and the states together are too large and represent a waste of savings.

But then the deficits are the price of the twin pillars of social conservatism and political democracy. Coalition politics and the patronage politics of social factions combine to make government expenditure a variable outside political control. Despite the misgivings of IFIs and credit rating agencies, Indian finance ministers carry on with the deficits as they are, knowing full well that any effective curbing of government spending would end any coalition. The same is the case with corruption and the crime/ politics nexus. The quality of public life has gone lower as India's democracy has become more inclusive. The costs of this democracy now constitute a non negligible burden on India's growth rate. If even half of the deficit now running at 10 per cent of GDP is avoidable, we are speaking of around 2 per cent per annum in GDP growth rate.

The Prospect

In one sense India is super stable and very resilient against drastic reform, social or economic. The strength of India's democracy vouches for its super stability. The revolutionary choice of the Constituent Assembly in 1946/1949 has had counter-revolutionary consequences, much as it happened in 19th century France following the French Revolution. The country is immune to radical change. If there is a danger anywhere it comes from the overarching ideology of nationalism. Let me spell this out.

There are as I said above three competing visions of Indian nationhood (Desai 2000). The Nehru vision of secularism, socialism and non-alignment is now moribund if not dead. The BJP Hindutva vision is in ascendance. It is non-secular, non socialist though uncomfortable with foreign capital. The third alternative is the confederate nationalist one which is deeply embedded in caste, language and religion. It is secularist and dirigiste if not socialist. (The Left parties — CPI, CPM — are a small presence in Lok Sabha and perhaps disproportionately large in India's political and intellectual life. They can be clubbed together with either the Congress or with the third cluster of confederationist parties.)

At present, Congress is secularist but against economic liberalization. This is partly because it is in opposition and partly because the older vested interests in the socialist model are housed in the Congress. The rhetoric is all about the poor and anti Western multinationals. The BJP and its parivar is split on economics. The RSS is anti foreign capital and anti reform. But the parliamentary wing of the BJP is led by people who have made their peace with economic reform. This is again because they are in office and not in opposition. But the old Jan Sangh was always derided as a party of shopkeepers and merchants. It has anti-dirigiste instincts. Of course being in electoral competition, the financing of patronage makes every party love the public sector. The third cluster is anti-capitalist in most of its rhetoric.

The dilemma facing India is that it can have a secular but anti reform coalition or a non secular but economically liberal coalition. The latter variant is in power now but it may lose the next election to a combination of Congress and a number of smaller parties. Only a Grand Coalition of the type German politics has seen, one between Congress and BJP may overcome this dilemma. I have been long an advocate of such a coalition which everyone considers quite utopian.

Such a coalition would become a reality only for one reason. If India is to be a militarily powerful force in Asia comparable to China then it does need to accelerate its economic growth. While the obsession with Pakistan lasts, China is not clearly perceived as a challenge. But sooner or later Indian nationalists of whatever cluster will realize that China is the only serious competitor for India – a rival not an enemy. To catch up with China could yet become a nationalist ambition. To achieve that India will have to set aside its fear of economic change and its parochial concerns with religious divisions.

Democratic Society and Democracy in India

The processes of formation of Indian state have rendered it a complex character. These processes contained various, often incongruent and contending moments that loom large over the career of the state. The state inherited two conflicting legacies at the time of its formation-the colonial and the nationalist. As a continuation of the colonial rule the post independence Indian state took over almost the entire colonial state apparatus. The Government of India Act of 1935 became one of the main sources of the new constitution and its institutional details. Colonial institutions like the army and the bureaucracy were accommodated within the new state system without much alteration in their structure and ideology.

The colonial logic sanctioned state interventions in social realm as part of regulatory functions of the state. The constitutional discourse and the state practices in the post independence period developed this logic in combination with their commitments to democracy and welfare. The regulatory role of the state was reinforced in the idea of a 'modern' Indian nation state to be established after independence. The modern character of the state emanated from both colonial as well as nationalist legacies. Essential features of the modern Indian state like rule of law, citizenship, sovereignty and the procedural norms of democracy arrived as a mix of these two legacies (Kaviraj, 2004). India was one of the few societies where political revolution preceded the social revolution. Legitimacy of the traditional social institutions stood challenged at the time of independence. Naturally the state acquired a central location in the overall social organization. At this level, the nationalist discourse prompted a blend of the state's regulatory capacities with its expected developmental role vis-à-vis construction of a modern, democratic, secular society in post independence India.

The transformative agenda developed as an inherent aspect of the nationalist movement due to its anticolonial character. And yet the nationalist legacy was not uniform. Plural and contending visions of the future state and society emerged from within the Indian national congress and from the movements challenging its legitimacy. The nationalist visions had two implications about the possible interventionist role of the state. One, the commanding, central role of the state in bringing about the desired (whatever it was) social change was acknowledged by different shades of the nationalist thought. It was stateness that gave to the new entity, at once, an encompassing, representative and transcendent quality (Kothari, 1995). At this level the role of the state as a public authority, acting beyond social contestations was acknowledged. The common, agreed upon agenda of transformation under state's leadership was shaped in terms of constructing a modern, democratic, secular society. It was strengthened in terms of two more transformative claims made on the state-those of social justice and economic redistribution. These expectations highlighted the second implied role of the state as an interventionist agency. At this level, inspite of its neutrality the state was expected to prioritise certain sectional claims over others. The public character of the state was defined in terms of its partiality towards the claims of the disprivilged. This created a possibility where the state, as a public authority, would take sides in social contestations in order to enrich the quality of public life. The twofold understanding of its interventionist role thus added to the complexities surrounding the state.

The socio-economic realities of Indian society legitimized the interventionist role of the state. At least four dimensions of these realities proved crucial in shaping the immediate and long-term strategies of the state's interventions. The first was the highly unequal and hierarchical nature of the society and the multidimensional, overlapping character of these hierarchies. Uneven patterns of regional development combined with plural nature of regional cultures formed the second important aspect of unequal nature of the society.

The immediate context of partition, rise of communal politics and the minority majority divide encouraged by the colonial rule influenced the nationalist thinking about state regulating the plural religious arena and acceptance of secularism (of a distinct variety) as a central aspect of the state ideology. Economic inequalities or the class reality provided the fourth crucial dimension of the social context in which the Indian state took shape. The nationalist movement had been instrumental in some ways in keeping the class inequalities latent in the course of development of the anti colonial discourse. Yet there was a clear awareness regarding the appropriational claims of dominant social sections over state power. Acceptance of intervention of state in economic arena resulted from both, elite perceptions of class inequalities and the modernizing mission of the state.

The constitutional discourse, that officially defined the procedural and ideological norms for the state becomes the final and the most important factor influencing state practices in the post independence period. Constitutional conceptions of Indian state are 'overlapping' in nature (Palshikar, 2001). These conceptions shape the character of the state both in terms of its ideology and in terms of its practices. As a legatee of colonialism and nationalism the Indian constitution accepts the twin logic of neutrality and instrumentality of the state as a central theme.

The exact balance of the two elements emerges more as a pragmatic, practical rather than a deliberate theoretical choice. The Indian constitution does not give us a clear-cut theory of state. Instead it develops a version of a democratic state that can take up multiple roles at the same time.

At the official level the state was expected to be a democratic and a welfare state. The constitution conveys the sense that simultaneous pursuit of these two goals may not be essentially congruent with each other. In the light of the contextual influences discussed above the constitution therefore, develops the idea of the state institutional domain at various levels. Constitutional provisions create possibilities where the state is insulated from its democratic responsibilities and takes up regulative role, where it intervenes in the social realm and therefore may become a possible party in social contestations (constitutional sanction to positive discrimination, group rights and minority rights), where the state creates possibilities of democratic resolution of these conflicts through its formal institutional set up and where the state rises above these contestations and asserts its publicness both through its neutrality (equal guarantees of political rights) and through its instrumentality (directive principles of state policy).

Besides, the constitution also provides internal checks and balances on the working of the state in its elaborate scheme of separation of powers. Tensions arising from several simultaneous expectations from the new state are thus clearly reflected in the shaping and outcomes of the constitutional discourse. In spite of these tensions and the resulting complications in the role of the state, the Indian constitutional discourse remains firmly embedded in the democratic logic. Its engagement with democracy results in democratic institutional set up that marked the procedural successes of the Indian state and also in possibilities of deepening of democracy at state and societal levels.

Contextual Democracy

The idea of democracy as it developed in India remained 'contextual' (Frankel, 2000:4) in many ways. The specific historical-social context or the contextual influences shaped the new democratic institutions in various ways. Reciprocally, social hierarchies and preferences for group rights were affected by the egalitarian and liberal principles of governance.

Elite perceptions and the resulting state discourses of democracy often invoked procedural aspects of the idea. In the context of multidimensional socioeconomic realities the emerging ruling classes saw democracy as a convenient, most suitable instrument for legitimizing their domination.

The very nature of class balance and heterogeneity made the proprietary classes somewhat more interested in maintaining the democratic process. This aspect of democracy was strengthened in the context of a rise of a bourgeois state engaged in the project of capitalist accumulation (Vanaik, 1990). It reinforced the regulatory functions that Indian democratic state was expected to perform.

However even the state discourses of democracy recognized its liberating potentials. The projects of individuation, modernization and economic transformation were seen as possible through democratic political processes. Anti-colonial legacies had posited a similar kind of faith in democracy among Indian masses. The faith was substantiated in successful nationalist political mobilizations. It opened possibilities of similar collective mobilizations in the post independence democratic politics. At this level democracy was seen as a space where movements of resistance to domination could be shaped. Although the meaning of substantive democracy (Jayal, 1999) was not clearly articulated, there was a definite hope towards achievement of the same. This aspect of democracy strengthened the welfare role of the state at one level. More than that it developed the idea of democracy as a fluid, layered concept.

Introduction of democracy into a highly rigid and inegalitarian social structure slowly but surely unleashed diverse patterns of mobilizations. They gave rise to very uneven democratic claims within Indian democracy. Presence of contending claims makes democracy a terrain of social contestations. It renders a contingent character to democratic politics. There is a definite expansion and deepening of democracy through contestations.

However these expansions take shape in an 'untidy' manner (Alam, 2004). The kaleidoscope of meanings, expectations and hopes that different sections of Indian society place on democracy, the various ways in which they contextualise it, renders any attempt to fix its meaning and scope futile (Mehta, 2004:3). There is every possibility that such untidy and noisy (Kohli, 1999) democracy may easily lose the element of public good and may lead to closure of substantive democratic option for many. On the other hand, the same democratic process remains the only arena in which a viable project for its substantiation can be imagined.

The Indian state as the main actor in the game interacts with such contextual democracy in its post independence practices. It is the essentially open and contentious democratic process that mediates the state society relationship in India. The process makes the state boundaries porous and opens the state institutional domain as a terrain of social contestations (Jayal, 1999). Commanding presence and centrality of state in social organization and multiple expectations from the state get combined with its democratic character to create such possibilities.

Both actors in the democratic play, the state and various social sections making claims on the state, try to invoke the elements of neutrality and instrumentality in the state in seeking the desired outcome. Selective uses of meanings of democracy, of the state institutional set up, of the democratic rights and of multiple roles of the state are often entertained by both sides. According to the constitutional design the post independence Indian state not only remains embedded in democratic logic but also has possibilities of directing it. The constitution places a high responsibility on the state to expand democracy in the social and economic sphere.

The idea of planning involved manifold negotiations of the state with the democratic process. As a modern, bourgeois state the Indian state was committed to rapid industrialization and capital accumulation.

Agrarian interests within and outside the Congress party opposed this agenda. Location of planning outside democratic contestations automatically provided a space for the state to push its economic agenda without entering into these contestations. At a more general level, the developmental ideology became a constituent part of the self-definition of post-colonial state in India. The state acquired representativeness by directing an economic programme on behalf of the nation. 'It was in planning that the post-colonial state would claim its legitimacy as a single will and consciousness-the will of the nation-pursuing a task that was both universal and rational: the well-being of the people as a whole. It is in its legitimizing role, therefore, that planning, constituted as a domain outside politics, was to become an instrument of politics.'

Failing the initial rationality of the Indian state the process of planning had many deep and long-term political repercussions. Economic changes resulting from the ten developments plans significantly altered the nature of political alignments of the dominant interests. Emerging political factors in the later years on the other hand also largely influenced the 'sacred' design of plans. The earlier omnibus role of the planning commission declined due to the changing political context. However the state continued with its logic of imagining economic arena and the state's powers to control the economic arena as a domain beyond contentious political process. It culminates, perhaps in a paradoxical manner, in the state's ability to create a consensus about the expansion of the market in the recent times.

It is with the same logic that the state executed another institutional expanse during its formative periodthat of bureaucracy as an instrument for implementation of the developmental goals. Role of bureaucracy in India originates in the colonial legacies.

Under the Macaulayan scheme a new class was formed that would serve as interpreters between the British and the millions whom they governed. The British system of the Indian Civil Services was one of the first to be deliberately constituted on the basis of recruitment by means of examination. The new state continued British practices to a large extent. The growth of the services had heralded a transformation of the British administrator from ruler to guardian. It is precisely this role of the bureaucracy that the new state needed for its consolidation.

Its operations as a developmental state added to the tasks of the bureaucracy. The bureaucracy had acquired professional competence and had emerged as a well-knit network in the colonial period. Thus a readymade institutional apparatus was made available to the new state. The centralizing, modernizing and developmental logic of the state underlined the importance of bureaucratic state institutions. The bureaucracy spread rapidly and became a crucial aspect of the post independence state. The constitution provided for a public service commission to ensure the professional competence and integrity of the bureaucracy. During the course of its development however the bureaucracy remained exposed to democratic pressures both internally and externally. Social composition of the civil servants became a prominent theme in discussions about bureaucracy. The idea of planning and its centralized implementation resulted in enormous expansions of bureaucratic power. At the same time the state emerged as the main employer with rapid growth of the public sphere. Precisely because of its developmental role, bureaucracy was expected to have a certain representative character. The discourse of reservations thus centred round the bureaucracy for a long time. In the initial period the upper castes were heavily represented in bureaucracy as well as in the political executive. With the introduction of caste reservations in services the composition of the services changed gradually. However the scheduled castes, scheduled tribes and other backward classes remained under represented in major way because of the non-implementation of the reservation policy.

External pressures arising from the complexities of democratic process resulted in 'politicization' of bureaucracy at various levels.

Political interference of the executive in the work of the civil servants must be seen as a very common phenomenon in any democracy. In the Indian context these interferences attained various expressions because of the widespread reach of the bureaucracy and its special role. Efforts to politically control the bureaucracy increased with gradual weakening of the state institutions. Indira Gandhi's loyalists during the emergency period put forward the notion of committed bureaucracy.

The civil servants were expected to be committed not to their professional ethics but to particular political interests. The changing social composition of the ruling elites in various states during the nineties saw yet another level of politicization of bureaucracy in terms of mass transfers of upper caste bureaucrats as a significant political strategy of the governing parties (Jafferlot, 2003). Perhaps the most recent and most perverse expression of this trend emerged in the state of Gujarat in the state led pogrom of the Muslims in 2002.

Even otherwise, the bureaucracy worked in close association with the dominant interests within and outside the government. The industrial bourgeoisie exercised greater authority on the bureaucracy at the centre while in the states the localized bureaucracy remained subordinated to the power of the rural rich. With the growing concentration of the governmental resources in its hands the bureaucracy entered into a complex nexus with these classes that resulted in nepotism and corruption on a major scale. Some scholars argue that, with its sharing of residues and access to resources the bureaucracy has become part of the dominant coalition of the ruling interests in India (Bardhan, 1984) and thus has intrinsically lost its transformative character. Bureaucracy's interactions with the democratic process rendered it a character of a large and ill-regulated machine that introduced numerous distortions in the policy making and implementation.

The state-bureaucratic organization and its developmental logic of planning along with the dominant position of the Congress as a ruling party ensured impressive achievements for the Nehruvian state in economic and political fields. Democratic contestations remained latent in this period. Instead, these acquired the form of inter-institutional conflicts. These conflicts originate in the ambivalent character of the Indian constitution. In its attempts to balance the elements of stateness with democratic promises, the Indian constitution provided elaborate schemes of separation of powers among the three branches of government and also for internal mechanisms of checks and balances. And yet it left open spaces where an appropriate reading of the constitution would be constructed only through its working in a concrete democratic context. It was about these spaces that initial conflicts over appropriation of constitutional powers emerged among the different agencies of the state.

11

The Challenges of Building a Democratic Developmental State

"A common factor among developmental states appears to be a committed leadership that is embedded in the 'right' context of demands. Developmental states are usually characterized by a leadership which is strongly committed to developmental goals, and which places national development ahead of personal enrichment and/or short-term political gains"

In Ethiopia, since the last seven years or so, the incumbent party and government have explicitly committed themselves to building a democratic developmental state that efficiently guides the national socio-economic and political development of the country by mobilizing the human and material resources of the state and directing them towards the realization of common goals. The current rulers place the needs of the poor and social issues such as health care, housing, infrastructure, education, poverty alleviation and reduction as well as a social safety net at the top of the national agenda. The country is led by a dedicated, radical and committed leadership bestowed with vision and strategy to fundamentally transform the socio-economic face and makeup of the nation in a relatively short period of time. Starting from a very dismal and pitiably low base of economic and human development as of 1991, considerable achievements in a large number of socio-economic and political spheres have already been registered throughout the country.

The tireless struggles to improve the living standard and overall well-being of the rural and urban populations across the country, to insure the rule of law and to safeguard human and democratic rights are continuing unabatedly. Although a lot remains to be done when compared to the constitutional democracy that the country and state boast of, today, peace and stability reign throughout the country, attracting many foreign and local investors to start new businesses in Ethiopia.

We also observe the current regime relentlessly striving to root out, rent-seeking, predatory behaviour, corruption and other malpractices in the public bureaucracy, to build an ethical, customer-friendly, efficient and meritorious public service, a well-functioning public-private sector alliance and collaboration, creating an investor friendly environment, supporting small business development and peasant agriculture productivity as well as commercialisation of small-scale agriculture, generating massive employment opportunities for the urban youth and women, encouraging export-led growth of the agricultural sector, and using state owned enterprises effectively and driving strategic investment initiatives. As a result, double-digit annual economic growth has been a characteristic pattern of the national economy since the last six or seven years, and now the government has formulated and launched a five-year Growth and Transformation Plan (GTP) with an over-ambitious aim of doubling the present national economy or gross domestic product with an expected yearly economic growth of 11-14% GDP, including doubling the agricultural production of the country at the end of the five-year period (2011-2015).

The State is also strongly committed to playing a big role in keeping our economy competitive and close to the leading edge in the global development of knowledge and technology by pursuing a democratic developmental state, akin to the current experiences of similar developmental states such as South Africa, Botswana, Mauritius, Ghana, Brazil, among others. But what do we mean by a 'democratic developmental state'? How is it possible to simultaneously tackle the twin challenges of socio-economic transformation: democracy and development? What is the relationship between democracy and development? Does democracy promote development or is it the vice versa? These vexing questions require succinct answers. Before going any further in the discussion of the topic, I believe, we must start with a definition of the concept because the term 'developmental state', amongst many circles of academics and business elites in Ethiopia today, is almost equated with the mere imposition of 'hard power' and authoritarian rule on the society with the sinister aim of perpetuating one-party rule under the guise of implementing socio-economic and political policies and programs in order to achieve fast and accelerated economic development and to extricate the poor masses from the scourges of poverty and depravation in a short period of time. This is because of the authoritarian political system that was prevalent during the developmental process of the so-called East Asian Tigers or Newly Industrialized Countries (NICs) such as Korea, Taiwan, Singapore, etc. in the 1960s and 1980s applying authoritarian politics to implement their developmental policies and agendas, and achieving spectacular economic growth rates and sustainable development in just three decades or so.

Yes, most developmental states in East Asia were initially authoritarian and applied heavy-handed approaches to implement their developmental policies and achieve fast growth in a short period of time. For these poor societies democracy in the short-term was considered a luxury they could ill afford, and thus they focused more on developing discipline than democracy, believing that the exuberance of democracy would lead to indiscipline and disorderly conduct which would be inimical to development. However, their integrity and commitment to achieve their developmental objectives and goals were unprecedented. This does not, however, imply that all authoritarian regimes are developmental and it also does not mean that states need to be authoritarian in order to be developmental. There have been many examples of anti-developmental or non-developmental authoritarian states in Africa and Latin America; Ethiopia of the pre-1991 era could be cited as an illustrative example in Africa. On the other hand, Brazil and South Africa today indicate that democratisation and a greater developmental orientation of the state can occur in parallel. In the case of Brazil, democratisation entailed a transition from military authoritarianism to democratic rule, while in the case of South Africa it was a transition from Apartheid to inclusive democracy.

However, building developmental states in a democratic context brings about particular challenges, which for the most part Asian success stories did not face. This issue has been neglected in much of the literature on developmental states. Brazil, India and South Africa, for example, have faced significant obstacles in managing their political economy with what Herring (1999) described as 'one arm tied behind [their] back by [their] commitment to liberal democracy'.

Definitions of a Developmental State

The term 'developmental state' does not enjoy any clear consensus about its meaning. Some even question the appropriateness of the term 'developmental state' contending that a 'state' as an abstract entity can neither be developmental nor non-developmental, and it is perhaps a 'regime', they contend, that may deserve such a label. Leaving aside this contention for further debate and scrutiny in the future, let us examine the views of other scholars on the issue. According to Castells: "A state is developmental when it establishes as its principle of legitimacy, its ability to promote and sustain development, understanding by development the combination of steady high rates of growth and structural change in the productive system, both domestic and in the relationship to the international economy... Thus, ultimately for the developmental state, economic development is not a goal but a means."

Chalmers Johnson contends that: "the developmental state was one that was determined to influence the direction of and pace of economic development by directly intervening in the development process, rather than relying on the uncoordinated influence of market forces to allocate economic resources."

Wikipedia, the Free Encyclopedia describes a 'Developmental state', or hard state, as "a term used by international political economy scholars to refer to the phenomenon of state-led macroeconomic planning in East Asia in the late twentieth century, In this model of capitalism (sometimes referred to as state development capitalism), the state has more independent, or autonomous, political power, as well as more control over the economy. A developmental state is characterized by having strong state intervention, as well as extensive regulation and planning. The other characteristics include (i) emphasis on market share over profit; (ii) economic nationalism; (iii) protection of fledging domestic industries; (iv) focus on foreign technology transfer; (v) large government bureaucracy; (vi) alliance between the state, labour and industry called corporatism; (vii) scepticism of neo-liberalism and the Washington Consensus; (viii) prioritisation of economic growth over political reform; (ix) legitimacy and performance; (x) emphasis on technical education. The term has subsequently been used to describe countries outside East Asia which satisfy the criteria of a developmental state. Botswana, for example, has warranted the label since the early 1970s. The developmental state is sometimes contrasted with a predatory state or weak state.

The first person to seriously conceptualise the developmental state was Chalmers Johnson. He wrote in his book "MITI and the Japanese Miracle":

In states that were late to industrialize, the state itself led the industrialization drive, that is, it took on development functions. These two differing orientations toward private economic activities, the regulatory orientation and the developmental orientation, produced two different kinds of business-government relationships. The United States is a good example of a state in which the regulatory orientation predominates, whereas Japan is a good example of a state in which the developmental orientation predominates.

Recent writing on developmental states has emphasized the importance of both infrastructural powers and political commitment. According to Ghani et al. (2005), a 'developmental' state project must possess at least two essential attributes. First, the state must have the capacity to control a vast majority of its territory and possess a set of core capacities that will enable it to design and deliver policies; secondly, the project must involve some degree of reach and inclusion, and have an institutional, long-term perspective that transcends any specific political figure or leader, and emphasizes commitment. In his view, an ideal-type developmental state is one that demonstrates a 'determination and ability to stimulate, direct, shape and cooperate with the domestic private sector and arrange or supervise mutually acceptable deals with foreign interests'. Thus, a developmental state is broadly understood as one that evinces a clear commitment to a national development agenda, that has solid capacity and reach, and that seeks to provide growth as well as poverty reduction and the provision of public services.

A regulatory state governs the economy mainly through regulatory agencies that are empowered to enforce a variety of standards of behaviour to protect the public against market failures of various sorts, including monopolistic pricing, predation, and other abuses of market power, and by providing collective goods (such as national defence or public education) that otherwise would be undersupplied by the market. In contrast, a developmental state intervenes more directly in the economy through a variety of means to promote the growth of new industries and to reduce the dislocations caused by shifts in investment and profits from old to new industries. In other words, developmental states can pursue industrial policies, while regulatory states generally cannot.

As in the case of Japan, there is little government ownership of industry, but the private sector is rightly guided and restricted by bureaucratic government elites. These bureaucratic government elites are not elected officials and are thus less subject to influence by either the corporate-class or working-class through the political process. The argument from this perspective is that a government ministry can have the freedom to plan the economy and look to long-term national interests without having their economic policies disrupted by either corporate-class or working-class short-term or narrow interests.

Models or Types of State and Their Role in Economy

Peter Evans of the University of California at Berkeley and a sociologist by profession categorizes states into three types (or models) based on their roles in economic development—the Minimal State, the Developmental State, and the Predatory State. Artikel Ilmiah adds another type: the Regulatory State. However these types of state are only ideal types. Given the complexity of reality, countries have historically applied a combination of them.

Other scholars categorize states into four models; these are: the democratic interventionist-welfare state, commonplace in many Western societies; the developmental state that evolved in the Soviet system, and spread with some modifications to many developing countries; the liberal, market-friendly state espoused by the World Bank, which has found a footing in most developing countries that have taken structural adjustment loans from the World Bank and IMF; and the business-like, managerial state promoted by Margaret Thatcher, Ronal Reagan and others. These types of states are not essentially at odds with or much different from the above state models. It is also contended that innovations in any kind of state can, with suitable modifications, be adapted in any other kind of state, and that innovations in governance systems and adaptive borrowings are powerful keys to state excellence.

When we analyse the state models, we come to understand that the Minimal State is a concept from Adam Smith. The supporters of this concept argue that market mechanisms know best and work more efficiently than governments. To have the most favourable conditions for business, the role of government should be kept as minimal as possible. Based on this framework, the role of government is restricted only to preventing monopoly and externalities, providing public goods, and enforcing the law. Government's help to business should be indirect and non-selective.

The Regulatory State goes one step further than the Minimal State. The supporters of the regulatory state argue that the government is also responsible for the welfare of society as a whole and may help business people by ensuring a better government. From this point of view, indirect help is not and never sufficient. Government should be more active in giving direct help and should sometimes be selective. Two variants of the regulatory state are the Associative State and the Welfare State. The Associative State frames government to work together with business people and labour to mobilize productivity and allocate distribution for welfare. The Welfare State frames government to distribute welfare programmes (e.g. housing, unemployment aid, healthcare, etc.) and sometimes, to protect small businesses from the threat of big business.

The Developmental State goes one step further than the Regulatory State. The supporters of the Developmental State argue that the government should direct the trend of national industries and pick the "winners" to become the leading industries (or business locomotives). To play this role powerfully, the government should manipulate industrial policy (protection, subsidies, lower tax), offer cheap loans, and give administrative guidance that can direct business people to choose certain business strategies. The assumption of this approach, contrary to the Minimal State, is that the government knows more than the market how to achieve the highest national economic growth. The last one is the Predatory State. The easiest way to describe the predatory state is as follows: "The predatory state is the developmental state without bureaucratic competence." As a developmental state, the predatory state also directs the trend of business and picks the "winners".

However, the criteria for the intervention is not technical competence based on assessments of expertise, but nepotism and corruption. The government's high officials act as rent seekers, giving government facilities and protection to business people, and getting personal benefits in return. The indirect role of government refers only to the Minimal State. In this category, the role of the government is only to protect market mechanisms and to build infrastructures for the economy. The government may spend much money to build railroads or highways. This role is considered indirect, since what is created is a part of public goods. The direct role of the government refers to the Regulatory State, the Developmental State and the Predatory State, since in these states the government's role is to be selective and more than just to protect market mechanisms. In the history of business, the governments of the United States and Great Britain play roles as Minimal States, Regulatory States and Developmental States interchangeably, from one point of time to another. Compared to the United States and Great Britain, Japan acts as a developmental state much more frequently.

The Relationship Between Model of State, Development and Democratisation

Although there has been considerable discussion in the

development economics literature on the role of the state, it is only in recent years that explicit attention has been paid to the model of state and its relationship to development. As development economics moved from a narrow definition of development confined largely to the growth of per capita incomes to a more holistic and needs-and-rights-based approach, the form of the state became relevant to the discussion.

While neo-classical economics was based on the implicit assumption of a minimalist state, all late-industrializing countries chose to deviate from the prescription, giving rise to the concept of a developmental state which played an active role in promoting the country's development. However, a developmental state was not preordained to be either democratic or dictatorial, nor destined to be either socialist or capitalist. The prototype of non-democratic developmental states with capitalist orientation were pre-War Japan and East Asian countries and that with socialist orientation were the former Soviet Union and East European countries.

Only the First World countries of Europe and North America had the distinction of combining developmental capacity with a democratic political regime. The basic characteristic of a developmental state was to promote the mobilization of economic surplus and its investment into new industries to ensure self-sustaining growth and rise in per capita incomes.

The developmental state used a large variety of instruments, both direct and indirect, to promote industrialization: general and targeted subsidies; tariffs; credit and direct finance; regulation of foreign investment and foreign capital inflows. Developmental states enlarged the size of the domestic market by unifying their countries politically and by investments in infrastructure.

The jury is still out on whether all countries can or should become a developmental state and whether a developmental state necessarily should be democratic. Historically, there was no strong positive correlation between the two.

The paradigm of a developmental state, which is largely based on the East Asian "miracle" economies is now facing a less hospitable environment as a result of the financial crisis faced by these economies during the late 1990s and the increasing pressures to open up the economies to foreign competition in all spheres. However, the basic idea of a developmental state with managerial capacity and leadership could still hold a country in good stead in facing the challenges of globalization.

With the change in the scope and objectives of development, the need for defining the form of government to achieve developmental goals has also become imperative. So long as development was defined narrowly as growth, it mattered little how it was achieved and often dictatorial and military regimes (such as in East Asia) performed better than democratic regimes.

However, with the inclusion of such objectives as social, political and institutional modernization; and widespread improvement in the human condition, including reduction of inequality of incomes, poverty incidence and gender gap, among others, the need for a democratic dispensation became unavoidable. However, the idea of democracy as a universal commitment is quite new, as it is quintessentially a product of the twentieth century.

Throughout the nineteenth century, theorists of democracy found it quite natural to discuss whether one country or another was "fit for democracy." This thinking changed only in the latter half of the last century, when it came to be realized that a country does not have to be deemed fit for democracy, rather it has to become fit through democracy. In fact, both democracy and development have rather steep and non-linear learning curves, climbing which is possible only through considerable investment of perseverance, patience and time.

In his recent work, Development as Freedom, Professor Amartya Sen has emphasized the link between democracy and development and has debunked the oft-repeated claim that undemocratic systems are better at fostering economic development. Sen finds no convincing evidence that authoritarian governance and the suppression of political and civil rights are really beneficial to economic development. Systematic empirical studies give no real support to the claim that there is a general conflict between political rights and economic performance. In fact, a harsher political system is often counterproductive in bringing out the full potential of the labour force.

What are Developmental States and Why do They Matter?

Again, what do we mean by the developmental state? And why do we believe that this concept contributes something useful to contemporary thinking on development policy?

According to Ghani et al. (2005), a 'developmental' state project must possess at least two essential attributes. First, the state must have the capacity to control a vast majority of its territory and possess a set of core capacities that will enable it to design and deliver policies; secondly, the project must involve some degree of reach and inclusion, and have an institutional, long-term perspective that transcends any specific political figure or leader, and emphasizes commitment. In his view, and ideal-type developmental state is one that demonstrates a 'determination and ability to stimulate, direct, shape and cooperate with the domestic private sector and arrange or supervise mutually acceptable deals with foreign interests'. Thus, a developmental state is broadly understood as one that evinces a clear commitment to a national development agenda, that has solid capacity and reach, and that seeks to provide growth as well as poverty reduction and the provision of public services.

Drawing on the work of Johnson (1982), Deyo (1987) and Evans (1995) among others, we understand a developmental state to exist when the state possesses the vision, leadership and capacity to bring about a positive transformation of society within a condensed period of time. To be judged developmental, a state does not need to be in control of everything and successful in all spheres. A transformation that is positive overall may be accompanied by a range of negative consequences, such as major environmental damage or greater social tension, which become problems that society and the state have to address in a subsequent phase.

The transformation can also take various forms. In the classic East Asian examples, it was aimed at speeding up growth, while at the same time enhancing opportunities to participate in the modern economy—most commonly through the expansion of public services such as education, health care and agricultural extension. The developmental state was associated with rapid processes of industrialization and/or the adoption of new technologies—that is, moving into higher value-added activities relative to the starting point. Typically, there was a shift from subsistence agriculture to more commercial, export-oriented farming, or to textile processing, or to tourism, or a mixture of these.

Clearly, not all social transformations are actively promoted by developmental states. There are many instances of private-sector-led growth in which the state's role has been quite limited. In addition, not all attempts at state-led transformations succeed.

In fact, in developing countries, ambitious attempts at state-led transformation have commonly met with failure, often with far-reaching negative consequences. Moreover, the developmental orientation of a state is not a permanent condition but rather a dynamic feature with a limited time horizon. Germany and Japan, for example, had developmental states at critical junctures in their history, which triggered considerable economic and social transformations, while also storing up unresolved issues for the future. Today the challenges are different and those countries' states [regimes] would no longer be considered developmental. Nor need the developmental condition be even across the entire state: a state may be characterized by the co-existence of sectors or institutional areas that have a clear developmental orientation with areas where significant anti-developmental factors are in play.

Developmental states have been the subject of research and analysis at various points in history. The roots of the idea of a developmental state reach back at least to List (1909) and Gerschenkron (1962), whose concern was the role of the state in rapid 'late' industrialization in continental Europe. The most recent experiences with successful transformations generated by developmental states have been those in East Asia between the 1960s and 1980s. Over a period of 30 years, a set of city-states and countries including Hong Kong, Singapore, South Korea and Taiwan underwent rapid economic growth and radical socio-economic change, moving from being poor agrarian societies in the 1960s to producers of high technology and high value-added goods by the 1990s. These so-called 'Asian Tigers' have generated a considerable literature. Since the 1980s, developmental states in

China and Vietnam have also overseen a remarkable process of social transformation. More limited examples of state-led development can be found in countries such as Brazil, India and Mauritius.

As this illustrates, we can with hindsight quite easily identify developmental states; that is, once the transformative outcomes have become visible. However, it is less easy to specify ex ante the key characteristics. Developmental states are marked by a combination of capacities, visions, norms and/or ideologies. They are not associated with specific policies; at different times and in different places, very different policies have ushered in social and economic transformations. At most, as Woo-Cummings (1999: 1-2) explains, the developmental state is 'neither socialist...nor free-market...but something different: the plan-rational capitalist developmental state...[which links] interventionism with rapid economic growth'.

A common factor among developmental states appears to be a committed leadership that is embedded in the 'right' context of demands. Developmental states are usually characterized by a leadership which is strongly committed to developmental goals, and which places national development ahead of personal enrichment and/or short-term political gains. Historically, many of the examples of the emergence of such a leadership have been associated with a severe crisis (the perceived threat that Japan posed to South Korea, for example), and the response that political elites have designed to overcome it. On the other hand, a degree of political stability is usually a precondition for such capacities to be sustained and to flourish. Aspects of the domestic context are important as well: demands arising from society, and in particular from wider elite groups, as well as international factors, may help or hinder the efforts of a national leadership in pursuing developmental goals.

Many of the original leaders in post-colonial developing countries had a developmental vision: Julius Nyerere of Tanzania and Kwame Nkrumah of Ghana are perhaps the best known African examples. Patrice Lumumba had the potential to become a visionary leader in the Congo. However, wider conditions were disadvantageous. Domestically, there were strong clientelist demands for spoils, and ethnic/tribal rivalries that needed to be managed. The international context of the Cold War was particularly unfavourable, providing the backdrop to the elimination of potentially good leaders (for example, the murder of Lumumba), as well as the imposition or tolerance of outrageously bad ones.

The importance of the structure of domestic demands is reflected in a fundamental characteristic of the developmental state: what Evans (1995) calls its 'embedded autonomy'. According to Evans, the developmental state is autonomous insofar as it has a rationalised bureaucracy characterized by meritocracy and long-term career prospects, traits that make civil servants more professional and detached from powerful rent-seeking groups. On the other hand, the state cannot be too insulated from society without running the risk of becoming excessively detached, unable to appreciate and act upon societal needs. Thus, it must also be embedded in society, that is, [connected to] a concrete set of social ties that binds the state to society and provides institutionalised channels for the continual negotiation and renegotiation of goals and policies'.

State capacities generally cannot increase if a developmental commitment among the state elite is missing or insufficiently resolute. This may be the main reason why so much donor-sponsored capacity building has proven ineffective. However, commitment at the elite level is insufficient on its own. It is usually necessary for the elite to expound a vision that connects the state and society in a mutually binding way, through some form of shared 'national project'. Another of the underlying requirements of the developmental state is thus the creation of a nation-wide public. A nation-wide public need not be rooted in a unified sense of 'nation' based on cultural and linguistic unity, but may well take the form of a more civic identity (as in the case of the US). The important issue is that all citizens see themselves as Ethiopians or Nigerians, Kenyans or Tanzanians as much as or more than as an Oromo or as Igbo or Kikuyu or Nyamwezi. Post-independence leaders in sub-Saharan Africa often understand this challenge, and their drive to expand primary education was in good part aimed at creating a national public consciousness.

Many African countries experienced some sort of big push for development during the early independence years. However, subsequently governance deteriorated too sharply for this to be followed through. The deterioration was due to a combination of domestic and external factors. On the one hand, clientelistic and/ or neo-patrimonial social structures strangled the potential of promising economic sectors and undermined attempts at state-led industrialisation. Efforts to spread education stalled, inter alia when increasingly authoritarian leaders found that those with some education, but lacking good employment opportunities (due to the clientelistic throttling of the economy), become politically dangerous. National armies discredited themselves through bloody coups and internal divisions along ethnic lines. The project of national integration failed.

Embedding State Autonomy

The big question for political economists in the 1990s was why the East Asian Tigers were growing so dramatically when other strong states were faring badly. Dictatorships and post-socialist states during the same period, for example, were creating the kind of economic and social ruin that caused their populations to detest them.

One answer came from Peter Evans, who identified two linked factors that distinguished successful 'developmental states' from economically failing ones, which he called 'embedded autonomy'. 'Embeddedness' he defined as good communication and ties with the private sector—the factor stressed by those promoting a 'developmental state' in Ethiopia regarding pro-poor inclusion. But this factor was bound up with 'autonomy', defined as political autonomy or insulation, which would simultaneously allow state officials to make policy professionally and independently of special private-sector interests.

In Evans' analysis, the interdependency of these factors was crucial. Social embeddedness without political autonomy would leave state officials vulnerable to private pressures, leading to corruption and cronyism. Autonomy without embeddedness would leave state officials isolated from real events, prone to bad decision-making and, in the worst scenarios, ruinous miscalculations. For embedded autonomy to work, Evans observed, the state must create a meritocratic bureaucracy of highly skilled people who can freely combine their close contacts with the private sector with their independent understanding of the global market to help steer economic planning in directions good for the national economy as a whole.

Notably, a meritocratic bureaucracy has nothing to do with democracy. South Korea, Taiwan and Singapore were, until recently, repressive dictatorships (as was Brazil). These states used the peasantry (as long as it lasted) for agriculture to drive growth; they did not look out for peasant interests or any interests that didn't serve central state growth. Not until the 1980s were the rising middle classes in these states able to launch effective struggles for greater political voice, precisely because the states were so strong.

Hence a tangential debate about developmental states is that if early authoritarianism enabled the East Asian Tigers to overcome entrenched private interests, then Ethiopia, for example, is hampered in this respect because Ethiopia today is a constitutional democracy where authoritarianism has no place whatsoever.

Money and Autonomy

While authoritarianism may be a necessary condition, it is not a sufficient one. Even pro-authoritarian development analysts admit that other necessary conditions are needed: notably, the financial power that supported strong states in Asia.

Where did that power come from? The answer clarifies that the key factor for the Tigers was not authoritarianism but yet another conspicuously neglected truth about the developmental-state model that should give its admirers pause: for several decades, the US Administration pumped billions of dollars straight to the East Asian Tigers' governments in order to consolidate their compliance and capacity in the Cold War. This massive external funding greatly strengthened these states in relation to their private sectors, allowing them to operate with unusual independence and autocracy. Yet, oddly, this enormous financial and political factor is entirely overlooked by many who enthuse about the capacity of least developed countries such as Ethiopia and other states to blossom economically simply by emulating some South Korean policy regarding the bureaucracy.

This massive external funding greatly strengthened these states in relation to their private sectors, allowing them to operate with unusual independence and autocracy.

The same factor explains why authoritarian Latin American states have been unable to follow the East Asian Tigers' model: because their states lacked that external funding and even by the late 1970s were running aground on debt. Instead, extensive direct foreign investment in Latin America (again mostly from the US) strengthened the private sector in relation to governments, and effectively made the 'developmental state' model unworkable on most of the continent. Generally, entrenched oligarchies and repressive landed elites stifled development in the rest of Latin America precisely because they were in control of the state.

In other words, these states were socially 'embedded' but profoundly lacked insulation from private elite interests—indeed, they were composed of those interests and existed entirely to serve them. In these conditions, which endure today, leftist revolutions and democratic reforms have had disappointing impact in improving the lot of the poor.

That this vital finding of the 'developmental state' literature is not even heard is perilous to the Ethiopian debate. For it boils down to this: it's no good including more people in the nation's development project (even poor people who clearly deserve more voice in state planning) if the state bureaucracy lacks sufficient political insulation, because otherwise this lauded 'inclusion' will just foster more savoury deals, clientelism and tender abuse.

The challenge for Ethiopia as a democratic developmental state in the making is the same challenge that faces countries everywhere: to develop institutions and policy instruments, to win the hearts and minds of the majority of the population around democratic developmentalism, to secure resources, particularly foreign savings, to build an efficient, meritocratic and meritorious public service, and to insulate the state from private political pressure enough to allow 'inclusion' to be a positive form of 'embeddedness' rather than just another distortion. Only then can the state play a genuinely positive role in relieving Ethiopia's endemic poverty and inequality and truly serve the nation as a whole. The future of Ethiopia surely lies in building a robust democratic developmental state where democracy and development co-exist as 'kissing cousins', because "bread without democracy is bitter and democracy without bread is fragile."

"If a country's problems require radical remedies, you need a radical government. But how can you have a radical government without radically-minded officials? Difficult problems are solved by people who desperately want to solve them: not by people who had been fully prepared until polling day to make those self-same problems worse, rather than better."

Bibliography

Anant, S. S.: *Changing Caste Hindu Attitudes Towards Harijans: A Follow Up After Four Years*, New Delhi, Vikas, 2019.

Barbara, R.: *Untouchable! Voices of the Dalit Liberation Movement*, London, Zed Books, 2016.

Bhagwat, Vidyut: *Dalit Women in India: Issues and Perspectives - Some Critical Reflections*, New Delhi, Gyan Publishing House, 2015.

Bose, N. K.: *The Scheduled Castes and Tribes and Their Present Conditions*, Calcutta, University of Calcutta, 2009.

Cohan, B. N.: *The Changing Status of a Depressed Class*, Chicago, The University of Chicago Press, 1995.

Dass Arvind and Sita Deulkar: *Caste and Communities in Conflict of Modernisation*, Dominant, Delhi, 2023.

David, H. : *Handbook of Regulation and Administrative Law*, New York, Marcel Dekker, 2014.

Dennis, L.: *Public Policy Management and Public Policy*, New York, Longman, 2019.

Dipak, K.: *Administration Report of the Political Agency*, Agartala, Tripura State Cultural Research Institute & Museum, 2015.

Francis, E.: *Bureaucratic Power in National Politics*, Boston, Little Brown and Company, 2008.

Garg, V.K. : *Caste and Reservation in India*, Alfa Publications, Delhi, 2023.

Gorhe, Neelam: *Social Development and Dalit Women*, Gyan Pub. House, New Delhi, 2015.

Gupta L.P. : *Administration for Educational Development of Tribes : A Study of Female Students in Darjeeling*, Classical, Delhi, 2022.

Haruka Yanagisawa: *A Century of Change : Caste and Irrigated Lands in Tamilnadu, 1860s-1970s*, Manohar, Delhi, 2016.

Hutton, J. H.: *Caste in India: Its Nature, Function and Origins*, London, Cambridge University Press, 1996.

James M.: *Untouchable : An Indian Life History*, CA, Stanford University Press, 2009.

Jogdand, P. G.: *Dalit Women in India: Issues and Perspectives*, New Delhi, Gyan Publishing House, 2015.

Jones, W.H.: *The Government and Politics of India*, London, Hutchinson, 2001.

Kshirsagar, R. K.: *Dalit Movement in India and Its Leaders (1857-1956)*, New Delhi, MD Pub. Pvt. Ltd., 2014.

Mayer, A.: *Caste in an Indian Village: Change and Continuity 1954-1992*, Delhi, OUP, 2016.

Morris, W.H.: *The Government and Politics of India*, London, Hutchinson, 2001.

Nath, Trilok: *Politics of the Depressed Classes*, Delhi, Deputy Publications, 2017.

Paranjpe, A. C.: *Caste, Prejudice and the Individual*, Lalvani Publishing House, New Delhi, 2010.

Rao, M. S. A.: *Social Movement and Social Transformation: A Study of Backward Class Movement*, New Delhi, Macmillian Press, 2008.

Riggs, F.: *Administrative Reform and Political Responsiveness*, Beverly Hills, Sage Publications, 2010.

Satyamurthy, T.V.: *Region, Religion, Caste, Gender and Culture in Contemporary India*, Delhi, OUP, 2016.

Shah, Ghanshyam: *Caste Association and Political Processes in Gujarat*, Bombay, Popular Prakashan, 2015.

Singh, Ekta : *Caste System in India : A Historical Perspective*, Kalpaz, Delhi, 2020.

Sunder, Prem : *Caste Class and Society : Then and Now*, Educational Pub, Delhi, 2023.

Verma, B. M.: *Development of Scheduled Castes and Administration*, New Delhi, Uppal Publishing House, 2013.

Whicker, L.: *Handbook of Research Methods in Public Administration*, New York, Marcel Dekker, 2019.

Index

❑❑❑